THE ATLAS OF
SACRED
PLACES

THE ATLAS OF SACRED PLACES

Meeting Points of Heaven and Earth

James Harpur

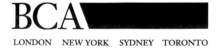

BCA

LONDON   NEW YORK   SYDNEY   TORONTO

CONTENTS

A Marshall Edition
Conceived, edited and designed by
MARSHALL EDITIONS
170 Piccadilly, London W1V 9DD

Copyright © 1994 by
Marshall Editions Developments Ltd.
This edition published 1994 by BCA
by arrangement with Cassell, London

CN 8721

EDITOR: James Bremner
ART EDITOR: Helen Spencer
MANAGING EDITOR: Lindsay McTeague
DTP EDITOR: Mary Pickles
PICTURE RESEARCH: Richard Philpott
RESEARCH: Simon Beecroft
COPY EDITOR: Isabella Raeburn
PRODUCTION: Janice Storr
                           Sarah Hinks

Films supplied by Dorchester Typesetting Group, UK
Origination by HBM Print, Singapore
Printed and bound in Spain
by Printer Industria Grafica, Barcelona

*Photographs shown on the preliminary
pages are a holy man at Varanasi, India,
and the Dome of the Rock, Jerusalem.*

*The symbols used in this book to
denote each place are: Mount Sinai,
tablets of the Law; Bodh Gaya,
the Bodhi Tree; Ephesus, statue of
Artemis; Iona, Celtic cross; Dome
of the Rock, the Dome;*

*Newgrange, spiral pattern;
Mycenae, "mask of Agamemnon";
Tomb Complex of Shi Huangdi,
terracotta soldier; Pyramids of
Giza, the pyramids; Oseberg,
carved animal head; Catacombs
of Rome, Christian fish symbol;*

The Olgas, domed rock; Temple of Karnak, ram-headed sphinx; Teotihuacán, face of Quetzalcoatl; Olympia, discus thrower; Cahokia, engraving of bird man; Pagan, pyramid-temple; Rock of Cashel, round tower and cathedral ruins; Caves of the Thousand Buddhas, bodhisattva;

Isfahan, iwan, or portal; Wat Phra Keo, guardian figure; Great Mosque of Córdoba, Moorish arch; Süleymaniye, dome; Golden Temple, Khanda symbol of Sikhism; San Vitale, head of Christ; Ise, wooden shrine; Cologne Cathedral, twin towers;

Varanasi, the ghats, or riverside steps; Delphi, omphalos stone; Mecca, Ka'aba; Mount Kailas, snow-capped peak; Lourdes, head of Virgin Mary; Canterbury Cathedral, medieval pilgrim.

INTRODUCTION

"PUT OFF THY SHOES FROM OFF THY FEET," THE LORD SAID TO Moses on Mount Sinai, "for the place whereon thou standest is holy ground." The idea that, like Mount Sinai, particular places in the world are holy or sacred can be found in different cultures, past and present, all over the world. But what makes such places sacred? Are there objective indicators that can be read like dials? Or is sacredness simply in the mind of the beholder?

Two 20th-century scholars who have shed light on the nature of the sacred are the German Rudolf Otto and the Romanian Mircea Eliade. Otto coined the word "numinous" to express the awe-inspiring power of a divine revelation or presence. And this sense of numinosity can be felt at many traditional holy places, such as Delphi in Greece, an oracular shrine set amid towering cliffs, or Mount Kailas, a symmetrical ice-capped peak rising above the plains of western Tibet.

Eliade contrasts "sacred space" with what he calls "profane space" – literally that which lies outside the temple – and uses the word "hierophany" to express a manifestation of the sacred. For animists, such as Shintoists – who believe nature is imbued with spirits – this could be a tree or rock; or, for Christians, the incarnation of God in Jesus. Certainly the sacredness of some places has stemmed directly from a hierophany: Mount Sinai, for example, where the Lord appeared to Moses; or Lourdes, where the Virgin Mary appeared to a peasant girl; or Iona, the island where Saint Columba saw visions of angels and performed various miracles.

Yet there are other reasons why a place may be considered holy ground. This book examines more than thirty examples, divided into five different sections. "In the Footsteps of Holy Men" includes monuments and landscapes that have become sacred because of their association with saints and spiritual teachers: Bodh Gaya in India, for example, where Siddhartha Gautama gained enlightenment and became the Buddha.

In ancient cultures, burial places were especially sacred because a dead person's journey to, and enjoyment of, the afterlife was felt to depend upon the sanctity of the grave and its funerary objects.

An Indian holy man welcomes the dawning of a new day at Varanasi, the country's most sacred city.

"In Honour of the Dead" looks at
ancient burial places, from the prehistoric passage grave of Newgrange in
Ireland to the pyramids of Giza, and
also the associated rites and beliefs.
The cult of the ruin reached its height
in the Romantic movement of 19th-century
Europe, when sightseers luxuriated in the aesthetics
of crumbling arches or solitary columns. "Eternal
Shrines" features places that evoke the sense of a distant or
mythic past, such as the Buddhist temples of Pagan in Myanmar
(Burma), which reinforces their original sacred dimension.

*ATLANTIC
OCEAN*

The combination of artistic skills
with an underlying religious spirit
has produced great creations – sacred space enclosed
by walls adorned with spires or tiles, glass
and gold leaf, or paintings or icons. "To
the Glory of God" looks at temples
worldwide, including the Safavid mosques
of Isfahan in Iran, with their iridescent
domes, and the Byzantine church of San
Vitale in Ravenna, whose mosaics are one of
Christendom's wonders.
"At the Journey's End" focuses on pilgrimage –
a journey toward a specific shrine, such as Mecca or
Canterbury Cathedral, as a central part of the religious
quest. On a physical level the pilgrimage can involve

*PACIFIC
OCEAN*

The locations of the places featured in
this book are shown on this map. Sites
are marked by numbers and dots which
correspond to the list of places below.

1 CAHOKIA *(U.S.)*
2 TEOTIHUACÁN *(Mexico)*
3 IONA *(Great Britain)*
4 NEWGRANGE *(Ireland)*
5 ROCK OF CASHEL *(Ireland)*
6 CANTERBURY CATHEDRAL
(Great Britain)
7 LOURDES *(France)*
8 GREAT MOSQUE OF
CÓRDOBA *(Spain)*

9 OSEBERG *(Norway)*
10 COLOGNE CATHEDRAL
(Germany)
11 SAN VITALE *(Italy)*
12 CATACOMBS OF
ROME *(Italy)*
13 SÜLEYMANIYE *(Turkey)*
14 DELPHI *(Greece)*
15 OLYMPIA *(Greece)*
16 MYCENAE *(Greece)*

17 EPHESUS *(Turkey)*
18 DOME OF THE ROCK *(Israel)*
19 MOUNT SINAI *(Egypt)*
20 PYRAMIDS OF GIZA *(Egypt)*
21 TEMPLE OF KARNAK *(Egypt)*
22 MECCA *(Saudi Arabia)*
23 ISFAHAN *(Iran)*
24 GOLDEN TEMPLE *(India)*
25 MOUNT KAILAS *(Tibet)*
26 VARANASI *(India)*

27 BODH GAYA *(India)*
28 CAVES OF THE THOUSAND
BUDDHAS *(China)*
29 PAGAN *(Myanmar)*
30 WAT PHRA KEO
(Thailand)
31 TOMB COMPLEX OF SHI
HUANGDI *(China)*
32 ISE *(Japan)*
33 THE OLGAS *(Australia)*

*PACIFIC
OCEAN*

*INDIAN
OCEAN*

hardships; on a spiritual plane, this is traditionally mirrored by
the soul's journey toward union with God.
    Whether certain places have an innate sacredness or whether
people sacralize them in their minds cannot be determined.
    However, that some places seem more numinous than others or are
the occasion for a hierophany or, through their holy art or
association with a shrine or saint, have accumulated a spiritual
energy has been established by tradition. And once sacred space
or holy ground is established, it is not easy to eradicate – as T.S.
Eliot wrote: "From such ground springs that which forever
renews the earth/Though it is forever denied."

IN THE FOOTSTEPS OF HOLY MEN

THE TOPOGRAPHY OF THE WORLD IS littered with places that are held in reverence because of their association with a great holy figure. In the Middle Ages, holy relics, such as the bones of saints, were believed to be charged with a power that would bring benefit – perhaps healing or good fortune. In a similar way, certain places are felt to have a holy aura as a result of being imbued with the energy of a saint or a spiritual teacher. Thus in the Sinai Peninsula the craggy mountain Jebel Musa, traditionally identified with MOUNT SINAI, is regularly climbed by those who want to stand where Moses encountered God and received the Law from him. In Buddhism, BODH GAYA in northern India is *the* holy site for the faithful, since it was here that Siddhartha Gautama, seated beneath the Bodhi tree, found enlightenment and became the Buddha. For Christians, the entire Holy Land, with its countless biblical associations, is a sacred place. Less well known, but holy all the same, is EPHESUS in present-day Turkey, which is chiefly associated with Saint Paul. He spent two years in this Greco-Roman city, teaching the gospel of Christ. Centuries after Paul, Christianity was brought to Scotland by the Celtic saint Columba. His spiritual base was on the tiny island of IONA, whose hills, fields and shores all bear his memory. Muslims also have sacred places associated with holy figures. One of the most revered of these is the DOME OF THE ROCK in Jerusalem, for it was from here that the Prophet Muhammad is said to have ascended to heaven and received instruction from God before returning to this world.

On the trail of the world's great spiritual figures

The Arcadian Way at Ephesus, a city which bears the imprint of Saint Paul, who taught there for two years.

MOUNT SINAI

"And Mount Sinai was altogether on a smoke, because the LORD descended upon it in fire...."

EXODUS 19:18

ACCORDING TO THE BIBLE, AFTER Moses had led the children of Israel out of slavery in Egypt, they made their slow tortuous way toward the promised land of Canaan, beset by thirst, hunger, and doubts about their new destiny. The wilderness through which they wearily travelled was that of the Sinai Peninsula, a vast sun-blistered triangle of barren plains and primeval mountains linking the continents of Africa and Asia. Here, in one of the most dramatic encounters between the divine and the mortal, Moses communed with God on a mountain known as Sinai, or Horeb, receiving from Him the Ten Commandments, the ethical corner-stone of Judaism and Christianity.

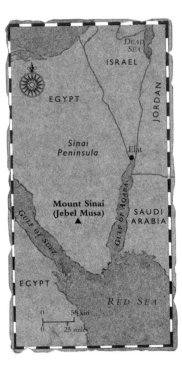

Although Mount Sinai's location cannot be known for certain, the strongest traditions identify it with the peak known as Jebel Musa (Mount Moses) in the south of the peninsula. In a terrain forged on the anvil of ancient volcanic action, Jebel Musa rises 7,500 feet above a sea of peaks stripped back to ore-rich rock, its summit a meeting place between God and man.

Moses and the Israelites had been wandering in the desert for three months before they came to the foot of Mount Sinai and pitched camp. In fact, according to Exodus 3, Moses had come to this mountain before while tending the flock of his father-in-law, Jethro, before the escape from Egypt. On that occasion, God had spoken to him out of the flames of a burning bush, which had miraculously remained uncharred, and had told Moses

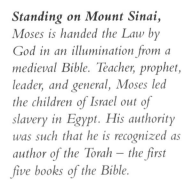

Standing on Mount Sinai, *Moses is handed the Law by God in an illumination from a medieval Bible. Teacher, prophet, leader, and general, Moses led the children of Israel out of slavery in Egypt. His authority was such that he is recognized as author of the Torah — the first five books of the Bible.*

to "put off thy shoes from off thy feet, for the place whereon thou standest is holy ground". Now once more Moses was about to tread this sacred terrain, this time to meet God in a more protracted and revealing encounter.

From the camp, Moses climbed up the mountain. There, God promised him that if the Israelites kept His covenant, they would be "a kingdom of priests, and a holy nation" (Exodus 19:6). He then warned Moses that three days later He would

appear on Mount Sinai to the people, who were to purify themselves for this awesome event and refrain from touching, on pain of death, the holy mountain until told to do so.

On the third day, ominous peals of thunder, zigzags of lightning, and the deafening blast of a trumpet alerted the trembling Israelites to God's presence. Before their eyes, a dense cloud cloaked the mountain top and God descended in the form of fire; smoke "as if from a furnace" rose into the sky as the mountain quaked: Sinai had

The summit of Jebel Musa,
a peak in the south of the Sinai Peninsula, is traditionally identified with Mount Sinai, the mountain where, according to the Bible, Moses received the Ten Commandments from God. Jebel Musa, with its panoramic views over a terrain of primordial grandeur, is sacred to Jews, Christians, and Muslims alike.

The Greek Orthodox monastery of St. Catherine lies below the northern slopes of Jebel Musa. It is possibly the oldest monastery in continuous existence. Apart from numerous chapels, the complex has a library, bakery, storerooms, wells, and visitors' quarters.

been transformed from an inert mass of rock to an interdimensional crossroads, a place suspended between mundane and heavenly realities.

As the trumpet rang out louder, Moses cried out to God, who answered him. "And the LORD came down upon...the top of the mount: and the LORD called Moses to the top of the mount; and Moses went up" (Exodus 19:20).

In what was a watershed moment in the world's spiritual history, God communicated to Moses the Ten Commandments, or Decalogue, whose injunctions, especially to worship God alone, and not to kill, steal, or commit adultery, laid the foundation of moral living in the Jewish and Christian religions. Then, in a number of further revelations, God prescribed for the Israelites specific ritual duties, and these, along with the Decalogue, became known as the Law, or Torah, which forms the heart of the Jewish tradition.

Eventually, after God had communed with Moses, He gave him two stone tablets "of the testimony" inscribed with His own finger. But as Moses walked back down the mountain with the tablets, he heard the hubbub of revelry in the camp, where he found his people dancing around a golden calf. For the Israelites, insecure in their faith and fearful of Moses' lengthy absence,

The huge cliffs of Jebel Musa, seen from its southern side, rise up from the plain in this painting by the British writer and artist Edward Lear (1812–88), who visited the area in January 1849.

This Christian chapel is perched on the summit of Jebel Musa, which it shares with a small mosque, and is sometimes used for services. These two Christian and Muslim shrines have as their literal and symbolic foundation a mountain sanctified by one of the great figures of Judaism.

had prevailed upon Aaron, Moses' brother, to melt down some gold earrings and make them an idol to worship.

Snatched from the sublimity of divine revelation to the reality of human frailty, Moses saw red – his "anger waxed hot" and he smashed the tablets. He then seized the golden calf, burned and ground it into a powder and, mixing this with water, made the Israelites drink it.

But with the people still out of control, Moses took a more radical measure. Rallying to his side members of the tribe of Levi, who were loyal to God, he told them to arm themselves and to slaughter "brother, companion, and neighbour". About 3,000 Israelites were put to the sword. Later, after the people had repented, God's covenant with them was renewed, and new stone tablets were inscribed.

Today, the gaunt creviced ramparts of Mount Sinai represent a place of tranquillity, remote from the stormy dramas of Exodus. It was the mountain's isolation and peaceful grandeur that attracted hermits to it and its environs from the earliest days of Christianity. Then, in A.D. 330, Helena, mother of the Roman emperor Constantine the Great, built a chapel at the foot of Mount Sinai where Moses' burning bush was held to have been.

This chapel became a focus for a monastic community and later, in 530, the Byzantine emperor Justinian ordered it to be fortified with strong walls for protection against attacks by nomadic tribesmen. He also built a new basilica, the Church of the Transfiguration, which has survived to the present. Now, with the rest of St. Catherine's monastery, it continues to welcome visitors, who come to savour the holy atmosphere, see the ancient icons, manuscripts, and other treasures, or share in the contemplative life of the monks.

For modern pilgrims, the highlight of a visit is to climb to the summit of Sinai in the footsteps of Moses, particularly to watch the dawn break. From behind the monastery, a route known as the "path of our Lord Moses" ascends past a number of holy landmarks, including a well, a chapel dedicated to the Virgin Mary, and two ancient gateways separated by a long flight of steps cut out of the rock.

The arduous journey to the top is rewarded by panoramic views over a landscape of pitted volcanic rock. As daylight glimmers on the horizon, a sea of lava flows away, and ridges and pinnacles guard deep shadow-filled gorges. In a still moment, even without the smoke, thunder, and lightning, it is possible to hear in the imagination the words that God uttered to Moses which would distinguish the Israelites from their pagan neighbors and set the course for monotheistic worship in the west: "I am the LORD thy God, which have brought thee out of the land of Egypt, out of the house of bondage. Thou shalt have no other gods before me."

TIMEFRAME

B.C.

1279–1213 REIGN OF THE EGYPTIAN PHARAOH RAMSES II, TRADITIONALLY IDENTIFIED WITH THE BIBLICAL PHARAOH WHO EVENTUALLY ALLOWED MOSES TO LEAD THE CHILDREN OF ISRAEL OUT OF EGYPT.

A.D.

106 THE SINAI PENINSULA COMES UNDER ROMAN CONTROL.

330 HELENA, MOTHER OF CONSTANTINE THE GREAT, BUILDS A CHAPEL BELOW MOUNT SINAI ON THE ALLEGED SITE OF THE BURNING BUSH.

530 JUSTINIAN ENCOMPASSES HELENA'S CHAPEL AND THE OTHER MONASTIC BUILDINGS WITH A WALL AND BUILDS THE CHURCH OF THE TRANSFIGURATION.

1517 THE SINAI PENINSULA BECOMES PART OF THE OTTOMAN EMPIRE.

1945 A LIBRARY IS BUILT IN THE MONASTERY TO HOUSE ITS MAINLY GREEK AND ARABIC MANUSCRIPTS.

1975 3,000 MANUSCRIPTS ARE ACCIDENTALLY DISCOVERED BEHIND ONE OF THE MONASTERY'S WALLS.

TO THE PROMISED LAND

After their dramatic escape from Egypt and the pharaoh's pursuing army, Moses and the Israelites pushed deep into the barren wilds of the Sinai Peninsula. To guide them, God appeared as a pillar of cloud by day and a pillar of fire by night – as shown below in a painting by the 19th-century British artist William West. The Israelites' ultimate destination was Canaan, the Promised Land, some 200 miles to the east. Their route is difficult to trace, since it is impossible to identify many of the places named in the book of Exodus. This map shows the traditional route, most favoured by scholars, and two alternatives. Of these, one passes directly across the peninsula via Jebel Helal, a peak sometimes put forward as an

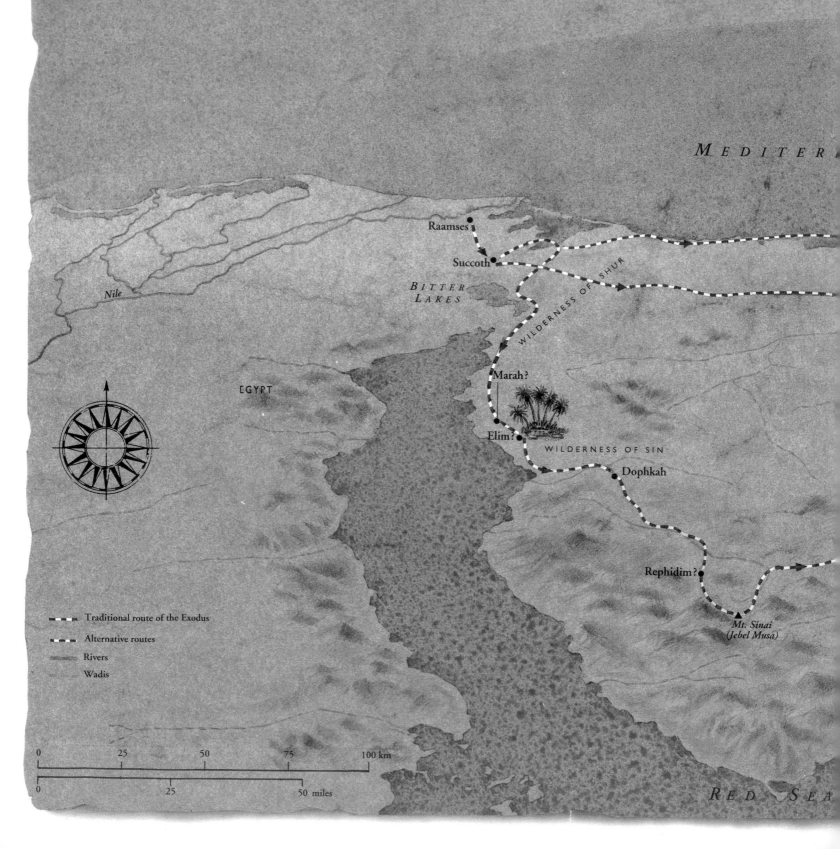

MEDITERR

Raamses

Succoth

BITTER
LAKES

Nile

WILDERNESS OF SHUR

EGYPT

Marah?

Elim?

WILDERNESS OF SIN

Dophkah

Rephidim?

Mt. Sinai
(Jebel Musa)

- – – – Traditional route of the Exodus
- – – – Alternative routes
- ~~~~ Rivers
- ~~~~ Wadis

| 0 | 25 | 50 | 75 | 100 km |

| 0 | 25 | 50 miles |

RED SEA

alternative to Jebel Musa (pp. 12–15) as the biblical Mount Sinai, while the other skirts the northern coast.

The traditional route leads southward toward the Wilderness of Sin and Jebel Musa, the most likely Mount Sinai. From here, a year after their flight from Egypt, the Israelites headed north for Ezion-geber and then the oasis of Kadesh-barnea. From there, they either trekked directly eastward or, more probably, returned to Ezion-geber and looped around Edom and skirted Moab to enter Canaan north of the Dead Sea. Moses, however, never set foot in the Promised Land: he died on Mount Nebo, reputedly aged 120, leaving his people in the hands of Joshua, who would lead the Israelites to victory at Jericho.

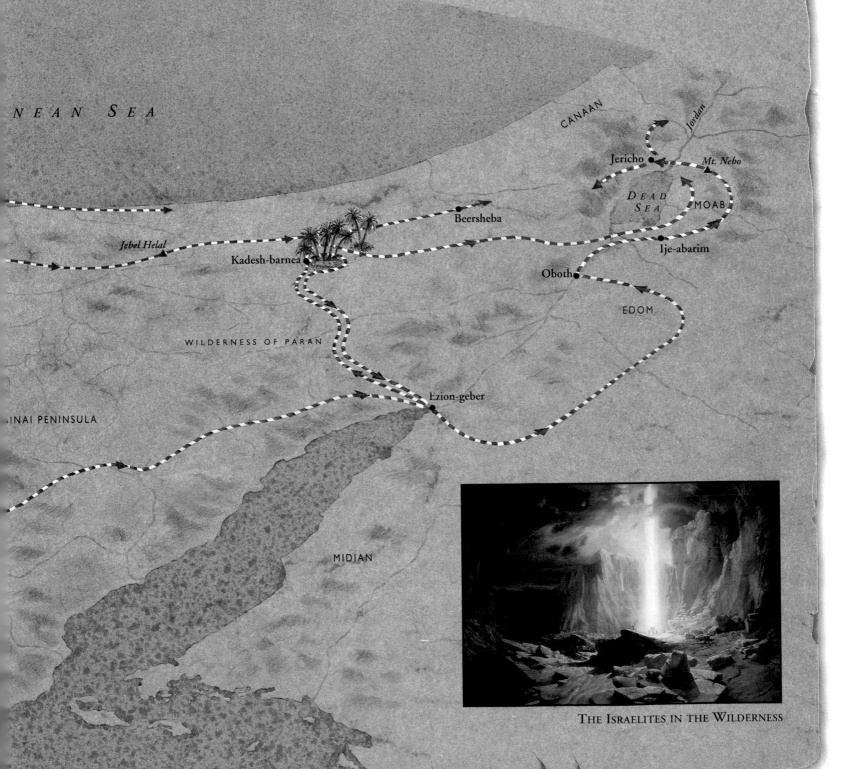

NEAN SEA

CANAAN

Jordan

Jericho

Mt. Nebo

DEAD SEA

MOAB

Beersheba

Jebel Helal

Kadesh-barnea

Ije-abarim

Oboth

EDOM

WILDERNESS OF PARAN

INAI PENINSULA

Ezion-geber

MIDIAN

THE ISRAELITES IN THE WILDERNESS

BODH GAYA

"The Sage thereupon collected fresh grass from a grass cutter, and, on reaching the foot of the auspicious great tree, sat down and made a vow to win enlightenment."

INDIAN POET ASHVAGOSA (C. FIRST CENTURY A.D.) DESCRIBING THE COMING OF SIDDHARTHA GAUTAMA TO THE PIPAL TREE AT BODH GAYA

A SPIRITUAL EVENT THAT ALTERED THE religious current of the world took place about 2,500 years ago in what is now Bodh Gaya, a small village in northeastern India. For here, below the spreading boughs of a pipal tree, an Indian prince named Siddhartha Gautama, after six fruitless years of seeking the ultimate meaning of life, sat cross-legged and entered a deep meditation. During the course of a moonlit night, he reached enlightenment, or Nirvana, and became the Buddha, the Awakened One, whose teachings would touch the lives of millions of people all over the world.

The tree under whose shady branches Gautama entered his fateful meditation became known later as the Bodhi or Bo ("Enlightenment") tree, and the place was soon recognized as sacred by the Buddha's followers. It was first revered officially by the great Indian Buddhist emperor Ashoka (c.265–238 B.C.), who marked it off from its surroundings with a railing. He also raised a shrine nearby which, later, became the site of the Mahabodhi Temple, whose grand 180-foot tower of honey-coloured stone now dominates the sanctuary.

Many smaller brick shrines and stone stupas, or reliquary mounds, were raised in succeeding eras. And in the 20th century Tibetan, Chinese, Thai and Japanese Buddhist schools have built temples around the shrine, making Bodh Gaya one of the great international Buddhist sites.

All these diverse monuments blend in with Bodh Gaya's natural setting, where shrubs and creeping vines, palm and pipal trees, sway in rhythm with the slowly flowing waters of the Falgu River, which borders the site to the east. At the hub is the pipal tree, said to be a descendant of the original Bo tree, which nestles in the Mahabodhi Temple's shadow – a constant reminder of Gautama's enlightenment.

Siddhartha Gautama was born, according to tradition, in 566 B.C. in Lumbini Grove, in what is now Nepal. The son of a local ruler, he grew up in great luxury, screened from the hardships and suffering of everyday existence. At the age of 29, however, his life reached a crisis point when he saw outside the palace confines, on four different occasions, an old man, a sick man, a corpse and a holy man.

The Mahabodhi Temple, *with its honeycomb of niches, is the most imposing shrine at Bodh Gaya, where, beneath a pipal tree, Siddhartha Gautama reached Buddhahood. According to the seventh-century Chinese pilgrim Xuan Zhang, the temple was once embellished with gold, silver, pearls and other gems. Near the temple is a descendant of the original pipal tree, below which stands a gilded Buddha statue* (ABOVE).

Tibetan monks of the Gelukpa, or Yellow Hat, school walk in procession during a festival at Bodh Gaya. The site has a number of temples belonging to Tibetan, Thai, Japanese and other Buddhist traditions.

This stylized carving of the Buddha's footprint is one of Bodh Gaya's numerous sacred objects and shrines. The footprint, lotus, spoked wheel, empty throne and Bodhi tree were the first symbols used by Buddhist artists to represent the Buddha before he was depicted in human form.

Consumed with a desire to find out the cause of and solution to human suffering, he left his wife and child and set out into the unknown.

For six years, Gautama sought out holy men and practised austerities without finding ultimate truth. Finally, rejecting severe asceticism, he sat down by a pipal tree at what is now Bodh Gaya and made up his mind to stay there until he gained enlightenment. During the next night, he was assailed by Mara, the Evil One, who tried to thwart him with his hordes of grotesque demons and seductive maidens. But Gautama remained unmoved, and Mara conceded defeat.

Then, in deep meditation, Gautama came to know his previous lives and saw how all living things died and were reborn. And, during the early hours of the morning, he realized the cause of human suffering and how it could be overcome. As the full moon shone, turning the pipal's leaves silver, Gautama became the Buddha.

For the next 45 years he travelled around northern India teaching his doctrine that the best spiritual way is a middle path between extremes of self-denial and self-indulgence. He taught until he was 80, when he died peacefully at Kushinagara (modern Kasia) northwest of Bodh Gaya.

This also became a place of pilgrimage, as did both Lumbini Grove and a park near Varanasi (Benares), where he delivered his first sermon. But for Buddhists, Bodh Gaya is still the most revered of the four sites.

From a distance, it is the Mahabodhi Temple that catches the eye, as it soars above Bodh Gaya's trees and its hodgepodge of shrines. The temple, which assumed its present form in about the seventh century A.D. but was subsequently much renovated, rises in a number of horizontal courses and resembles a narrow, truncated pyramid.

Within the temple compound, other monuments associated with the Buddha include a small, whitewashed brick shrine, just inside the entrance to the right. This marks the spot where the Buddha is said to have stood gazing in rapture at the Bo tree with unblinking eyes for a whole week. And parallel to the temple's northern side is the Jewelled Walk, a raised, elongated platform where the Buddha paced back and forth debating whether or not he should reveal the fruits of his enlightenment to the world. Carved lotus flowers mark his footsteps.

South of the temple lies the Muchalinda Lake, its entrance guarded by a pipal. The Buddha was meditating beneath an ancestor of this tree when a torrential thunderstorm struck. But just as the rain began to pour down, Muchalinda, king of the serpents, rose from the waters of the lake, coiled himself around the Buddha and extended his seven hoods to shelter the Lord's head. Northeast of the temple lies the Rainbow shrine, a roofless monument where the Buddha, just after his enlightenment, irradiated a brilliant light that separated into distinct bands of white, yellow, blue, red and orange colour.

Bodh Gaya, however, is greater than the sum of its parts. All its monuments are subsumed by the unifying presence of the Bo tree and revolve around it, like planets orbiting the sun. To this spiritual magnet Buddhists are drawn from all over the world, their saffron or wine-coloured robes standing out like exotic flowers against the green bushes and shrubs.

To watch a monk sitting cross-legged by the Bo tree, his eyes shut and spine erect, is to travel back in time to the moment when Gautama understood the nature of *dukka*, or suffering. From then on, his teaching became a great tree of enlightenment, its roots spreading into the depths of human hearts, its branches reaching out to touch unborn generations of the future.

Coloured flags festoon Bodh Gaya's pipal tree (LEFT), *reputedly descended from the original Bo tree. Pilgrims also tie scarves to its branches, burn incense, and lay cut flowers and small lamps at its foot. Near by is a red sandstone block known as the* vajrasana, *the diamond throne, which, according to tradition, is the seat of the Buddha's meditation. For Buddhists, this spot is the centre of the universe.*

TIMEFRAME

B.C.

566   TRADITIONAL DATE OF SIDDHARTHA GAUTAMA'S BIRTH.

531   GAUTAMA REACHES ENLIGHTENMENT BENEATH THE BODHI TREE AND BECOMES THE BUDDHA.

c.265–238   REIGN OF EMPEROR ASHOKA DURING WHICH BODH GAYA IS OFFICIALLY RECOGNIZED AS A BUDDHIST HOLY SITE.

A.D.

c.7TH CENTURY   THE MAHABODHI TEMPLE IS BUILT IN THE FORM IT NOW RESEMBLES.

c.15TH CENTURY   BODH GAYA BECOMES A HINDU SHRINE, BUT IS ABANDONED AS A PILGRIMAGE CENTRE.

LATE 19TH CENTURY   EXTENSIVE RENOVATIONS OF THE SITE.

1891   BODH GAYA BEGINS TO BE A CENTRE FOR BUDDHIST PILGRIMS AGAIN.

1958   CELEBRATION AT BODH GAYA, AMONG OTHER SACRED SITES, TO COMMEMORATE THE BUDDHA'S 2,500TH BIRTHDAY.

EPHESUS

"Moreover ye see and hear, that not alone at Ephesus, but almost throughout all Asia, this Paul hath persuaded and turned away much people, saying that they be no gods, which are made with hands."

EPHESIAN SILVERSMITH DEMETRIUS REFERRING TO SAINT PAUL (ACTS 19:26)

A BUSTLING PORT OF 250,000 SOULS, Ephesus, situated on the western coast of what is now Turkey, was the home of the temple of Artemis – one of the seven wonders of the ancient world. It was also the chief banking and commercial centre of Asia Minor and one of the great metropolises of the Greco-Roman world.

Apart from being a focus for the cult of Artemis, the city was a magnet for practitioners of magical arts, such as fortune telling, astrology and exorcism. In the first century A.D., it became a seedbed of the new Christian religion, which in centuries to come would blossom as the established religion of the Roman Empire.

According to one tradition, Saint John the Apostle came to Ephesus after the crucifixion, accompanied by Mary, the mother of Jesus, who lived out her days in the city. And according to the book of Acts in the New Testament, Saint Paul stayed in Ephesus for two years, teaching the gospel of Jesus Christ.

Ephesus was first settled by Ionian Greeks from across the Aegean about 1,000 years before the birth of Jesus. These new arrivals found that the local inhabitants worshipped Cybele, a version of the great mother goddess revered throughout the Middle East and western Asia, and they amalgamated her with their own goddess Artemis. Thus they created the powerful hybrid Artemisia Ephesia, a deity associated with wild nature and fertility.

In time, as a result of its strategic location at the head of the Cayster River

The bearded figure *of Saint Paul looms out of a background of gold mosaic from the interior of a Greek Orthodox Church. Paul spent two years in Ephesus teaching the gospel of Jesus Christ during his third missionary journey in the mid-50s A.D. His stay there was the crown of his ministry; at this time his theological development was at its peak, and he wrote some of his major letters to the fledgling Christian churches.*

and its fine harbour, Ephesus developed into an important trade centre. It provided a valuable link between the Near East and Greece and, during the Roman period at the end of the first millennium B.C., with Spain, Sicily and Egypt.

In 550 B.C., the city was captured by King Croesus of Lydia, whose capital of Sardis lay some 60 miles to the east. Croesus, famed for his legendary wealth, set about rebuilding the city. He also presented columns and golden cows for a new and bigger temple of Artemis, or Artemisium. This structure lasted until 356 B.C., when it was burned down by

an egocentric maniac called Herostratus, whose act of arson was inspired solely by a desire to perpetuate his name.

Undaunted by this vandalism, the Ephesians set about creating a new temple that would become one of the wonders of the ancient world. It was completed in the first half of the third century B.C. and had an area four times that of the Parthenon in Athens. Its forest of 127 gleaming marble columns raised its roof nearly 60 feet above the ground. And its sanctuary was filled with magnificent sculptures. The shrine lasted 400 years until it was razed in A.D. 263 by the Goths, a barbarian tribe

***The setting sun** casts a rose light over the stone theatre of Ephesus – the scene of a riot against Saint Paul some 2,000 years ago. Beyond the theatre, the paved Arcadian Way stretches toward the area of what was once the ancient harbour and the sea, which has receded since biblical times.*

originally from northern Europe. Although partially rebuilt, it never regained its former status as Christianity began to take a grip on the Roman world.

In the sixth century, columns from the temple were filched by the Byzantines of Constantinople (modern Istanbul) for use in the construction of Christian cathedrals. And in the course of the following centuries, silting of the Cayster River ruined Ephesus's harbour, ending its days of glory and finally sealing the fate of the temple. Now only the foundations of the Artemisium remain, uncovered by the British engineer J.T. Wood in 1869.

If the citizens of Ephesus in the years before Christ were chiefly devotees of Artemis, it was followers of Christ who came to exert their influence increasingly during the first millennium A.D. And it is Christians who make regular pilgrimages here today. They come to venerate two people in particular: Mary, the Blessed Virgin, and Saint Paul.

The Temple of Hadrian, *the second-century Roman emperor, was one of a number of shrines reflecting the diversity of worship in Ephesus before Christianity tightened its grip on the city in succeeding centuries.*

This footprint *carved into a street was the sign for a brothel, one of the many fleshpots in Ephesus during Paul's time.*

After the crucifixion of Jesus, Saint John the Apostle is said to have taken Mary with him to Ephesus, an event that was referred to by Pope Celestine in the fifth century. But perhaps the most extraordinary substantiation for Mary's presence in Ephesus was provided in more recent times by an invalid German visionary named Katherina Emmerich (1774–1824). For she described in detail the Virgin's house at Ephesus in her *Life of the Blessed Virgin*, even though she had never left Germany.

Toward the end of the 19th century, Catholic priests resident in Smyrna (now Izmir) read her story and in 1891 organized an expedition to Ephesus to see whether there was any truth in it. To their amazement, they found a small chapel-like building perched on a hillside four miles south of the ruins of the city. Its location, structure and setting were almost identical to Katherina's description.

Also, they found that every year, on August 15, local Orthodox Christian pilgrims came to this shrine, which they called Panaya Kapula ("Doorway to the Virgin"), to celebrate the Dormition of the Virgin. In 1892, the archbishop of Smyrna pronounced the building a place of pilgrimage; and, in 1967, its sanctity was endorsed by a visit by Pope Paul VI.

The other major Christian figure at Ephesus was Saint Paul. His lengthy stay in the city was made in the mid-50s, during his third missionary journey around Asia Minor and Greece. A Roman citizen who had formerly persecuted the followers of the nascent Christian religion, Paul had been converted to the way of Jesus Christ after a literally blinding vision on the road to Damascus (Acts 9:1–19).

At Ephesus, Paul taught for three months in the synagogue of the Jewish community until they became hostile to his message. According to Acts, he then moved to the lecture room of a teacher named Tyrannus and, for the next two years, preached to both Jews and Gentiles.

So powerful was Paul's presence that handkerchiefs and aprons that he had touched were given to the sick, who were apparently cured by them. His reputation

Rows of egglike breasts sprout *from the chest of the goddess Artemis in this statue found at Ephesus. Their shape has prompted suggestions that they may be the ova of bees — the bee was the symbol of Ephesus — dates, or testes. Whatever they are, the suggestion of fertility is clear. Artemis, or Diana in Roman mythology, was an earth goddess associated with wild nature and worshipped at the Artemisium, which was one of the largest temples of the ancient world.*

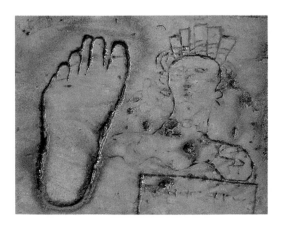

spread – even to the extent that some itinerant Jewish exorcists invoked his name and that of Jesus to rid a madman of an evil spirit. However, these healers were re-buffed when the evil spirit tartly responded to their invocations with the words: "Jesus I know, and Paul I know, but who are you?" Whereupon, the sick man flew at them, ripped their clothing to shreds, and promptly dismissed them.

Reports of this incident spread like wildfire, adding to Paul's authority. It also deeply impressed many dabblers in magical arts, who brought out their books of secret spells, known as Ephesian Letters, heaped them up, and burned them. As Acts puts it: "So mightily grew the word of God...."

The most famous and dangerous incident that befell Paul at Ephesus happened as he was planning to leave the city for Greece (Acts 19:23–40). The trouble started when a silversmith named Demetrius called a guild meeting about the threat Paul was posing to their craft of making small silver copies of Artemis's shrine to sell to pilgrims. A fiery dema-gogue, Demetrius stirred up the gathering, accusing Paul of destroying their trade with his assertion that gods made by hand were not gods at all and with his contempt for the goddess's shrine. The silversmiths, worked up into a frenzy, began to shout "Great is Artemis of the Ephesians".

Soon the town was in uproar. Filled with the fury of a lynch mob, a crowd rushed into the 24,000-seat theatre drag-ging with them two of Paul's companions,

Bristling with ancient buildings, *Ephesus* (ABOVE LEFT) *is one of the major sites of Turkey. Its more notable monuments include the library of Celsus (**1**) and the Arcadian Way (**2**), which led to the ancient harbour (**3**). The theatre (**4**) lay at the heart of the city, south of the stadium (**5**), while the Artemisium (**6**) stood to the northeast. A road (**7**) leads south to the House of the Virgin Mary.*

26

Dappled with sunlight and enclosed by trees, the House of the Virgin Mary stands a few miles south of the main Ephesus site. It has become a major pilgrimage place for Christians.

Gaius and Aristarchus. Paul immediately leaped to their aid, but was restrained by friendly officials, who feared that the apostle would be torn limb from limb. Meanwhile, the theatre was a scene of total chaos, with people milling around shouting, many having no idea why they were there in the first place. A Jew named Alexander attempted to address the crowd. But seeing that he was of the same race as the accursed Paul, they shouted him down and began to chant "Great is Artemis of the Ephesians" in hypnotic unison for two solid hours.

An end to the madness came only when the town clerk stood up and coolly pointed out that Paul and his companions had not actually blasphemed against Artemis and that there were perfectly good law courts in which to bring grievances. More to the point, he raised the spectre of severe Roman reprisals if rioting broke out in the city. The clerk's words brought the people to their senses, and the crowd dispersed. Any doubts Paul may have had about leaving Ephesus must have vanished, for he set out for Macedonia immediately.

Today, visitors can wander around the massive site of Ephesus along streets that Paul – and possibly the Virgin Mary – would have trod. Of all the monuments still recognizable from Paul's time, the theatre best evokes the apostle's memory. Here, sitting on its stone seats, it is possible to imagine the silversmiths' chanting resounding around the tiers. It symbolized, in effect, the death cries of paganism becoming increasingly desperate before the deafeningly still voice of Christianity.

TIMEFRAME

B.C

c.1000	FIRST GREEK SETTLERS ARRIVE AT EPHESUS.
550	CROESUS OF LYDIA CAPTURES THE CITY.
356	THE TEMPLE OF ARTEMIS IS BURNED DOWN.

A.D.

c.55	PAUL COMES TO EPHESUS.
c.65	PAUL DIES A MARTYR'S DEATH IN ROME.
263	THE GOTHS DESTROY THE ARTEMISIUM.
1841	PUBLICATION OF KATHERINA EMMERICH'S BOOK DESCRIBING THE VIRGIN'S HOUSE AT EPHESUS.
1869	J.T. WOOD DISCOVERS THE REMAINS OF THE ARTEMISIUM.
1892	THE VIRGIN'S HOUSE IS PRONOUNCED A PLACE OF PILGRIMAGE BY THE ARCHBISHOP OF SMYRNA.
1967	POPE PAUL VI VISITS THE HOUSE OF THE VIRGIN.

PAUL'S THIRD JOURNEY

Convinced that the Christian Gospel was intended by God to reach all humanity, Gentiles as well as Jews, the apostle Paul made a series of long, arduous missions in the mid-first century A.D. to spread the teachings of Jesus Christ. Paul's third journey is shown here, along with a few of the major sacred monuments of his day: the Temple of Herod the Great in Jerusalem; the Temple of Artemis in Ephesus; and the Temple of the Divine Julius Caesar in Rome. Paul started at Antioch in Syria. His route took him west, through various towns in which congregations had already been founded, and then to Ephesus (pp. 22–27). There he stayed for over two years before crossing from Asia to Europe via Troas.

Paul then made his way to Corinth, a port with a reputation for moral laxity but also a centre of Greek

ITALY

Danube

MACEDONIA

Philippi

Thessalonica

Rome *(Temple of the Divine Julius Caesar)*

AEGEAN SEA

Athens

Corinth

SICILY

MALTA

MEDITERRANEA

THE RUINS OF ANCIENT CORINTH

culture. Paul stayed there for three months and wrote his important letter to the Christians in Rome. But he also met with opposition, and when a plot by resident Jews prevented him from sailing direct to Syria, he set off overland via Macedonia and then by boat – Roman transport vessel – to Tyre, thus ending his mission.

Although he was given a prophetic warning that he would be arrested if he proceeded to Jerusalem from Tyre, Paul still went. But the prophecy was fulfilled: some Jews rioted against him because they thought he had broken Jewish law by taking a Gentile into the Temple. Paul was arrested by the Romans and, after interrogation, claimed his right as a Roman to be tried in Rome, which was respected; but his journey to the greatest city in the western world was his last: in about A.D. 65, he was, according to tradition, martyred.

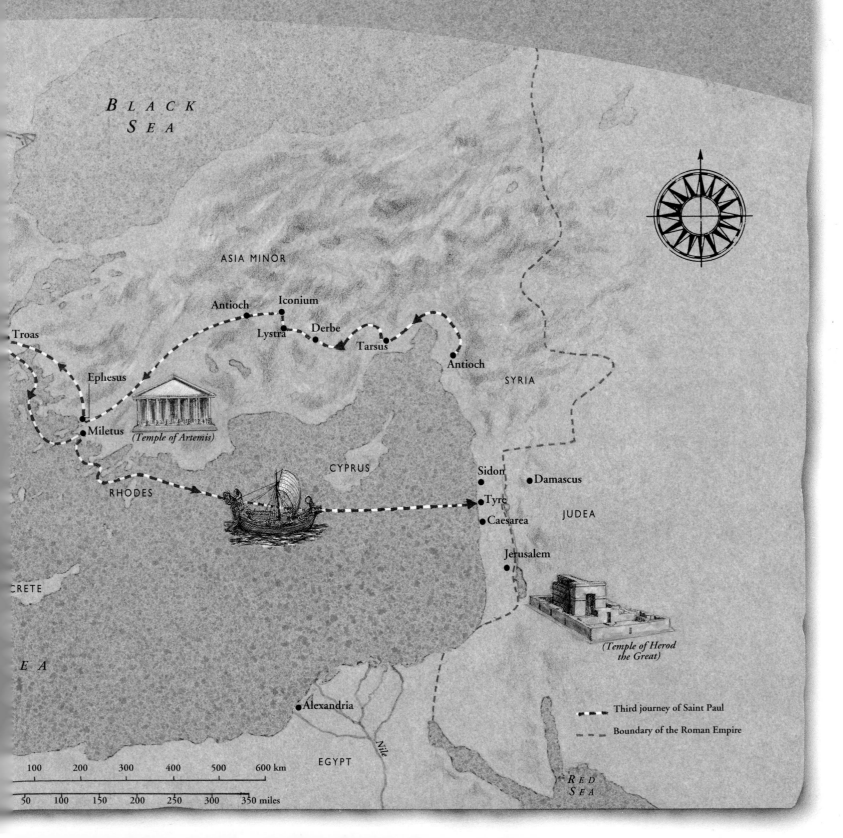

BLACK SEA

ASIA MINOR

Antioch Iconium
Troas
Derbe
Lystra
Tarsus
Ephesus
Antioch
SYRIA
Miletus
(Temple of Artemis)

CYPRUS

Sidon Damascus

RHODES
Tyre
Caesarea JUDEA

Jerusalem

CRETE

(Temple of Herod
the Great)

E A

Alexandria

Nile
EGYPT

| 100 | 200 | 300 | 400 | 500 | 600 km |

| 50 | 100 | 150 | 200 | 250 | 300 | 350 miles |

RED SEA

- - - Third journey of Saint Paul

- - - Boundary of the Roman Empire

IONA

"That man is little to be envied, whose patriotism would not gain force upon the plain of Marathon, or whose piety would not grow warmer among the ruins of Iona."

BRITISH WRITER DR. SAMUEL JOHNSON, WHO VISITED IONA IN 1773

A SMALL ELONGATED ISLAND LYING OFF the western coast of Scotland, Iona has an unrivalled place in the spiritual history of Britain. For it was from this windswept, mostly flat strip of land that the great saint Columba (521–597) brought the bright light of the Christian faith to the pagan Picts of Scotland.

Although it lacks the majestic glens and forests of the mainland, Iona has its own special charm. Its low-lying terrain and slender girth make the visitor constantly aware of its island status. To the west, the silvery Atlantic flecked with small islands stretches away to the horizon; unseen to the south lie the mist-enshrouded hills of Ireland, Columba's homeland; and to the east the damson-hued mountains of Mull

rise across a sound so narrow that monks used to shout across it to attract the attention of the ferryman.

Nor is Iona's enchantment one of purely natural beauty, although the clarity of its light, its secret coves, white sands washed by foaming waves, and its exposure to the elements and the night's canopy of stars are conducive to an "atmosphere of miracle". For its topography is sacred, inextricably bound up with the life and actions of Columba and his monks.

At the southern tip of the island, for example, there is the spot where Columba and his 12 companions first landed by boat from Ireland in 563. And on a hill nearby, Columba looked back toward his homeland, since he had vowed to settle only in a place where Ireland was completely out of sight. There is also Cnoc an t-Sidhein, a small hillock where the saint had a vision of angels, and, in a more sinister vein, the White Strand of the Monks, where later Ionan monks were massacred by raiding Vikings in 986.

After Columba's death in 597, the island remained famous for its Celtic Christian spirituality for centuries. Missionaries of the Columban Church continued to make converts in northern Britain and farther abroad, and it was only with the start of raids by Viking marauders in 794 that its influence began to wane. There were further Viking attacks in the 9th and 10th centuries, these bellicose Scandinavians finding rich pickings among the sacred treasures of the pious and scholarly monks.

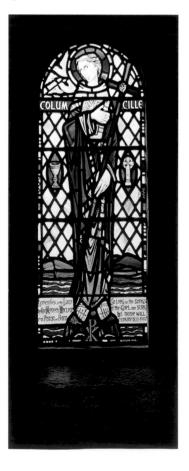

Saint Columba, "the morning star of Scotland's faith", is famous for bringing Christianity to pagan Scotland in the sixth century A.D. This modern stained glass window in Iona Abbey shows his Celtic name Columcille, meaning "Colum of the church".

The medieval abbey of Iona, *set against a backdrop of the mountains of Mull, stands on the site of Columba's original settlement. From the 9th to the 11th centuries, the abbey graveyard was the burial place of 48 kings of Scotland, including Macbeth, later immortalized by William Shakespeare.*

During the Middle Ages, a Benedictine abbey was built on the island, in 1203, confirming its place as part of mainstream Roman Catholic Christianity, as opposed to the Celtic Christianity that Columba had practised. (The two types differed only in certain practical matters, such as the date of Easter and the type of tonsure monks should adopt.) However, from this time on, Iona was never influential beyond its immediate locality. Gradually, over the

centuries, especially after the Reformation in the 16th century, the abbey church and other buildings fell into decay, becoming a picturesque ruin for travellers. Major restoration work finally took place in three phases, from 1874 to 1876, 1902 to 1910, and from 1938 onward.

Although the medieval abbey is the main attraction for visitors, it is the presiding spirit of Columba that makes the island unique. He was born in a wild and

Sunlight gilds the elegant columns of the cloisters that form the peaceful heart of the abbey. Clustered around them are the chapter house to the east, the refectory to the north, and the medieval abbey church to the south.

mountainous region of Donegal in northwestern Ireland in 521. Royal blood flowed in his veins, since his father was descended from Niall of the Nine Hostages, high king of Ireland from 379 to 405. Christianity had come to Ireland through the evangelizing of Saint Patrick (*c*.389–461) and the young Columba received a sound Christian education in monastic schools under a number of learned churchmen. At the age of 25, he was self-confident and well-trained enough to found the monastery of Derry (now officially called Londonderry) in present-day Ulster, or Northern Ireland.

Columba then went on to preach up and down the country for about 15 years, founding hundreds of churches and monasteries, including those of Durrow and also Kells, which is famous for its illuminated gospels. All this time, he was able to hone the organizational skills and powers of leadership that would later serve him well.

The reason for Columba's mission to Scotland is shrouded in mystery. According to one tradition, he may have played a part in provoking an intertribal battle between his kinsmen – the northern Uí Neill clan – and the southern Uí Neills. Filled with remorse, Columba was charged by a church synod to go into exile and convert as many souls to Christianity as those who had fallen in battle. This account, however, does not appear in the biography of Columba by the later Ionan monk Adamnan (*c*.628–704), who simply states that the saint left Ireland for Britain at the age of 42, "desiring to seek a foreign country for the sake of Christ".

In any event, in 563, with his 12 companions, Columba set sail northward toward the islands of Scotland, braving the seas in a coracle, a small boat made of animal skins bound to a wicker framework with leather thongs and sealed with pitch. He first landed on the tiny island of Oronsay, but, determined that his beloved Ireland should not be visible from his new home, he set off again and reached Iona. Here, near the gravelly beach and cliffs of what is now called Port of the Coracle, he climbed a small hill and, gazing in the

Waves sweep into the Port of the Coracle on the southern tip of Iona, where Columba and his 12 companions landed in 563. Flanked by heather-clad cliffs and divided in two by a large humpback rock – the end of which is visible on the left – this small secluded bay is one of the sacred spots visited by pilgrims. A grassy mound near the bay was once believed to conceal Columba's coracle; however, excavations have been unable to substantiate this.

direction of Ireland, found the horizon empty. This, he decided, was the place he would make his spiritual base for the rest of his life.

Columba and his companions set to work to make Iona their home. For food, they fished, grazed cattle, and grew crops on the light lime-enriched sandy earth on the west of the island. They hunted seals for meat and for oil, which they used in lamps. And they surrounded their wood and wattle huts, as well as their oaken church, kiln, kitchen, stables, mill, and guesthouse with a vallum – a bank and a ditch.

None of these structures has survived the combination of Viking sword and fire and centuries of rain and fierce Atlantic winds. However, the abbey and other ruins, which all date from the Middle Ages, partly occupy the site of Columba's dwellings and thus perpetuate the sacred tradition of the place.

In time, as Columba's reputation for saintliness grew, more young followers came to Iona and the community prospered. After some two years of a strict monastic regime, which included farming and copying manuscripts as well as prayer and austere living, Columba set out to accomplish his real vocation – the conversion of pagan Scotland to Christianity.

At this time, what is now Scotland was split between four peoples. In the northern regions were the Picts, a fierce Celtic people who were once feared by the Romans; in the southwest were the Celtic Britons of Strathclyde; in the southeast lived the Angles, or English, who had originated from Germany; and in the west there was a colony of Irish Celts known as the Dal

Saint Martin's cross stands next to the abbey and dates from the ninth century. Here, its west side shows the Virgin and Child in the centre surrounded by animals and human figures; serpents and round bosses adorn the lower part of the shaft.

Riada, who had come from Antrim in northeastern Ireland in the fifth century. These Irish Celts, to whom Columba was related by blood, were also known as Scots, and it was this name which later became applied to the whole of the country.

Columba's plan of conversion was to target first the top man: King Brude of the northern Picts, whose kingdom lay in Inverness in the northeast. So, setting out with a few companions, Columba travelled on foot along the Great Glen, the continuous loch-filled valley that stretches diagonally across the country from southwest to northeast. But when they reached Brude's fortress, the king refused to open the gates. So Columba, making the sign of the cross, knocked on the gates, which flew open of their own accord. Impressed by this piece of magic as well as by Columba's preaching of the one true God, Brude accepted the new faith.

That was only the beginning. In the following years, Columba spent much time among the Picts, challenging the power of their Druid priests. And Columban monks continually crossed over from Iona to consolidate their leader's work. Building churches and preaching the gospel, they turned Scotland into a Christian nation. Columba himself gained a reputation for being a strong, pragmatic statesman as well as a wise and good man, and clan chiefs and kings sought him out for advice.

But despite his travels and adventures – including a successful confrontation with the Loch Ness monster in what was perhaps the first recorded sighting – Columba always returned to Iona. Here, he

Dr. Samuel Johnson visited Iona in 1773 and spent the night in a barn. He referred to the place as the "luminary of the Caledonian regions".

guided his monks, prayed and meditated, copied manuscripts (an art for which he was famed), and studied.

And it was on this secluded island especially that the saint had mystic encounters with the divine and performed miracles. On the small hillock named Cnoc an t-Sidhein, for example, Columba was reputedly visited by angels. According to his biographer Adamnan, "holy angels, the citizens of the holy country, clad in white robes and flying with wonderful speed, began to stand around the saint while he prayed; and after a short converse with the blessed man, the heavenly host, as if feeling itself detected, flew speedily back again to the highest heavens."

On another occasion, a monk named Colga was praying by the gate of the church on Iona when suddenly he saw it

"filled with heavenly light, which more quickly than he could tell, flashed like lightning from his gaze. He did not know that Columba was praying at that time in the church…."

Columba's time on earth ended in the summer of 597. By this time, the saint was too frail to walk any distance, and so, one day, sensing his imminent death, he asked to be taken in a cart to the fields in the west of the island to tell his brethren tilling the soil that he would soon die.

About a week later, while he was resting on his way back from the granary to the

A crown of doves forms a snowy aureole above the abbey church. The bird is emblematic of Columba, whose name is Latin for "dove". Early churchmen also pointed out that "Iona" is the Hebrew word for dove.

monastery, Columba's old white packhorse came up to him and rested its head on the saint's chest, uttering cries of distress and weeping like a human. When Diarmaid, Columba's attendant, tried to shoo it away, the saint forbade him, saying that God had obviously made known to the animal that its master was about to leave it.

Columba then climbed a hill overlooking the monastery and blessed his foundation, saying: "On this place, small and mean though it be, shall not only the kings of the Scots and their people, but also the rulers of foreign and barbarous nations and their subjects confer great and unusual honour; the saints also of other churches even shall regard it with no common reverence." And returning to his hut, he took up his pen and continued his task of transcribing the psalter (the book of Psalms) until he reached Psalm 34, verse 10: "They that seek the Lord shall not want any good thing...." Here he stopped.

That night, as the church bell tolled at midnight, Columba went to the church to pray for the last time. The faithful Diarmaid, followed by other monks holding blazing torches, entered soon after and found Columba lying before the altar, dying. Held in Diarmaid's arms, Columba feebly raised his right hand to bless them and then gave up his last breath. After three days of mourning, the saint's body was buried in a simple grave. By tradition, the site of this grave is now occupied by the small chapel known as Saint Columba's shrine beside the main door of the abbey.

"When in some future time I shall sit in a madly crowded assembly... and the wish arises to retire into the loneliness, I shall think of Iona..." wrote the German composer Felix Mendelssohn. Scotland's wild nature and the sound of waves breaking on the rocks inspired his well-known Hebrides Overture, *written between 1830 and 1832.*

Thus ended the life of one of the greatest Christian figures of his age, whose charisma seems to have permeated the natural fabric of the island. For visitors to Iona have long been impressed by its sacred atmosphere, among them the British writer and wit Dr. Samuel Johnson (1709–84) and the German composer Felix Mendelssohn (1809–47). In a letter written from Glasgow dated August 10, 1829, Mendelssohn expressed the enchantment of Iona's romantic history and ruins and, most of all, its isolation: "If I had my home on Iona, and lived there upon melancholy as other people do upon their rents, my darkest moment would be when in that wide space, that deals in nothing but cliffs and sea-gulls, suddenly a curl of steam should appear, followed by a ship and finally by a gay party in veils and frock-coats, which would look for an hour at the ruins and graves and the three little huts for the living, and then move off again."

Although modern day-trippers would seem to have fulfilled Mendelssohn's fears, Iona's tranquillity still remains unimpaired. And perhaps in the future there will come a time when this little island will once again become a preeminent centre of monasticism and scholarship, just as a prophecy, which is traditionally ascribed to Columba, predicts: "In Iona of my heart, Iona of my love, instead of the chanting of monks shall be the lowing of cattle. But before the world comes to an end, Iona shall be as it was."

TIMEFRAME	
A.D.	
521	SAINT COLUMBA IS BORN IN DONEGAL, IRELAND.
563	COLUMBA AND HIS 12 COMPANIONS LAND ON IONA AT THE PORT OF THE CORACLE.
597	COLUMBA DIES.
794	VIKINGS ATTACK IONA FOR THE FIRST TIME.
986	IONAN MONKS ARE MASSACRED BY VIKINGS.
1203	THE BENEDICTINE ABBEY IS BUILT ON THE SITE OF COLUMBA'S ORIGINAL SETTLEMENT.
1561	AS A RESULT OF THE REFORMATION, THE SCOTTISH PARLIAMENT PASSES AN ACT TO SUPPRESS MONASTERIES; IONA'S BUILDINGS ARE DISMANTLED.
1874	RESTORATION OF THE ABBEY CHURCH BEGINS.
1938	THE REV. GEORGE MACLEOD FOUNDS THE IONA COMMUNITY, AFFILIATED WITH THE CHURCH OF SCOTLAND, WHICH RESTORES THE REMAINING ABBEY BUILDINGS.

ISRAEL

THE DOME OF THE ROCK

"At the dawn, when the light of the sun first strikes the Dome and the drum catches the rays, then is this edifice a marvellous sight to behold...."

MUSLIM CHRONICLER MUQADDASI (*FL.*10TH CENTURY)

FROM THE MOUNT OF OLIVES LOOKING southwest, the tawny landscape around the old city of Jerusalem stretches away, encrusted with the white rectangles of buildings and patches of dark green cypresses. In the foreground a honey-coloured stone wall draws its crenellations along in a rough trapezoidal shape, cordoning off the area known as Temple Mount from the rest of the old city.

The Mount is sacred space *par excellence*. Here, King Solomon built his magnificent temple in the 10th century B.C., in whose holy of holies the ark of the covenant was kept, watched over by sphinxlike cherubim. Solomon's temple and the two later ones that occupied the site have long since been consigned to history and the imagination. But their place has been taken by the shrine of another faith: the Dome of the Rock, revered by Muslims as the embarkation point of the Prophet Muhammad on his legendary ascent to heaven.

Setting suns have burnished the Dome a deeper shade of gold for 1,300 years, ever since the shrine was completed in A.D. 691 by Caliph ("Successor") Abd al-Malik of the Umayyad dynasty, whose power base was the city of Damascus in Syria. With its golden curves that seem beaten to "airy thinness", the Dome rises from a circular drum encircled by a sloping roof and an octagon of walls sheathed in marble and predominantly blue glazed tiles.

From afar, the harmonious proportions and the transitional movement upward from octagon to drum to dome give this

A bud of gold bursting forth over Jerusalem, the Dome of the Rock is one of Islam's holiest shrines. Built in the seventh century A.D., the Dome encloses an outcrop of rock held sacred by Muslims, Jews, and Christians. Muslims believe it was the departure point for the Prophet Muhammad's legendary journey to heaven.

36

Inside the Dome, *the rock is encircled by arches supported by columns taken from the ruins of Jerusalem churches destroyed by the Persians in 614. The rock is reputedly marked by Muhammad's footprint – left as he pushed off upward toward heaven – as well as by the grip marks of the Angel Gabriel as he thwarted the rock's desire to follow the Prophet.*

Temple Mount *is shown in its context within the old city of Jerusalem in this aerial view. In front of the golden cupola of the Dome of the Rock is the dome of the Aqsa Mosque. This was built in the early eighth century, but only reached its final form in 1035 after being rebuilt following its destruction by an earthquake. The Crusaders used it as a church and, in 1168, Saladin donated a pulpit of ivory and mother-of-pearl. This, however, was burned in a fire in 1969.*

ISRAEL

jewel of Islam a sense of lightness, almost as if the Dome could expand and rise gently into the skies like a golden hot-air balloon. Its simple interconnecting lines and hard, light-reflecting surfaces suggest a structure of the space age as much as a shrine of antiquity. For a shrine it is – not a mosque as is commonly supposed – and the third holiest in Islam, after the Ka'aba at Mecca and the Great Mosque at Medina. And the focal point of its sacredness lies not so much in the golden dome, but in what it artfully conceals: an oblong mass of rock, 56 feet by 42 feet, which, according to tradition, is the peak of the biblical Mount Moriah, where Abraham offered up his son Isaac for sacrifice.

Although Muslims hold Abraham to be a great prophet, their pious regard for the rock stems from Muhammad's night journey. This is briefly referred to at the beginning of *sura* (chapter) 17 of the Qur'an: "Celebrated be the praises of Him who took his servant on a journey by night from the Sacred Mosque [i.e. the Ka'aba] to the Remote Mosque [i.e. the temple at Jerusalem], the precinct of which we have blessed, to show him our signs!"

Popular tradition has fleshed out the bones of the Qur'anic verse to give a more vivid version: one night, while the Prophet was at Mecca, some time before his emigration to Medina in 622, he was woken by the Angel Gabriel. He presented Muhammad with a strange celestial winged creature called al-Buraq ("Lightning"), which had the face of a woman and a peacock's tail, and was somewhere between a horse and donkey in size. Riding the steed through the skies to Jerusalem, Muhammad met Abraham, Moses, Jesus, and other prophets and prayed with them at the site of the temple of Solomon – the sacred rock of Temple Mount.

Then, from the rock, Muhammad climbed a supernatural ladder of light through the seven heavens to come

In a blaze of glory, *the Prophet Muhammad leaves the rock below the clouds as he soars heavenward astride al-Buraq – a strange hybrid winged steed with the head of a woman. Angels fly around him bearing* *witness to his celestial voyage. This Persian miniature was painted during the reign of the 16th-century Safavid king, Shah Tahmasp. The artist has followed the convention of not depicting the Prophet's features.*

eventually before Allah, who instructed the Prophet about prayer. Muhammad returned to earth by the same ladder and flew back to Mecca on al-Buraq, arriving before the night was over.

Today, the rock – the launching place for Muhammad's celestial journey – is softly lit by windows whose symmetrical patterns of coloured glass are set in the walls of the drum and octagon. It is enclosed by an intricately carved wooden screen into which has been inserted a rectangular shrine crowned with a cupola and containing relics of the Prophet, including a hair from his head. Two circular arcades of marble columns and piers create an inner and outer walkway, or ambulatory, allowing pilgrims to perform the ritual circumambulation (*tawaf*) which also occurs at the Ka'aba at Mecca.

The chief glory, however, is the interior of the dome. Its gold and red arabesques subtly decrease in size from the outer rim, converging on the centre and drawing the eye upward to a seventh heaven of artistic sublimity. From the irradiating sunlike centre hangs a chain, which once supported a chandelier; and, in a band near the apex, a Qur'anic inscription proclaims in Kufic script: "God, there is no god but He, the living, the selfsubsistent. Slumber takes Him not, nor sleep. His is what is in the Heavens and what is in the earth."

The dome works in tandem with the rock. Without the rock, the dome would be merely a virtuoso work of art totally devoid of a spiritual *raison d'être*. Conversely, without the majestic dome soaring above it, the rock's ancient power would be dissipated, uncontained, its connection

A mesmeric kaleidoscope of gilt and plaster, the dome, which stands 70 feet above the ground, presents a vision of cosmic harmony.

The Dome's oblong rock (3) *lies at the heart of its octagonal structure. The eight-sided form was not original to Abd al-Malik's architects, since the Romans had used it. But its combination with drum and dome was new. Four of the eight sides have doors that face the cardinal points. And the columns create inner and outer walkways (**1** and **2**) for ritual circumambulation.*

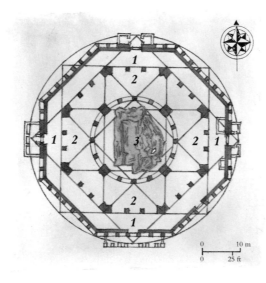

with the Prophet's heavenly journey visually undermined.

The Muslims first gained access to Temple Mount in 638 when an Arab army under Caliph Omar Ibn al-Khattab forced Sophronius, the patriarch of Byzantine-ruled Jerusalem, to surrender the city. The devout and austere Omar entered the city with his men as the inhabitants held their breath, fearing for their lives. But the bloodbath that had occurred in Jerusalem 24 years before when the Persians sacked the city was not to recur this time.

Instead, the caliph asked to be taken around the city and be shown the sacred places, including the Church of the Holy Sepulchre, Christendom's holiest temple. Invited by Sophronius to pray at the church, the caliph showed his respect for Christianity by refusing the offer,

41

THE DOME OF THE ROCK

explaining that if he prayed there, it would encourage his followers to convert the church into a mosque. Omar was later taken to Temple Mount, where he found the holy rock neglected and covered in litter. He ordered it to be cleaned up and forbade prayers there until it had been purified by rainfall.

It was another 53 years before Muslim pilgrims to Jerusalem would be greeted by the golden dome flashing with sunlight in the distance. The shrine was finished in 691, its structure based on traditional Byzantine architectural elements that were embellished with distinctive Islamic decoration. It was paid for with seven years of

Jerusalem lies at the centre of the stylized continents of Europe, Asia, and Africa in this 16th-century German engraving. *The idea of Jerusalem as a holy city at the hub of the world helped to inspire the Crusaders' campaigns to recapture it from the Muslims.*

revenue from the Muslim province of Egypt, where enough gold was collected to guarantee that the entire dome was gilded.

No description of the Dome exists from the period of the Umayyad caliphs (which ended in A.D. 750). However, an early 11th-century Muslim writer named Ibn al-Faqih recorded that 300 lamps lit the shrine every night and that it was covered in white marble, with its roof in red gold. It is also said that the shrine was cleansed and purified by water perfumed with attar of roses, musk, and saffron. An atmosphere conducive to higher thoughts was created by the burning of incense and fragrant wood, and by lamps filled with sweet-smelling oil.

From the time of its construction to the present day, the Dome has undergone repairs, renovations, and alterations. Even so, its basic structure and decoration are largely the same as when it was first completed. The dome itself collapsed in

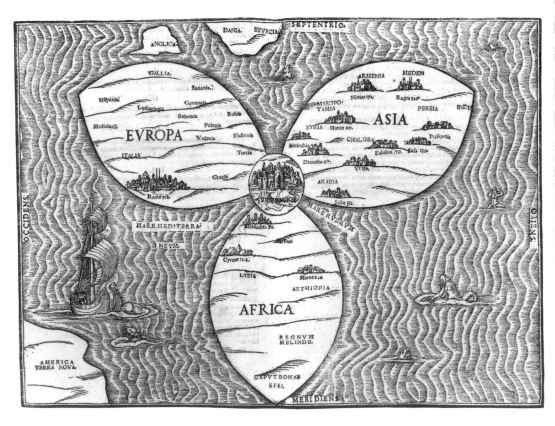

42

1016, during the rule of the Fatimid dynasty, but was soon rebuilt. When the Christian Crusaders stormed Jerusalem in 1099, massacring its inhabitants, they converted the Dome to a Christian shrine, naming it *Templum Domini* ("Temple of Our Lord").

The Crusaders replaced the Muslim crescent on top of the dome with a gold cross and set up an altar on the rock, before which they cut out steps. Nor did mutilation of the rock end there: because Christian pilgrims were disposed to chip off bits of it for souvenirs or to sell as holy relics, it had to be protected by a marble panel. This was removed after the capture of Jerusalem in 1187 by the great Muslim general Salah al-Din, known to the west as Saladin. Twelve years later, the wooden screen which can be seen now was erected.

Other work on the Dome included replacing the mosaics on the drum and upper walls with brilliantly coloured tiles from Kashan in Persia during the reign of the Ottoman sultan Süleyman the Magnificent (1520–66); and the repair of the wooden ceiling and mosaics, and the releading of the dome in 1874 by Sultan Abd al-Aziz. In the 20th century, a complete restoration of the monument was carried out from 1956 to 1962, when the lead outer dome was replaced by a lighter one of gold-coloured aluminium.

Withstanding the ebb and flow of history, the Dome of the Rock is still the golden hub of Jerusalem, itself a city that in the eyes of medieval writers lay at the centre of the world. In its inspired lines and proportions, the shrine transcends narrow sectarian religiosity and points toward a universal divine principle. It still remains as much a wonder of the world as when the medieval Muslim chronicler Muqaddasi watched the light of dawn strike its golden surface a thousand years ago and proclaimed it a sight "that in all Islam I have not seen equalled...."

With the serene Dome lifting *their hearts, devout Muslims on Temple Mount face Mecca as they perform one of the five daily prayers prescribed by Islam. The Dome continues to provide a spiritual focus for Muslim Arabs living in and around Jerusalem, especially since the Six Day War in 1967, when the Israelis captured the city.*

TIMEFRAME

B.C.

*c.*950	THE TEMPLE OF SOLOMON IS BUILT IN JERUSALEM ON WHAT IS NOW CALLED TEMPLE MOUNT.
587/6	THE BABYLONIANS SACK JERUSALEM AND DESTROY THE TEMPLE.

A.D.

70	THE ROMANS CAPTURE JERUSALEM AND RAZE THE TEMPLE OF HEROD THE GREAT.
570	MUHAMMAD, THE PROPHET OF ISLAM, IS BORN.
638	JERUSALEM SURRENDERS TO A MUSLIM ARAB ARMY.
687–691	THE DOME OF THE ROCK IS CONSTRUCTED.
1099	THE CRUSADERS CAPTURE JERUSALEM.
1537	SÜLEYMAN THE MAGNIFICENT RESTORES THE DOME.
1948	FOUNDATION OF THE STATE OF ISRAEL.
1967	DURING THE SIX DAY WAR, ISRAELI TROOPS SEIZE THE OLD CITY OF JERUSALEM, INCLUDING TEMPLE MOUNT.

IN HONOUR
OF THE DEAD

IN ANCIENT CIVILIZATIONS, THE BURIAL place or tomb was not only a repository for the dead, but also an entrance into another world. Here the deceased could enjoy the afterlife and, it was hoped, confer manifold blessings upon the living. In many cultures, when the bodies of the deceased, especially those of royalty and nobles, were laid to rest, they were accompanied by household and precious goods – objects thought to be of use in the after-life. In Grave Circle A at MYCENAE in Greece, for example, the German archaeologist Heinrich Schliemann found an array of golden funerary objects, including a face mask he thought had belonged to the legendary Greek warrior-king Agamemnon. In a similar vein, the Viking ship burial at OSEBERG in Norway has yielded a hoard of richly carved wooden objects; and the TOMB COMPLEX OF SHI HUANGDI, the first Chinese emperor, is famous for the grand army of terracotta soldiers that were unearthed in pits around the emperor's unexcavated burial mound, which promises to contain further treasures. The belief in the afterlife is perhaps most strikingly evident in two burial places of the contrasting cultures of ancient Egypt and Christianity: the PYRAMIDS OF GIZA are the grandest funerary monuments in the world and housed the bodies of the pharaohs who, the Egyptians believed, would in death travel to the sun god. On a somewhat more intimate scale, the CATACOMBS OF ROME were the tombs of early Christians, and the sacred art depicted on their walls proclaims the sovereignty of Jesus Christ over death.

Sacred burial grounds and treasures of the afterlife

The pyramids of Giza near Cairo, the final resting place of the pharaohs, and one of the seven wonders of the ancient world.

NEWGRANGE

"When one considers the multitude of hands, the length of time…which conspired to form this stupendous monument…one cannot but repine at the caprice of fate and fame…that the name, which it was to perpetuate, is gone."

ANTIQUARIAN SIR THOMAS POWNALL, WHO VISITED NEWGRANGE IN 1769

ON DECEMBER 21, 1969, THE IRISH archaeologist Michael O'Kelly stood inside the dark cavelike chamber within the prehistoric grave mound of Newgrange in northeastern Ireland. Ready to record his impressions on tape, O'Kelly waited for the sun to rise on the shortest day of the year. For, during his excavations on the mound, begun in 1962, O'Kelly had heard local traditions that at particular times of the year, a beam of sunlight penetrated the mound's 60-foot-long passage, illuminating the chamber at the end.

Minutes before 9 A.M., O'Kelly was rewarded with a scene that must have been familiar to the builders of Newgrange, 5,000 years ago: "At exactly 8.54 hours GMT the top edge of the ball of the sun appeared above the local horizon and at 8.58 hours, the first pencil of direct sunlight shone through the roof-box and along the passage to reach across the tomb chamber floor… As the thin line of light widened… the tomb was dramatically illuminated…."

In fact, O'Kelly had witnessed this solar revelation in 1967. But it was only two years later that he recorded his impressions for posterity, confirming that, like the ancient megaliths of Stonehenge in Britain, Newgrange had been deliberately aligned with a key moment in the solar calendar.

For the builders of Newgrange, the winter solstice would have marked the lengthening of the day in the year's cycle and the dawning of a new year and, at a symbolic level, the conquest of light over darkness, life over death.

Faced with sparkling white quartz and rising about 30 feet, Newgrange is one of Europe's finest prehistoric passage graves. The mound was built with some 200,000 river stones, about the size of grapefruits, interspersed with layers of turf that helped to stabilize the structure. A circle of standing stones, one of which is shown here at left, surrounded the mound.

Eerily lit by candles,

Newgrange's corbelled chamber lies at the end of a 62-foot-long passage. The remains of human bones, both cremated and unburned, as well as steatite "marbles", pendants, beads, and a bone chisel – thought to have been funeral offerings placed with the dead bodies – were found within the chamber. However, the life and culture of the mound's prehistoric builders remains shrouded in mystery.

Newgrange, Ireland's finest prehistoric monument, is one of the best examples of a passage grave in western Europe. About 30 feet high and 250 feet in diameter, the mound resembles a flying saucer that has landed on a low ridge overlooking a coil of the Boyne River. It is surrounded by more than 20 smaller satellite graves dotted around, as well as by the impressive mounds of Dowth and Knowth, which lie less than a mile away. Together, they form a Stone Age burial ground dating from about 3200 B.C.

Inside the mound, a narrow passage, about 3 feet wide and 62 feet long, roofed and lined with slabs of stone, leads into a main chamber off which are ranged three

recesses like the leaves of a shamrock. The chamber's vault, recognized as one of Newgrange's marvels, is corbelled: each horizontal stone course slightly overlaps the one below until, 20 feet above the ground, the structure is plugged with a single capstone.

The exact nature and function of the mound and the culture of those who built it some 5,000 years ago is still debated. However, early Irish folk traditions refer to Newgrange as Bru na Boinne, the abode, or mansion, of the Boyne, and link it with the Irish god Dagda, the "Good God". Dagda belonged to a supernatural people known as the Tuatha De Danaan, who are said to have inhabited Ireland until the

arrival of the Celts in the latter half of the first millennium, when they mystically melted into the country's "fairy mounds". Ownership of the Bru passed to Dagda's son Oengus who, in the romantic legend *The Pursuit of Diarmaid and Grainne*, bade fairy horsemen carry the dead body of Diarmaid from Ben Bulben mountain in County Sligo to the Bru.

Apart from the mound's association with death in folklore, there is also a tradition that in historical times it was used for burials of the Irish high kings of Tara, which lay about 12 miles southwest of Newgrange, before the country was Christianized from the fifth century onward. One of these kings, Cormac mac Airt (*c.* fourth century A.D.?), is said to have given strict orders for his body not to be buried in the Bru, which he called "a cemetery of idolators". But the king's retainers ignored his command and carried the royal corpse to the Bru. However, as they approached the Boyne, it magically swelled up three times, preventing them from crossing. As a result, they interred Cormac on the south side of the river as he had requested.

In more recent times, Newgrange was first rediscovered in 1699 as a result of the local landowner, Charles Campbell, removing stones from the mound for road building. In so doing, he discovered the

entrance to the passage. One of the first to investigate was the Welsh antiquarian Edward Lhuyd (1660–1708), who happened to be in the area. Lhuyd described it as the "most remarkable curiosity", and over the following years, a succession of antiquarians came to explore it.

In the early 18th century, Thomas Molyneux, a "Professor of Physick" at Trinity College, Dublin, said the mound had been built by Danish invaders in the Middle Ages. Subsequent antiquarians in

A golden blaze of sunlight illuminates the interior of the mound via the "roof box" on December 21, the winter solstice.

Newgrange's corbelled chamber and passageway are shown in cross-section in this engraving by the 18th-century soldier and antiquarian Charles Vallency.

Guarding the entrance of the mound *is the huge, richly carved curbstone, which measures more than 10 feet long and 4 feet high. Its spiral and lozenge patterns are recurrent motifs in passage grave art.*

the 18th and early 19th centuries also ascribed its construction to races other than the native Irish, citing, for example, the Egyptians and the Indians.

In this century, scholars have proposed that Newgrange, Dowth, and Knowth and other passage graves were the work of invader-colonists from Brittany or Iberia, where megalithic building techniques and engravings resemble those found in Ireland. But although the inspiration for the Irish mounds may have ultimately derived from settlers or invaders from the continent, scholars now tend to think they were built by native Irish people.

Whether or not Newgrange and other mounds were simply tombs is also unresolved. They may, for example, have provided a spiritual focus for a community in the way that the great medieval cathedrals of the west were always more than houses of worship. There may be, too, some significance in the abstract symbols, including spirals, ellipses, lozenges, and circles, that are carved on the stones at Newgrange and other Irish passage graves.

The contemporary Irish-American art historian Martin Brennan has put forward the case that Newgrange and other mounds were not primarily for burial at all. His investigations have shown that mounds other than Newgrange, for example Knowth, are also aligned with solstitial and equinoctial sunrises and sunsets. He also found that at certain times moonbeams penetrated the mounds in a seemingly significant way.

This evidence convinced Brennan that the mounds were primarily solar or lunar temples or observatories. To support his claim he has pointed to the number of carved symbols, such as sunlike rayed circles and lunar crescents, that appear to be lunar and solar motifs. He also noted that Dagda, once the owner of Newgrange, has been identified as a sun god.

The mystery of Newgrange can never be resolved for certain. Perhaps those who built it wanted the year's newborn sun to pour its rays into the dark womblike chamber where the remains of their royal ancestors lay. And perhaps, by this mystical alchemy, they hoped for a union between the sun god and the deceased, possibly to ensure the preservation of the dead's existence in the afterlife and therefore perpetuate on earth the blessings of their spirit kings.

TIMEFRAME

B.C.

c.3200   NEWGRANGE IS BUILT ON THE BANKS OF THE BOYNE RIVER.

A.D.

c.4TH CENTURY   KING CORMAC MAC AIRT IS SAID TO HAVE BEEN BURIED OPPOSITE NEWGRANGE ON THE SOUTH BANK OF THE BOYNE.

1699   THE MOUND IS REDISCOVERED: IT IS FIRST INVESTIGATED BY WELSH ANTIQUARIAN EDWARD LHUYD.

1725   THOMAS MOLYNEUX WRITES THAT NEWGRANGE WAS BUILT BY THE DANES BETWEEN THE 8TH AND 9TH CENTURIES.

1890   IRISH ARCHAEOLOGIST GEORGE COFFEY BEGINS HIS PIONEERING WORK ON NEWGRANGE.

1962–75   NEWGRANGE IS EXCAVATED AND RESTORED BY MICHAEL O'KELLY.

1967   O'KELLY FIRST WITNESSES THE SUN'S PENETRATION OF THE TOMB CHAMBER ON DECEMBER 21, THE WINTER SOLSTICE.

1983   MARTIN BRENNAN'S BOOK *THE STARS AND THE STONES* SUGGESTS THAT NEWGRANGE IS A SOLAR TEMPLE RATHER THAN A BURIAL MOUND.

THE MEGALITHIC WORLD

Prehistoric Europe stretched from the Atlantic seaboard in the west to the shores of the Black Sea in the east. The many peoples who inhabited this vast area were preliterate: their story is told through their material remains, of which the megalithic ("big stone") monuments are the most impressive. These powerful structures – often set in brooding and desolate landscapes – were erected principally from about 4500 to 1500 B.C. Some, such as passage graves, were built as tombs. But by the late fourth millennium, circles of standing stones, rows of stones known as alignments, and single dressed stones, or menhirs, began to appear, particularly in France and the British Isles.

The religious beliefs and rituals of the megalith builders is still shrouded in mystery. Some of the

HEBRIDES

Callanish

SCOTLAND

Knebel
DENMARK

IRELAND
Knowth
Dowth
Newgrange
Castlerigg

ENGLAND

ATLANTIC
OCEAN

NETHERLANDS

Borger

Avebury
Stonehenge

Wéris

GERMANY

La Chaussée-
Tirancourt

Barnenez
Carnac
Gayr'inis

FRANCE

Arles-Fontvieille

PORTUGAL

Cova d'En Daina

CORSICA
Filitosa

SPAIN

Els Tudons

SARDINIA

MINORCA

Anta do Silval

Monchique   Soto   Cueva del
Romeral

Los
Millares

Cueva de Menga

MEDITERRANEAN

structures, however, seem to have been aligned with seasonal and astronomical events, involving the rising and setting of the sun, moon and certain stars, such as Sirius. At Stonehenge in Britain, for example, at the summer solstice, the rising sun is aligned with the circle's axis. And the 12 avenues of almost 3,000 stones at Carnac in northern France may be connected with the phases of the moon.

This map shows the general distribution of megalithic sites in prehistoric Europe, with some of the more important ones named and illustrated. They include Stonehenge; Newgrange (pp. 46–49); the passage grave of Anta do Silval; the burial structure, or *naveta*, of Els Tudons; and the long stone chamber known as a *hunebed* near Borger. The extensive alignment of Carnac is photographed below.

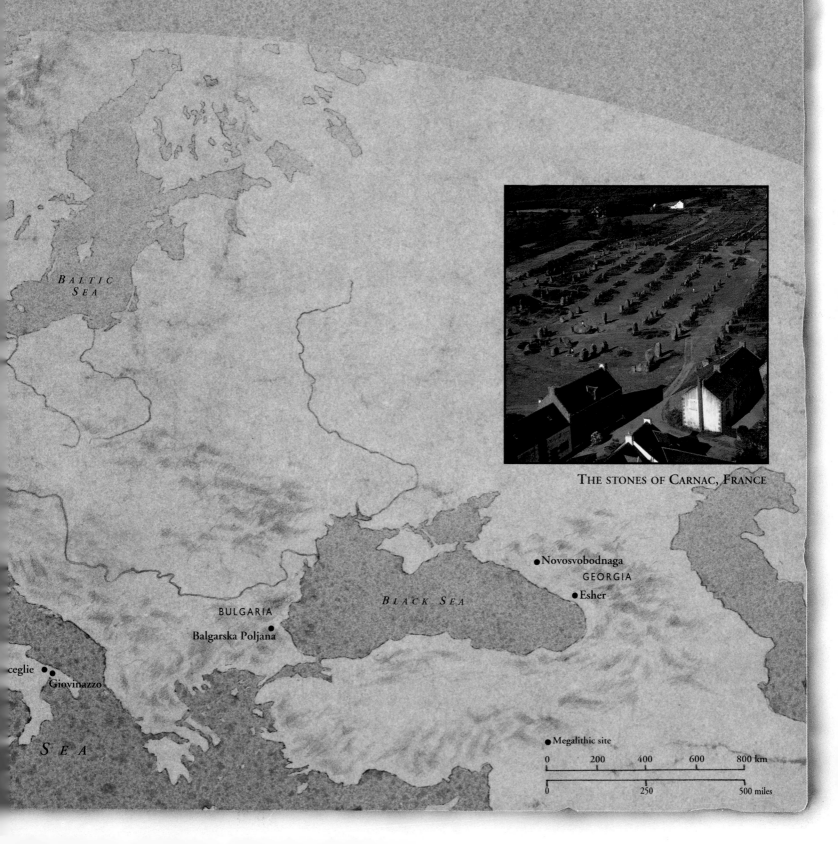

THE STONES OF CARNAC, FRANCE

BALTIC
SEA

Novosvobodnaga
GEORGIA
Esher

BLACK SEA

BULGARIA
Balgarska Poljana

ceglie
Giovinazzo

SEA

● Megalithic site

0   200   400   600   800 km

0   250   500 miles

MYCENAE

"With extreme joy I announce to Your Majesty that I have discovered the tombs which tradition, echoed by Pausanias, has designated as the sepulchres of Agamemnon, Cassandra, Eurymedon...." CABLE FROM HEINRICH SCHLIEMANN, GERMAN EXCAVATOR OF MYCENAE, TO THE KING OF THE HELLENES IN 1876

A HEAVY, BROODING ATMOSPHERE HANGS over the ancient city of Mycenae more tangibly than at any other place in Greece. For death haunts these Bronze Age ruins, dating back some 3,500 years, like a spectre, casting a shadow over the innocuous sunlit stones and the tawny, giraffe-skinned countryside. Death dominates the legends surrounding the city. And the material evidence of death, in the form of graves, tombs and funeral goods, has long been the focal point of the various teams of archaeologists who have excavated at the site from the third quarter of the 19th century up until the present.

Mycenae's citadel encrusts a small hill that rises between two craggy peaks in the Peloponnese, southern Greece. Its huge grim walls, once believed to have been built by the legendary one-eyed Cyclopes giants, follow the contours of their rocky

eminence. Above them rises the summit of the acropolis, crowned by a battered ground plan of masonry where a fortress-palace once stood. Below them, to the south, the dusty plain of Argos, dotted with olive trees, sweeps away several miles to the sea.

According to legend, Mycenae was the stronghold of the family of Atreus, the son of Pelops, from whom the Peloponnese ("Island of Pelops") takes its name. The bloody saga of the Atreid dynasty, with all its interfamily killings, incest, and canni-balism, makes the Mafia look positively angelic in comparison. For example, it was Atreus who, to avenge the seduction of his wife by his brother Thyestes, served his brother a dish of food consisting of Thyestes' own children.

The most famous member of the family was Atreus's son Agamemnon, king of Mycenae. According to the *Iliad*, written by the great epic poet Homer (*c.*800 B.C.), Agamemnon led the Greek expedition to Troy in Asia Minor to rescue his sister-in-law, the beautiful Helen, who had been abducted by the Trojan prince Paris. At the end of the 10-year war and the destruction of Troy, Agamemnon returned home,

Dubbed "broad-streeted" and "golden" *by the epic poet Homer, Mycenae was the capital of the legendary hero Agamemnon. The top of the Lion Gate* (RIGHT) *shows two rampant headless lionesses. Beyond lies Grave Circle A, where a wealth of gold objects was unearthed by Heinrich Schliemann.*

Clytemnestra, her hand gloved in red to signify her bloody deed, stands over the netted corpses of her husband Agamemnon and his Trojan slave Cassandra. The scene comes from Aeschylus's Oresteia *in a production by the British National Theatre in the early 1980s.*

During Agamemnon's absence at the Trojan war, Clytemnestra took a lover named Aegisthus; when Agamemnon returned home to Mycenae, she murdered him. However, she later paid for her crime by being killed by their son Orestes.

anticipating, perhaps, the equivalent of a returning hero's welcome.

What this great warrior, a "leader of men", did not know was that during his absence overseas, his wife Clytemnestra, the "Lady Macbeth" of Greek legend, had taken a lover: Aegisthus, Agamemnon's cousin. And both were secretly plotting to kill the returning hero, not least because Agamemnon had previously sacrificed his daughter Iphigenia to make the winds blow and set in motion the becalmed Greek fleet bound for Troy. Clytemnestra would probably also have been goaded by the sight of her husband parading his Trojan slave Cassandra, a fascinating wild-eyed creature who uttered strange and ominous prophecies.

In any event, the unsuspecting Agamemnon was warmly received by his dissembling wife and later cut down, either in his bath or, in another version of the legend, at the dinner table. But the cycle of bloodshed did not end there. For, in time, Agamemnon's son Orestes, urged on by his sister Electra, avenged the death of his father by killing both his mother Clytemnestra and her lover Aegisthus.

Tales of Troy, Agamemnon, and his bloody homecoming fascinated Homer as well as the Greeks of the classical age (*c.*500–300 B.C.) and continue to do so worldwide, not least through the plays of ancient dramatists such as Aeschylus and Sophocles, authors, respectively, of the *Oresteia* and the *Electra*. Until the 19th century, scholars generally believed that the Homeric heroes of Troy and Mycenae had no historical foundation.

However, the German archaeologist Heinrich Schliemann (1822–90), taking Homer's *Iliad* and *Odyssey* literally and using them as a geographical guide, confounded current opinion by digging at the site of Hissarlik in modern Turkey and unearthing the remains of a great city, now acknowledged to be Troy. He also found a quantity of golden treasures which he thought (mistakenly) had belonged to the Trojan king Priam.

Heinrich Schliemann, *a self-made millionaire and brilliant linguist, began excavating Mycenae in 1876, having previously discovered the site of Troy. When he died in 1890, one scholar was heard to remark that "the spring had gone out of the year".*

It was a spectacular find for one of the great romantic figures of archaeology. The son of a poor pastor, Schliemann was first employed as a grocer and then a cabin boy. Later, he became a military contractor during the Crimean War (1853–56) and, helped by his flair for languages (he was fluent in a dozen), he amassed a vast fortune. Then, at the age of 36, he threw himself passionately into archaeology and, 15 years later, made the discoveries at Troy that gained him wide fame.

Still fired with the Homeric tales, Schliemann next turned his attention to the Greek mainland and Mycenae. In August 1876, he began digging just inside the walls of the citadel, for he had read that the ancient traveller Pausanias (*fl.* A.D. 143–176) believed Agamemnon's grave lay inside the city's gates, while those of Clytemnestra and Aegisthus were outside. Again, Schliemann struck gold. Within a circle of stone slabs, his workmen dug up five shaft graves from which a dazzling array of gold objects emerged, fully justifying Homer's description of Mycenae as being a city "rich in gold".

Resting with the decayed bodies of 16 people were gold goblets and plates; gold crowns, diadems, and necklaces; gold discs and plaques bearing motifs of lions, griffins, cuttlefish, deer, eagles, and swans; gold vases with lids attached with gold wire; and a flower with a silver stem and petals of gold. Most fascinating of all were the golden death masks that had covered the faces of the deceased. One mask in particular, whose noble features, trimmed moustache and beard, and serene smile have the air of kingliness, convinced Schliemann that he was gazing at the face of Agamemnon himself.

But was Schliemann correct? Did his finds really support the historical veracity of the Homeric legends? In fact, modern scholars reckon the shaft graves and their gold contents predate the likely time of Agamemnon by some 300 years. The fall

Schliemann's excavation *of Grave Circle A is shown in this contemporary engraving. Here, within the limit of upright stone slabs, his team uncovered five shaft graves (a sixth was found later) containing a cornucopia of gold objects buried with 16 bodies. Behind the circle rises the unexcavated mound of the citadel.*

of Troy to the Greeks, if it happened at all, is dated to about 1250 B.C. But the graves go back to about the 16th century. Whoever it was that inspired the makers of the masks, it was not proud Agamemnon.

More than 70 years after Schliemann's discovery of what became known as Grave Circle A, another, earlier cemetery, known as Grave Circle B, was found outside the city walls. But this contained nothing like the gold riches found in the first circle. Both cemeteries apparently formed one continuous burial ground in which graves were marked by upright stone slabs carved with figures – sometimes shown hunting – and abstract motifs.

Circle A, however, must have been particularly hallowed ground because it was incorporated within the city when the great stone walls visible today were built to fortify the acropolis in the 13th century B.C. This sacred burial area was then cordoned off from the secular parts of the citadel by a double circle of limestone slabs.

The two grave circles are not the only evidence of royal burials at Mycenae. More spectacular in architecture, though less so in grave goods, are the great domed *tholos* tombs, whose first appearance at Mycenae began in about 1500 B.C., perhaps marking a change of dynasty.

Tholos tombs, which are found at other Mycenaean sites on the Greek mainland, typically consist of a circular chamber cut into a hillside, resembling in shape an old-fashioned beehive or a conical helmet. Their internal walls are corbelled, with successive courses of stone, each overlapping the one below, narrowing in diameter as they rise to a final aperture plugged by a capstone. A ceremonial passage known as a *dromos*, which is open to the skies and flanked either side by rising stone walls, leads to the entrance.

There are nine *tholoi* at Mycenae, of which the most magnificent is the misnamed Treasury of Atreus. Carved out of the hillside west of the citadel, the Treasury dates from the mid-13th century. At the end of its 120-foot *dromos* beckons the dark rectangle of the open entrance, once flanked by slender carved stone pilasters and still surmounted by a long lintel stone weighing over 100 tons. Above this stone is a triangular space designed to relieve it of excessive weight and originally blocked up by a sculpted stone, perhaps in the manner of the frieze of stylized lions in the famous Lion Gate of the citadel.

Inside, the bright sunlight is suddenly eclipsed by a cavernous, sepulchral dark, a

The citadel of Mycenae is barnacled on a craggy eminence isolated by ravines and flanked by the hills of Elias and Zara (out of the picture). Its strategic position overlooking the plain of Argos was strengthened by forbidding walls up to 40 feet high and 20 feet thick.

Carved out of a hillside, *the Treasury of Atreus is the largest* tholos *tomb at Mycenae. A 120-foot-long passage, or* dromos, *leads to the entrance, once flanked by pilasters. The triangular space above the doorway was originally plugged by a stone.*

cooling of temperature, and the whispering reverberations of sound. As the shock of darkness recedes, it is possible to pick out 33 courses of stone rising to a height of nearly 45 feet. On the curving walls bronze nails have been found, suggesting that the tomb may have been decorated with gold or bronze rosettes, which would have gleamed resplendently in torch or firelight. No body was found here or in the small side chamber leading off the *tholos.* However, the size and grandeur of the tomb suggest that its anonymous occupant was probably a king, perhaps an ancestor of Agamemnon, possibly Atreus.

Knowledge of *tholos* tomb burial rites is difficult to glean, since most of them were plundered in ancient times. However, the 20th-century British archaeologist Lord William Taylour, using evidence from a number of *tholos* sites, has speculated how a king might have been buried at the Treasury of Atreus. First, according to his

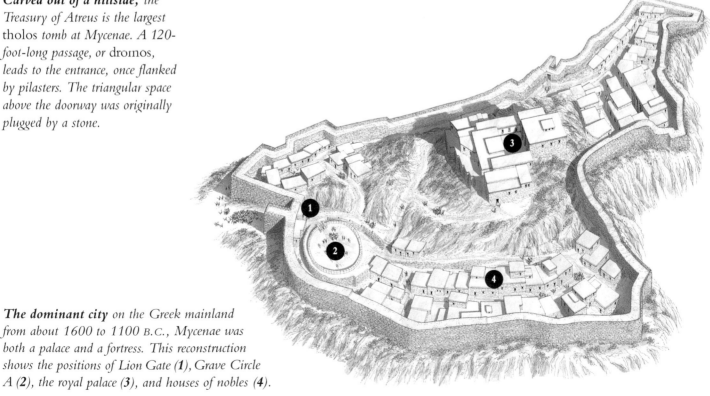

The dominant city *on the Greek mainland from about 1600 to 1100* B.C., *Mycenae was both a palace and a fortress. This reconstruction shows the positions of Lion Gate (1), Grave Circle A (2), the royal palace (3), and houses of nobles (4).*

view, the dead king's body was brought along the tomb's *dromos* on a bier on a chariot that was pulled by a team of horses and accompanied by a procession of mourners. The bronze doors of the entrance were open, allowing natural light to gleam on the bronze-clad wall within the beehive chamber.

The king's body was carried inside, laid on a carpet of gold, and surrounded by food, wine, unguents, swords, daggers, rapiers, spears, a bow and arrow, and a huge shield shaped in a figure of eight – items deemed necessary for the journey to the afterlife. The horses that drew the chariot were then ritually slaughtered and other animals, including rams, were sacrificed and roasted for a funeral feast in the tomb. After the mourners had eaten, paid their last respects to the dead, and left, the tomb was sealed and the *dromos* filled with stones.

Mycenaean beliefs in the afterlife are also hard to fathom. It is tempting to turn to Homer for help, since the names of the Homeric and, later, the classical gods, such as Zeus, Poseidon, Hera, and Artemis, have been found in the Mycenaean script known as Linear B. However, Homer's epics reflect more the conditions of his own time or the immediately preceding Dark Age (*c*.1100–800 B.C.), and it would

The glare of sunlight *frames the entrance of the Treasury of Atreus, Mycenae's largest tholos, or "beehive tomb". During his excavations, Schliemann entertained Emperor Dom Pedro II of Brazil here, decking out the tomb with a table, carpets, silver, sofas, flowers, and lamps.*

Mycenaean warriors *prepare to kill a lion on the bronze blade of a dagger found in Shaft Grave IV in Grave Circle A. The blade is inlaid with gold, amber, and niello – a blackish alloy of sulphur, silver, and other metals.*

The pride of Athens's archaeological museum, this gold mask was thought by Schliemann to bear the face of Agamemnon; however, it is now known to predate the Mycenaean king by about 300 years. Nevertheless, the strong nose, thin enigmatic mouth, and carefully etched eyebrows and moustache suggest the powerful features of a Mycenaean ruler.

be wrong to treat them as historical documents of the late Bronze Age. For example, whereas the Mycenaeans buried their dead, in Homer they are cremated. Nevertheless, there are echoes in Homer, corroborated by archaeology, of the Mycenaean era.

The Mycenaeans may well have believed in the Homeric concept of Hades, a gloomy underworld realm to which the immaterial spirits of the dead journeyed; and in the need to conduct proper funeral rituals to dispatch the spirit and thus prevent it from lingering on earth as a malevolent presence. For example, in Book XXIII of the *Iliad*, the Greek hero Achilles is reproached by the ghost of his dead friend Patroclus for not conducting his funeral rites. As a result, Patroclus says, he has been held at bay at the gates of Hades by disembodied spirits. If Achilles were to cremate him, however, he would not return from this underworld realm to haunt him.

The modern Greek scholar G.E. Mylonas speculated that the Mycenaeans believed the final decaying of flesh on the bones of the deceased meant that his spirit had completed the journey to Hades and would haunt this world no longer. This, he believed, explained why shaft graves, *tholos* tombs, and chamber tombs (simple tombs cut out of hillsides) were re-used for burials and that scant regard was given to the original occupants' skeletons and grave goods, which were often roughly handled or even ruined.

Although the grave goods of Mycenae's *tholos* tombs have long since been destroyed by the ravages of time or plundered by robbers, at least the shaft graves have yielded a golden cornucopia – a fitting reward for Schliemann's ardent faith in the Homeric classics. The prize of all his treasures, the "mask of Agamemnon", now holds pride of place in the National Archaeological Museum in Athens. It greets visitors with its gold visage and secretive smiling lips that doubtless could reveal tales of heroic deeds and bloody killings, if not of Troy and the glories and tragedies of Mycenae.

TIMEFRAME

B.C.

c.1600	MYCENAE IS NOW THE DOMINANT CITY ON THE GREEK MAINLAND.
c.1600–1500	SHAFT GRAVES ARE BUILT AT MYCENAE.
c.1500	THOLOS TOMBS FIRST APPEAR AT MYCENAE.
c.1300–1200	HUGE DEFENSIVE WALLS ARE BUILT AROUND THE CITADEL.
c.1100	MYCENAE IS BURNED, PERHAPS BY INVADING DORIANS.
468	NEIGHBOURING ARGOS DESTROYS MYCENAE.

A.D.

c.160	GREEK TRAVELLER PAUSANIAS VISITS THE SITE AND FINDS IT IN RUINS.
1876	HEINRICH SCHLIEMANN EXCAVATES GRAVE CIRCLE A AND DISCOVERS A NUMBER OF SHAFT GRAVES.
1954	GRAVE CIRCLE B IS DISCOVERED.

THE TOMB COMPLEX OF SHI HUANGDI

"As soon as the First Emperor became king of Qin, work was begun on his mausoleum at Mount Li…more than 700,000 conscripts…laboured there."

HAN HISTORIAN SIMA QIAN (C.145–90 B.C.)

BENEATH THE SHADOW OF MOUNT LI, near Xi'an in north-central China, there stands a broad, hill-like burial mound that may contain one of the greatest treasure troves yet to be discovered. For this artificial eminence, more than 2,000 years old, covers the tomb of one of the greatest figures of Chinese history: Shi Huangdi, the First Emperor.

A man haunted throughout his life by the fear of death, Shi Huangdi ordered the building of his tomb after he had become king of the state of Qin in 247 B.C. at the tender age of 13. He directed more than half a million workers to create the most magnificent mausoleum in China. Time alone will tell whether his aim was achieved. For the moment, the tomb remains unexcavated below its grassy, tree-tufted mound.

The tomb's satellite burial pits, however, have already yielded extraordinary finds. In 1974, in what is now called Pit 1, about a mile east of the mound, peasants digging a well accidentally discovered an army of some 6,000 terracotta soldiers, all larger than lifesize. Drawn up in battle formation and once holding real weapons, they had guarded the emperor's grave for more than 20 centuries. Their faces – no two of which are alike – eerily show the idiosyncratic stamp of actual individuals.

The magnificence of this clay army has whetted scholars' appetites for the tomb itself, despite the fact that robbers may have looted it in ancient times. Expectation has also been intensified by a description of the

A modest path flanked by crops leads to what might prove to be the richest tomb in China. The as yet unexcavated mound, bristling with apricot trees, rises over the burial place of China's First Emperor, Shi Huangdi, who died more than 2,000 years ago.

Ghostly warriors *from the mists of China's past rise again from a pit discovered near the emperor's tomb in 1974. These terracotta soldiers, who were buried to guard Shi Huangdi's tomb, all have individual faces. Here, a charioteer is followed by his officers. Neck scarves were used to prevent their armour from chafing their skin.*

mound's interior by the Han historian Sima Qian, writing about 2,000 years ago.

According to Qian, hundreds of thousands of workers laboured on the tomb. No expense was spared. Artists depicted the glittering heavens on the ceiling; while a three-dimensional map of the imperial domains was created on the ground, with models of palaces, towers and other buildings. These were set in a landscape veined with silver rivers of mercury – also used to

represent the ocean – with an ingenious mechanism to keep the mercury flowing between its miniature banks.

To deter potential grave robbers, crossbows were primed to shower deadly bolts if triggered by an intrusion. To maximize security, the luckless artisans were sealed up in the tomb once it was completed, as were the emperor's concubines. Finally, the mausoleum was planted with trees and shrubs to make it look like a hill.

Clutching their spears, Qin foot soldiers, with their elegantly attired officer on the right, lead a four-horse chariot and other infantry in this reconstructed scene from Pit 2.

Shi Huangdi carried out extensive reforms during his reign, but was vilified by later intellectuals for his infamous Burning of the Books in 213 B.C., an act designed to strike at the heart of Confucian scholars critical of his regime.

It was a final resting place fit for one of the most ruthless, dynamic and influential rulers of Chinese history. Born in about 258 B.C., Shi Huangdi, then known as Zheng, became king of Qin at a time when China was a cauldron of feuding states. Qin, however, became the most powerful, owing to its brutal militarism and disciplined way of life based on the principles of Legalism. This was a contemporary philosophy that stressed the virtues of autocratic rule, strict laws and severe punishments. By 221, "as a silkworm devours leaves", Zheng had led Qin to victory over its enemies.

Then, as Shi Huangdi, China's First Emperor, Zheng set about refashioning the kingdom in his own image. Advised by his shrewd grand councillor, Li Si, he created a strong central government, abolished the country's feudal system, and forced noble families to move to his capital of Xianyang, now part of Xi'an. He standardized weights, measures, coinage and even the widths of carriage axles. In the north, he joined up and strengthened local defensive barriers to create the Great Wall, designed to keep out barbarian nomads.

Although pragmatic and single-minded, Shi Huangdi was also highly superstitious, employing some 300 astrologers to scan the heavens. His fear of death continued to grip him remorselessly – not an entirely irrational phobia, as three attempts on his life showed. His search for the elixir of immortality led him to sponsor an expedition to a legendary island off China's eastern coast said to be inhabited by immortals who possessed the potion. The expedition, however, never returned.

In 210, without a magical brew to preserve him, the emperor eventually died of an illness while touring his eastern provinces. To procure the accession of Shi Huangdi's weaker second son, councillor Li

Si and Zhao Gao, the chief eunuch, at first hid their master's death. They managed to return his body to the capital, disguising the stench of decaying flesh by arranging for a cart of rotting fish to accompany the imperial litter.

Although the plot succeeded, Shi Huangdi's death effectively spelled the end of the Qin dynasty. It rumbled on for four more years amid various uprisings; but it eventually collapsed in 206 and was replaced by the Han dynasty.

For more than two millennia, Shi Huangdi's tomb complex lay buried. But since 1974, excavations of Pit 1 and two others close by have revealed not only thousands of clay warriors, but also chariots, bows, arrows, spears, swords, iron farm tools, bronze horses and leather and bronze bridles. The soldiers themselves were fashioned from local clay, their hollow torsos resting on solid legs. Their heads and arms were made separately and later attached to the bodies.

To gaze on this phalanx of phantom warriors *en masse* is to realize the vast resources and martial discipline of the Qin army, as well as the lengths to which one man went to safeguard his resting place and journey to the other world. For it is no accident that the soldiers face east, toward most of the emperor's enemies on earth.

Now, more than 2,000 years after their ruler's death, the terracotta army has brought worldwide fame to the Tiger of Qin – some compensation, perhaps, to a man who believed his dynasty would last "10,000 generations", but which in fact lasted only 15 years. Yet should his fame prove immortal, it will not have been due to any elixir, but to the magic of the spade and the alchemy of archaeology.

Their empty hands *once holding real weapons, clay soldiers stand four abreast in Pit 1. Now housed in a hangar, the pit consists of 11 parallel passages, each some 650 feet long.*

TIMEFRAME

B.C.

247   THE 13-YEAR-OLD ZHENG IS CROWNED KING OF THE STATE OF QIN AND BEGINS THE BUILDING OF HIS TOMB.

221   ZHENG UNITES CHINA AND RULES AS SHI HUANGDI, THE FIRST EMPEROR.

210   SHI HUANGDI DIES OF NATURAL CAUSES AND SO PRECIPITATES A POLITICAL CRISIS.

206   THE HAN DYNASTY REPLACES THE QIN DYNASTY IN POWER.

A.D.

1974   WHILE DIGGING A WELL NEAR MOUNT LI, PEASANTS FIND TERRACOTTA SOLDIERS IN WHAT IS NOW CALLED PIT 1.

1976   TWO MORE PITS, WITH YET MORE LIFESIZE POTTERY FIGURES, ARE DISCOVERED.

1979   THE EMPEROR'S TERRACOTTA ARMY IS OFFICIALLY OPENED TO THE PUBLIC FOR THE FIRST TIME.

1980   A PAIR OF BRONZE FOUR-HORSE CHARIOTS, EACH WITH A CHARIOTEER FIGURE, IS FOUND TO THE WEST OF THE TOMB MOUND.

THE PYRAMIDS OF GIZA

"A stairway has been set up to the sky that you may ascend..."

FROM PYRAMID TEXT 619

CAIRO'S SPRAWLING SUBURBS ARE AN unpromising start for a journey leading 4,500 years back in time to the only one of the seven wonders of the ancient world to have survived. Yet, as modern buildings abruptly end and the vast stretches of desert on the plateau of Giza beckon, the sight of the pyramids rising dramatically into the sky is indeed a wonder to behold. From afar, when their sharply angled facades are split between bright sun-burnished gold and crisp dark shadow, they resemble gigantic diamonds half buried in the desert sands.

There are three pyramids at Giza, all built by kings of the Fourth Dynasty during the period known as the Old Kingdom (*c.*2575–2130 B.C.). The oldest and largest is the Great Pyramid, which rises more than 480 feet and was built for King Khufu, who is better known by his Greek name, Cheops.

Just to the south lies the pyramid of Khufu's son and successor, Khafre (Greek Chephren), which, although marginally lower than the Great Pyramid, rises higher since it was built on raised ground. The third pyramid, substantially smaller than the other two, was built by King Menkaure (Greek Mycerinus) – probably a brother of Khafre. Together they form the greatest assemblage of building stones in the world and remain a potent symbol of ancient Egypt and its god-kings, or pharaohs.

In other cultures, ancient and modern, great monumental buildings are more often than not temples, palaces or places of

Symbols of eternity, the pyramids of Giza lie a few miles west of the River Nile on the edge of Cairo, Egypt's capital. Built in the middle of the third millennium B.C., the pyramids were as ancient to the Romans as Roman civilization is to the modern world. They are named after the pharaohs who built them – respectively, from right to left, Khufu, Khafre and Menkaure.

entertainment, such as the Colosseum in Rome. The pyramids, however, eschew such temporal functions. They are houses of eternity, giant tombs built so that the king could pass into and enjoy the afterlife. To many observers throughout history, including the Roman naturalist Pliny the Elder (A.D. 23–79), the scale of such funerary monuments has seemed a testament to rampant egomania.

Indeed, the much-vaunted statistics graphically illustrate what may seem a pharaonic *folie de grandeur*. Scholars have calculated, for example, that the Great Pyramid was originally composed of about 2,300,000 blocks of stone weighing on average two and a half tons each. It has been estimated that this single pyramid could house the cathedrals of St. Peter's in Rome and St. Paul's and Westminster Abbey in London, as well as those of Florence and Milan.

Another statistical comparison was allegedly made by Napoleon Bonaparte during his military campaign in Egypt, which began in 1798. While a number of his officers toiled up to the top of the pyramid's precipitous slope, Napoleon sat in the shade, apparently performing comparable mental exertions. For when the officers returned to base, the emperor coolly told them that there was enough stone in the three pyramids to build a wall the equivalent of 10 feet high and 1 foot wide around the whole of France.

Pliny judged the pyramids to be "idle and frivolous pieces of ostentation". It can be said in their favour, however, that they provided work for tens of thousands of labourers, especially during the three-month period of the annual Nile inundation when farmwork in the river valley became an impossibility.

Since the Egyptians believed the tombs were crucial to the well-being of the deceased in the afterlife and that they, the living, stood to gain from the blessings of their semi-divine pharaohs in the next world, the building of the pyramids had practical benefits. Also, they were undoubtedly a source of civic pride, in the way that the Parthenon was to the ancient Athenians, or cathedrals were in medieval Christian Europe.

Little is known of the three pharaohs for whom the pyramids were built, and none of their bodies has been found. Archaeologists have shown that the burial chambers

King Khafre *was the fourth ruler of Egypt's Fourth Dynasty and the builder of the second of the Giza pyramids. This black diorite statue shows him enthroned, with the falcon god Horus perched behind his head, giving him protection with outstretched wings.*

The eerily lit Grand Gallery *leads into the heart of the Great Pyramid. More than 150 feet long and nearly 30 feet high, the gallery was built of limestone walls topped by a corbelled vault. It connects the Ascending Corridor with the King's Chamber, where the body of the king was deposited.*

Although its beard and nose *have fallen away, the sphinx's* *face still evokes a sense of* *mystery and serenity. The* *19th-century French writer* *Alexandre Dumas remarked* *that it was a "gigantic dog that* *watches this granite flock".*

Cut from a limestone outcrop, *the Great Sphinx rises 65 feet* *and represents an aspect of the* *sun god. It bears the face of a* *Fourth-Dynasty pharaoh,* *commonly believed to be that of* *Khafre, since it stands next to* *the valley temple and causeway* *of Khafre's pyramid, shown* *here behind it.*

inside the pyramids had long been plundered by robbers, possibly within three centuries of being built. This was despite builders' attempts to conceal entrances and plug passageways with blocks of granite. Throughout Egyptian history, tomb robbers risked their lives to steal the grave goods, especially precious ornaments and jewellery, which were placed in the tomb in the belief that the deceased could have, after death, the material things that had been enjoyed during life.

It is not clear what form the dead pharaohs were believed to have taken in the afterlife. Egyptian texts speak of an immaterial spirit known as the *ba*, which left the body at death but was dependent for its well-being on the preservation of the physical body – which explains the need to embalm and protect it.

There was also an entity known as the *ka*, a sort of personal life force, sometimes rendered as "soul" or "personality" or the "self", which came into existence with a person's birth and remained after death. Regular offerings of food and drink, or their representations on tomb walls, were intended to give sustenance to the *ka*, and one Egyptian name for a tomb was "house of the *ka*". Thus the tomb was not merely a receptacle for the dead, but also a means of safeguarding the king's body and providing him with the necessary equipment to continue his existence in the afterlife.

Ironically, the very objects that were placed in the tomb for the benefit of the king after death attracted intruders, who would usually pillage the tomb and destroy the corpse. These robbers were undeterred by physical obstacles and unfazed by

The "solar boat" of King Khufu, the world's oldest surviving ship, was found dismantled in a pit near the Great Pyramid in 1954. About 138 feet long, it was probably intended to carry the king to the afterlife.

magical protective spells on tomb walls. In fact, they showed callous disregard for the dead. For example, they would readily hack to bits the bandaged embalmed body, or mummy, to get at any body jewellery. And, in a multiburial tomb at Thebes in southern Egypt, archaeologists have surmised that robbers set the mummies of

children alight simply to give themselves enough light to work by.

The method by which the pyramids were constructed is still debated. Granite, it seems, was brought down river by boat from Aswan in the south. Local quarries provided stone for the bulk of the buildings. Gleaming white Tura limestone blocks, from the Muqattam Hills across the Nile, opposite Giza, were used to provide a smooth pale "skin" for the pyramids. Over the centuries, this casing has been stripped away by successive generations of local builders so that only a small patch at the top of Khafre's pyramid remains. This gives an inkling of how the pyramids must have once shone in the sunlight.

It seems the stone blocks were dragged to the building site by teams of men with ropes, sledges and rollers (the wheel was not used). The stones were then hauled along mud ramps that had been lubricated with water and fitted into position. Once the main body of the pyramid had been completed, working from bottom to top, the casing of Tura limestone was fitted from top to bottom; at the same time, the ramps were demolished.

In all three pyramids, passageways lead to the pharaohs' burial chambers. In those of Khafre and Menkaure, the chambers were cut out of the rock foundations, while in Khufu's, the King's Chamber lies at the centre of the building. It is reached by the so-called Descending Corridor, which leads down from the original entrance in the pyramid's northern face, about 55 feet above the ground. (Today, visitors enter by an entrance carved out by medieval intruders.)

From this passageway, another, known as the Ascending Corridor, branches off at an angle toward the centre and leads into the 153-foot-long Grand Gallery. Rising 28 feet, the gallery has polished limestone walls and a corbelled vault of progressively overlapping stones.

The Step Pyramid of Saqqara,
a few miles south of Giza, was a
precursor of the true smooth-sided
pyramid. The tomb of Djoser, the
second king of the Third Dynasty
(c.2650–2575), the Saqqara
pyramid is the oldest stone
building of its size in the world.
Its form evolved over a period
of time from the mastaba *tomb,*
which was a simple oblong
structure covering a burial chamber
dug into the ground beneath it.

How the Great Pyramid was
built is still a matter of debate
among scholars. A massive ramp
(1), such as the one shown here,
may have been used to drag the
huge numbers of stone
blocks into place.

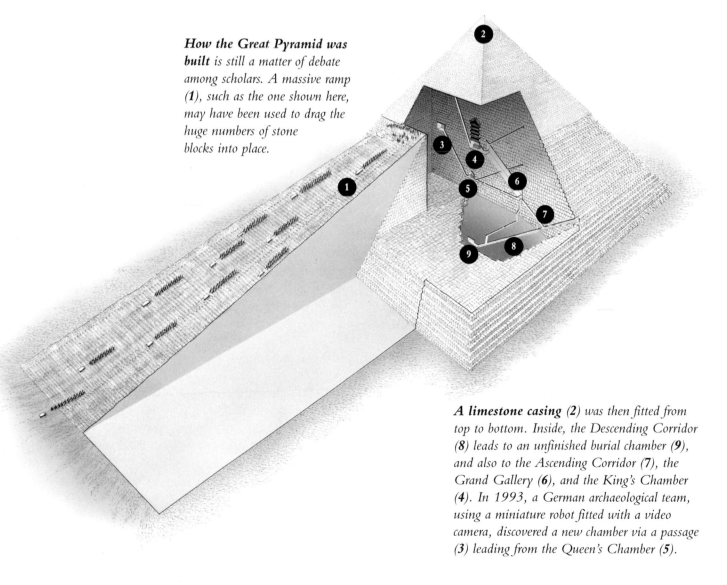

A limestone casing (2) was then fitted from
top to bottom. Inside, the Descending Corridor
(8) leads to an unfinished burial chamber (9),
and also to the Ascending Corridor (7), the
Grand Gallery (6), and the King's Chamber
(4). In 1993, a German archaeological team,
using a miniature robot fitted with a video
camera, discovered a new chamber via a passage
(3) leading from the Queen's Chamber (5).

The gallery, in turn, finally leads to the King's Chamber, a granite room about 34 by 17 feet and almost 20 feet high. The granite sarcophagus that once held the king's body stands near the west wall. Its stark emptiness is a poignant reminder of the unknown fate that the body suffered at the hands of intruders.

The question still remains as to why the Egyptians chose the form of the pyramid. Archaeologists have shown that in architectural terms, the true pyramid, which has smooth sides, may be the natural development of the step pyramid, the best example of which is that of Djoser, the second king of the Third Dynasty (c.2650–2575), at Saqqara, several miles south of Giza. The stepped pyramid, in turn, seems to have been an enlarged variation of the type of tomb known as the *mastaba*, which consists of a low rectangular mud-brick structure covering a rock-cut tomb, to which it is connected by a vertical shaft.

However, as the modern British Egyptologist I.E.S. Edwards has argued, it is likely that the pyramid also, if not primarily, had a powerful symbolic resonance. This was connected with the pyramid's triangular shape, suggestive of a staircase leading up to the heavens, and to the Egyptian cult of the sun.

Although it took various forms, the sun cult essentially focused on the god Re, who was believed to sail across the sky each day in his boat – a highly appropriate vessel in a country so dependent on the Nile for transportation. Every night, Re was thought to continue his nautical journey through the underworld in order to reappear at the first light of dawn.

In time, this solar cult absorbed elements of, and was eventually superseded by, the cult of the god Osiris. Central to this deity is the myth of his murder by his brother Seth. According to one version, Isis, Osiris's wife and sister, recovered his body and kept watch over it. However, Seth found the corpse and cut it into pieces which he scattered all over Egypt. But Isis combed the country and found all the

The sphinx and pyramids, painted here by the British artist David Roberts in 1849, captured the imagination of many 19th-century travellers. A number made the climb to the top of the Great Pyramid to enjoy the panoramic views. In 1843, the German Egyptologist Richard Lepsius even lit a bonfire on its pinnacle to celebrate Christmas.

Shafts of sunlight bursting through clouds (RIGHT) may have helped to inspire the form of the pyramids. Support for this conjecture comes from the Pyramid Texts, in one of which is written: "I have laid down for myself this sunshine of yours as a stairway under my feet on which I will ascend...."

pieces except for the genital organs. In another version, Isis restored her husband's body to life, and Osiris became king of the region of the dead. Meanwhile, Horus, son of Osiris and Isis, set out to kill his uncle, Seth, to avenge his father. Eventually, after a long struggle, Horus triumphed and became the new king.

Both Re and Osiris symbolized for the Egyptians the possibility of personal survival after death, provided that the appropriate tomb and funerary rituals were followed. In the solar cult, survival of death was at first a privilege only of royals. After death, the king would have to travel to a celestial region in the east, where he would join Re on his daily journey across the skies.

According to one of the Pyramid Texts (inscriptions found on the walls of burial chambers and corridors of late Old Kingdom pyramids), access to the heavenly realm was by a "staircase", so that the king might "mount up to heaven". This being the case, it might be that the step pyramid

was designed specifically to provide a stone stairway to heaven.

In addition, it has been shown that the form of the true pyramid to some extent imitated the conical shape of the sun-god's stone symbol known as the *benben*, which was housed in his temple at Heliopolis, just east of Giza. As Edwards has pointed out, both the pyramid and the *benben* may derive their shape from the phenomenon, sometimes seen at Giza especially in winter, when triangular shafts of sunlight burst through the clouds on to the desert sands so that "the immaterial prototype and the material replica are here ranged side by side".

Nor should this be seen as too fanciful. For there are Pyramid Texts that speak of the king ascending to heaven on a "ramp" of sunlight. Perhaps, as an ancient Egyptian architect pondered how to make tombs safer from robbers and more grand in aspect, a literal shaft of inspiration appeared from the sky, from Re himself, a revelation of a form that would become one of the world's most enduring monuments.

OSEBERG

"Now they took her to the ship. She took off the two bracelets she was wearing and gave them both to the old woman called the Angel of Death who was to kill her...."

ARAB DIPLOMAT IBN FADLAN DESCRIBING A VIKING FUNERAL IN RUSSIA IN A.D. 922

To step inside the Viking Ship Museum near Oslo, Norway's capital, and see the sleek longship unearthed from a burial mound at Oseberg, 40 miles to the south, is to realize in an instant the power and beauty of the vessels that made the Viking Age (*c.* A.D. 800–1100) one of the most extraordinary epochs in European history. More than 70 feet long, 17 feet wide, and 5 feet deep, wrought predominantly from oak and adorned with intricate carvings, the Oseberg ship would have skimmed through the icy foaming seas of the north, its proud prow rearing up from the hissing waters like a sea dragon.

The Vikings, or Norsemen, were pagan warriors from Norway, Sweden, and Denmark, who, from about 800, exploded out of the fjords and harbours of their homelands in sea-going vessels and, for almost three centuries, terrorized western Europe. The basis of their maritime power was the *langskip*, the long ship, the pride of their navies.

Fitted with both a strong square sail and rows of oars, the long ship was quick and manoeuvrable. And its shallow draft allowed it to negotiate rivers and bring Viking warriors inland to make attacks on cities such as Paris and London. The ship

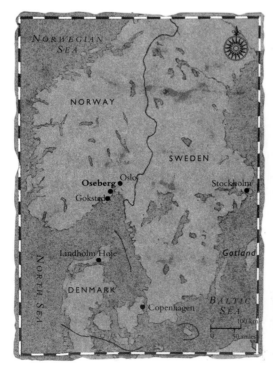

The Oseberg ship, shown here in all its restored splendour in the Viking Ship Museum, is more than 70 feet long and some 1,200 years old. This "surf dragon", which could be sailed or rowed, was used in the burial rites of a woman, possibly a Viking queen.

A snarling animal's head, which once formed the finial of a wooden post found in the Oseberg ship, captures the fierce spirit of the Viking soul. The head's highly intricate carving has led scholars to name its unknown creator the "academician".

not only played a crucial part in Viking life, but also had a significant role in funeral practices. Although Viking burials vary from region to region, the use of a ship, either real or symbolic, large or small, interred or cremated, as a last resting place for the dead is a recurrent feature in their society.

Some burials, such as those of Oseberg and nearby Gokstad, involved real boats buried within earth mounds. Elsewhere, on the island of Gotland off Sweden, for example, or Lindholm Høje in Denmark, the graves are marked by stones set upright in the shape of ships. Some grave boats were burned before burial; others were left intact and filled with goods for the deceased to take into the afterlife.

The Oseberg ship first came to light in 1903, when local farm workers dug into a grassy mound, about 20 feet high and more than 120 feet in diameter, protruding

from a plain beside a river. Reports of a suspected ship mound reached Gabriel Gustafsson, director of the Archaeological Museum in Oslo; on August 8, his 50th birthday. Without delay, he set to work on preliminary excavations.

To Gustafsson's amazement, he found not only a magnificent ship more than 1,000 years old, but also a wealth of grave goods, many of them examples of the finest craftsmanship. During the following summer of 1904, with a team consisting of a botanist, engineers, geologists, artists, and photographers, he set about excavating the mound in earnest.

Despite the intrusion of medieval robbers, the peat and blue clay that enclosed the ship had preserved it and its contents to a remarkable degree. Walnuts, wheat, and a chest of wild apples were found, as well as the largest collection of wooden objects

How the Oseberg ship would have looked afloat is shown in this modern reconstruction. Described by Viking poets as an "oar steed" or "ocean-striding bison", the Viking ship was a dreaded weapon.

As one ninth-century Irish monk noted in the margin of his manuscript, only the weather seemed to deter a Viking attack: "The wind is fierce tonight, whipping the waves to white; I need not fear the Viking host crossing the sea to this coast."

ever found in a Viking grave. These included a sturdy, finely carved, four-wheeled cart, buckets, casks, beds, sledges, chests, boxes, and a chair. Most striking of all, however, were wooden posts whose ends had been carved into the snarling heads of animals.

The excavators found the remains of two bodies in a burial chamber at the stern end of the ship along with pillows, blankets, and eiderdowns. The bones belonged to two women, one of them elderly, the other aged between 25 and 30. Since the robbers had paid more attention to the younger woman – evidenced by the state of her

remains – scholars surmise that she was the high-born, probably royal, recipient of this splendid burial.

Some people even believe she may have been Queen Asa, grandmother of Harald Finehair, who gained control of most of Norway in the late ninth century. If this were so, the older woman would probably have been her handmaid, accompanying her mistress into the afterlife.

The Oseberg burial rites cannot be inferred from the archaeological record; however, they may have been akin to those described by the 10th-century Arab diplomat Ibn Fadlan, who witnessed a

burial ceremony of Swedish Viking settlers by the Volga River in southern Russia in 922. According to Ibn Fadlan, the dead man's ship was dragged ashore and prepared to receive his body. The deceased was taken from his temporary grave and dressed in special funerary clothes. The corpse was laid in the ship along with fruit, meat, bread, drink, and weapons.

One of the dead man's slave women was then ritually killed on the ship by an old woman known as the Angel of Death, while men beat their shields to drown her cries. Next, the ship was set on fire with burning brands. With a strong wind whipping up the flames, the vessel and its voyagers were quickly reduced to ashes.

Although the Oseberg ship was not cremated, it, like the Volga vessel, was provisioned with food, and two people,

Gabriel Gustafsson, third from the left, poses with his team in a photograph taken on September 21, 1904, during the excavation.

one probably a servant, were involved. The Oseberg ship, which is thought to have been built around 800, had been repaired and given a new rudder and 15 pairs of pine oars just before its burial 50 years later, possibly indicating an overhaul for its last voyage to the other world.

Nothing is known for certain about the Viking belief in the afterlife. But the preponderance of ship burials, as well as those involving wagons and horses, suggest that death was the first stage of a journey to another world. For Viking heroes who died on the battlefield, this other world was Valhalla, an abode presided over by the supreme god Odin, where the order of the day was endless drinking and feasting.

However, the Oseberg ship was moored to a rock, suggesting to some scholars that rather than setting out for the afterlife, the deceased were waiting safely at anchor for a future day of resurrection. In one sense, with Gustafsson's excavation, that is exactly what happened.

Among the objects buried with the two skeletons in the Oseberg ship was a double-edged sword whose hilt is shown above. Axes and spears are other weapons that the Viking dead took with them to the afterlife.

TIMEFRAME

A.D.

c.800–1100 THE PERIOD OF THE VIKING AGE.

c.800 THE OSEBERG SHIP IS FIRST BUILT.

c.850 THE SHIP IS THOUGHT TO HAVE BEEN REFITTED BEFORE ITS BURIAL WITH THE BODIES OF TWO WOMEN.

922 IBN FADLAN WITNESSES A VIKING BURIAL BY THE VOLGA RIVER.

1903 REPORTS OF THE OSEBERG SHIP BURIAL REACH GABRIEL GUSTAFSSON ON AUGUST 8.

1904 EXCAVATION OF THE MOUND TAKES PLACE FROM MAY 6 TO DECEMBER 16.

THE VIKING AGE

In an explosion of energetic enterprise from the late 8th to the 11th centuries, the Vikings streamed out of Scandinavia for foreign lands. For these fierce maritime Norse warriors, the sea was like a bridge that connected them with Christian western Europe and farther abroad. Their motives were mixed. Some engaged in savage raids for plunder, often taking rich pickings from defenceless monasteries and other Christian sacred places. Others were more concerned with exploration and trade, ready to exchange their slaves, furs, ivory walrus tusks, salted fish and sealskins. And yet others found places to settle, such as Iceland, Greenland, islands off Scotland, and a part of northwestern France, which was ceded to the

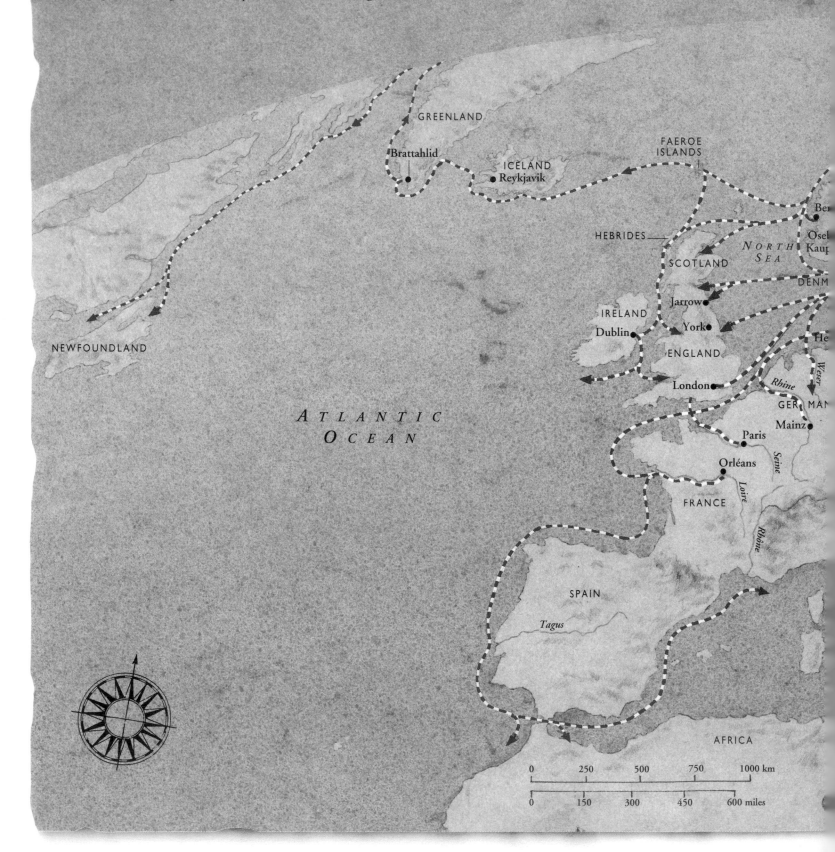

Norsemen in 911 and became known as Normandy. They even reached North America in the late 10th century, hundreds of years before Christopher Columbus "discovered" the New World.

Owing to the shallow draught of their ships, the Vikings were able to utilize Europe's network of rivers and penetrate its interior along, for example, the Loire, Seine and Rhine. Swedish Vikings also crossed the Baltic Sea to Russia, trading as far as the Caspian Sea and forming dominant communities in the cities of Novgorod and Kiev. Some even reached the Byzantine capital of Constantinople, where they served as mercenaries and even eventually formed the emperor's elite Varangian Guard.

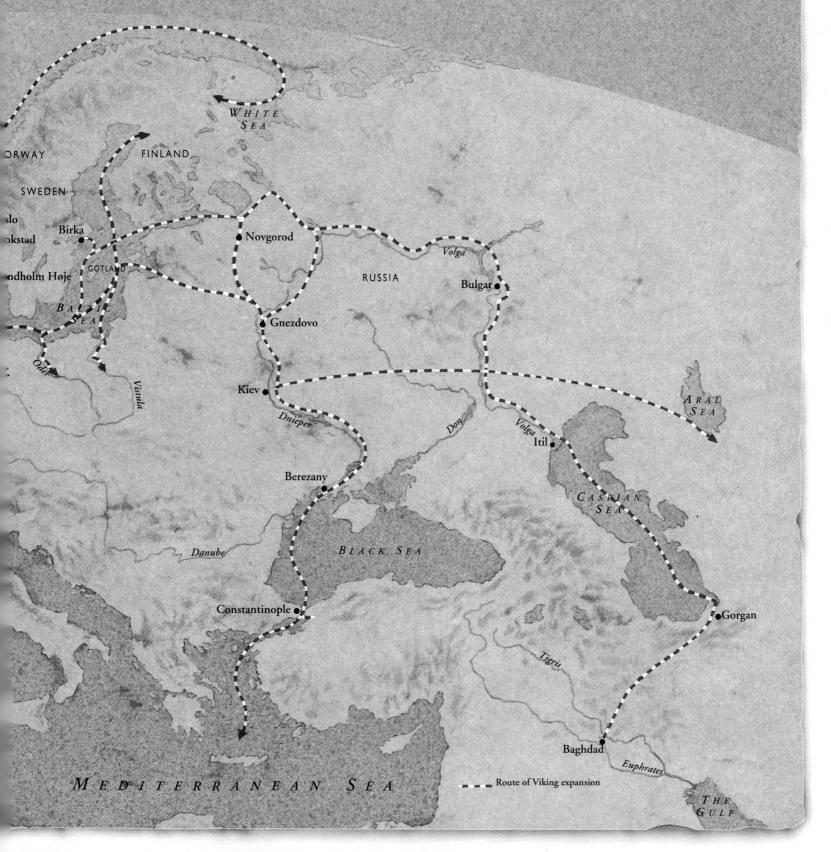

Route of Viking expansion

ITALY

THE CATACOMBS OF ROME

"I often entered the crypts, dug deep into the earth, their walls lined on either side with the bodies of the dead...."

SAINT JEROME (C.342–420), REFERRING TO THE CATACOMBS OF ROME

ITALIAN ARCHAEOLOGIST G.B. DE ROSSI had good cause to remember 1849. For that year, he made a discovery that rolled back 16 centuries of history to the time of the early Christians. Outside the walls of Rome, he discovered an underground cemetery, or catacomb, which had held the bodies of several early popes. Informed of this amazing find, Pope Pius IX hurried to the cemetery and, his eyes filled with tears, asked de Rossi: "Are these really the tombstones of my predecessors who were buried here?"

De Rossi had been alerted to the existence of the cemetery while looking around an old Christian chapel near the Via Appia. Here, he spotted a marble slab

inscribed with the broken letters NELIUS MARTYR and deduced that the stone had once marked a Christian tomb. And he was aware from literary sources that in the vicinity lay the undiscovered catacomb of Saint Callistus – in which several third-century popes, including one named Cornelius, were interred.

De Rossi's subsequent excavations were a spectacular success. In the flickering gloom within a labyrinth of underground passages, he found not only a marble slab with the letters COR, which fitted with NELIUS MARTYR, but also a crypt in which the popes had been buried.

A catacomb typically consists of a maze of underground galleries, often carved out

Carved out of ground lying south of ancient Rome, the cavelike crypt of the popes forms part of a third-century catacomb named after Saint Callistus. Sanctified by the bodies of early Christian clergy and martyrs, the catacombs were underground cemeteries. They also served as meeting places for Christians, especially before their religion was adopted by the Roman emperors in the fourth century A.D.

Shouting the words "Come forth", Jesus raised Lazarus from the dead, an episode recounted in Saint John's Gospel (11:1–46) and depicted in this mural from the Roman catacomb of Jordani. The miracle, which demonstrates Jesus's power over death, was popular in catacomb art – more than 50 depictions have been found in the Roman cemeteries. According to John's Gospel, Lazarus was buried in a cave; here, a Roman-style boxlike tomb is shown.

on more than one level and connected to chambers. These burial places have been found in other parts of Italy, as well as in Asia Minor, Egypt, Tunisia and Malta. However, the term "catacombs" has become virtually synonymous with the Christian cemeteries in Rome, which are the most famous and extensive – about 40 of them have been found. The earliest date back to the second century A.D. and are situated mainly near the ancient roads that radiate from the city, since Roman law forbade burial within the walls.

In spite of periodic persecutions of Christians from the time of Emperor Nero (54–68) to the early fourth century, the catacombs, like all burial places, were considered sacrosanct by the Romans and rarely plundered or damaged. The best known and most visited are those named after saints Callistus, Sebastian and Domitilla, all of which are situated on or near the Via Appia that leads south from the city. Their narrow passages are lined with rows of rectangular niches, or *loculi*, in which the shrouded and lime-coated bodies of saints, martyrs and ordinary Christians were placed.

Elsewhere in their dark confines are sizable tomb chambers, or *cubicula*, that housed generations of the same family. Pious inscriptions and Christian symbols, such as the fish and the anchor, and delicate murals of Adam and Eve, the raising of Lazarus from the dead, and other scenes from the Bible add colour and warmth to the walls. They show that the tombs were places of devotion, lovingly tended.

Jesus looks after his flock in his role as the Good Shepherd in this painting from a catacomb ceiling. The most popular theme in catacomb art, the Good Shepherd is often depicted in a lush idyllic setting with birds, plants and trees. The figure has echoes of classical art, in which a shepherd is typically shown bearing on his shoulders an animal for sacrifice. For the early Christians, however, the shepherd's task was to save his sheep, just as Jesus saved people from their sins.

The early Christians considered the burial of the dead a sacred duty. According to the early church father Tertullian (*c.*160–225), some of the money collected every month by Christian communities was spent on burials for the poor. And Ambrose, the fourth-century bishop of Milan, advised that, if necessary, church vessels should be sold in order to raise money to finance Christian burials.

This Christian concern for the dead was influenced by the belief in bodily resurrection and by the doctrine of purgatory. This is a place or state in which the dead must expiate their sins and undergo punishment before encountering the divine vision of God; and in this they can be helped by the prayers of the living. Conversely, the prayers of those in the afterlife were considered beneficial to the living. Thus, the catacombs were places where a communion between the living and the dead could take place.

Christians gathered in the tombs especially on the anniversary of the death of a saint, martyr or loved one. Together, they partook of a *refrigerium* – a memorial "refreshment meal" – and celebrated the Eucharist. In this way, a sense of sanctity pervaded these holy warrens which, with their sacred art, were always more than just tombs. In later centuries, pilgrims from northern and other parts of Europe came to Rome especially to visit them. The large number of visitors can be judged by the fact that special guide books, or *Itineraria*, were produced.

The catacombs were mostly created by *fossores*,

80

The dark rectangles of loculi *fill the central gallery of the catacomb of Priscilla. The bodies of the deceased were inserted in these niches and then sealed in with stone slabs or tiles.*

professional diggers, who dug them out of the soft volcanic tufa around Rome, often on private plots of ground owned by wealthy individuals. Corridors were frequently carved at right angles from an initial passage and then linked by a passage running parallel to the first. Because space was usually at a premium, further galleries were excavated down to five levels.

Catacomb burials began to decline in the fifth century as Rome became threatened by barbarian tribes. The tombs suffered at the hands of the Goths in 537 and were plundered by the Lombards in 755. Unable to protect the holy bones of martyrs and saints from marauders, later popes in the eighth and ninth centuries transferred the relics to churches within the city walls.

During the Middle Ages, the tombs were virtually forgotten. Interest in them was rekindled in the 16th century, especially after 1578, when workmen uncovered on the Via Salaria a multi-galleried catacomb in a good state of preservation. The discovery attracted the attention of a certain Antonio Bosia, whose meticulous explorations of cemeteries earned him the sobriquet "the Columbus of the Catacombs". However, scientific excavation and recording began in earnest only in the middle of the 19th century.

Today, the catacombs still preserve their mystique and sanctity. It takes little imagination to conjure up the figure of a *fossor*, wearing a short tunic, carving out a *loculus* with his pick, or putting chippings in his bag, or spiking a lamp into a wall. Or to see a group of Christians gathered together, murmuring their prayers or sharing a meal as they gaze at a fresco of Jesus, perhaps raising Lazarus from the dead or tenderly carrying a lamb on his shoulders. As one early pilgrim scribbled on a catacomb wall: "There is light in this darkness; there is music in these tombs."

ETERNAL SHRINES

MANY OF THE WORLD'S MOST SACRED sites are ancient shrines of the past, whose holy atmosphere – frequently intensified by dramatic landscapes – has not dissipated during the course of centuries. For although a great deal of their original splendour has crumbled, their roofless temples, solitary columns and broken walls continue to conjure up a real sense of mystery and stimulate the imagination. Some places, such as CAHOKIA in the United States, PAGAN in Myanmar (Burma) and TEOTIHUACÁN in Mexico, were huge religious and political centres, their cityscapes dominated by great monumental sacred structures. Other holy places consisted solely of a grand temple whose impressive architecture proclaimed the might of its patron deity – and the priesthood associated with it. The TEMPLE OF KARNAK at Thebes, for example, was the largest sanctuary in Egypt, built to glorify the god Amun. The locations of some shrines were obviously shaped by their natural settings. OLYMPIA in Greece, famous for being the home of the Olympic Games, grew up next to a prominent hill within a lush river valley. The OLGAS – great domes of rock lying at the very heart of Australia – are entirely natural and are impregnated with Aboriginal Dreaming lore. The medieval Christian ruins of the ROCK OF CASHEL in Ireland rise up from a grassy eminence and look out on to a panoramic landscape. And at Dunhuang in China, the CAVES OF THE THOUSAND BUDDHAS were carved out of cliffs in wilds in the northwest of the country by early Chinese Buddhists, who adorned them with sacred murals and statues.

Great sanctuaries of the past hallowed by the present

Buddhist temple pyramids in Pagan form the greatest collection of shrines in Myanmar and Southeast Asia.

THE OLGAS

"Time the old, the dim magician has ineffectually laboured here, although with all the powers of ocean at his command; Mount Olga has remained as it was born."

EXPLORER ERNEST GILES, WHO FIRST SAW THE OLGAS IN 1872

LIKE MASSIVE HUMPBACKED WHALES rising from a sea of desert, the Olgas are a group of more than 30 rocky domes that form one of Australia's great natural sights. Situated in the Northern Territory, the Olgas, like their famous neighbour Uluru, or Ayers Rock, are sacred to the Aborigines, to whom they are known as Katatjuta – the place of "many heads". They are a storehouse of Aboriginal legends which relate how they came into being during the Dreaming, the time of creation.

Stripped of their mythological clothing, the Olgas are masses of conglomerate – a rock often likened to a plum pudding because it is a mixture of boulders fused with pebbles. Once part of a prehistoric sea bed, the Olgas were raised and folded by movements of the earth's crust some 500 million years ago. They were then gradually sculpted by the forces of erosion into a huddled group of giant rocks.

Some of these rounded stone ramparts are bunched together, their precipitous flanks defined by narrow crevices. Others are spaced apart, their smooth bulwarks polished by the constant winds. Highest of all the peaks is Mount Olga, the

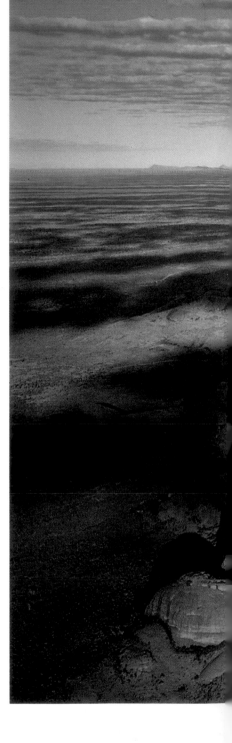

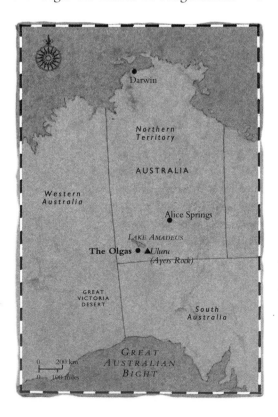

The sheer pock-marked sides of the Olgas are riddled with Aboriginal Dreaming legends. These great rocks, which are spread over an area of 11 square miles, rise up to an impressive 1,500 feet. They were discovered by white explorers only toward the end of the 19th century.

westernmost sentinel of the group, which rises sheer about 1,500 feet above the desert floor and from which the rest of the group take their name.

The first white man to set eyes on the Olgas was the explorer Ernest Giles, in October 1872. He was unable to reach them, however, because his horses could not cross a lake that blocked his path. He named the lake and distant domes Amadeus and Mount Olga, respectively, after the king and queen of Spain, who were notable patrons of science. Giles actually

made his way to the Olgas the following September but found there, to his shock and dismay, the tracks of another explorer named William Gosse. As Giles wrote afterward: "Had the earth yawned at my feet, for ever separating me from this mountain, or had another of similar appearance risen suddenly before my eyes, I could not have been more astonished...."

For Aborigines, Katatjuta has been a sacred site since time immemorial and can be understood only in relation to the Dreaming. According to Aboriginal belief,

The ribbed formations of clouds seem to mirror the bulging configurations of the Olgas, which lie at the centre of Australia and are sacred to the Aborigines.

Scattered like the fossilized bones of a huge dinosaur, the Olgas are a three-dimensional Dreaming map. The snake Wanambi lives on Mount Olga *(8)* and retreats to a waterhole *(7)* during the dry season. Elsewhere are food *(6)* prepared by the mice women; the dying kangaroo man *(5)*; Pungalunga men *(1, 2* and *3)*; and the Valley of the Winds *(4)*.

this was when their "ancestors", in the form of humans and totemic animals, emerged from the depths of the earth into daylight. As they journeyed across the land, they created hills, waterholes, caves, lakes and other natural features through everyday actions such as hunting, fighting, marrying, thinking and singing.

The paths the ancestors took are known as Dreaming tracks, or songlines. When Aborigines follow trails belonging to their totemic group and sing the songs and tell

Glowing like great ruby spheres, the Olgas' conglomerate domes are fired to a deep red by the rising and setting sun, a phenomenon also experienced at Uluru (Ayers Rock).

the stories handed down from their ancestors, they enter into the world of the Dreaming and become symbiotically at one with the ancestor and the landscape.

The Dreaming refers not only to the original act of ancestral creation, but also to a dimension of time continuous with the present. Thus, the western concept of history as a series of events irrevocably consigned to the past is alien to the Aborigines. For them, the Dreaming and the journeys of the ancestors are an ever-present reality in which they can actually participate by ceremonial singing, storytelling and dancing. The land is a living text, its topography printed with Dreaming lore, and the songlines that criss-cross the continent are sacred paths leading the initiated into an eternal dimension.

Katatjuta, with its myriad crevices, fissures, gullies, striations and waterholes, is impregnated with Dreaming stories.

A green carpet of trees and shrubs lines the floor of the narrow Valley of the Winds that leads into the heart of the Olgas.

Mount Olga, for instance, is the home of a snake named Wanambi who, during the rainy season, lies curled in a waterhole on the mountain's summit, but moves to another one in the gorge below during the dry season.

Mount Olga's caves are believed to be Wanambi's various camp sites, and black lines created by water on its eastern end are the hairs of his beard. Wanambi's breath is the wind that blows through the gorge, reaching hurricane force when he is angry. No one must transgress tribal law; otherwise Wanambi, taking the form of a rainbow, will wreak mortal revenge.

On the eastern side, a number of domes are connected with ancestors known as the mice women. Two large rocks near the end of Mount Olga are great mounds of food prepared by them, while monoliths nearby are their camp sites. And on the south-western tip are domes where the Liru, poisonous snake men, made their camp

before setting out to attack the harmless carpet snakes at Uluru. East of these stands a distinctive pinnacle which is the transformed body of Malu, a kangaroo man, dying of wounds inflicted by dingoes. The rock on which he leans is his sister Mulumura, a lizard woman, who cradles her brother in her arms.

Also important are the stone bodies of giant cannibals known as the Pungalunga, which can be seen on the northwestern side. Taller than trees, powerful-jawed, and sharp-toothed, the Pungalunga killed, dismembered and cooked their human victims. The last of these savage giants was eventually killed by two kangaroo men, who speared him in the back while he was crouched in the scrub ready to ambush them. As the Pungalunga fled howling in pain, the two men tracked him down to a cave near a spring, where they managed to finish him off.

Although non-Aborigines are mostly unaware of the Olgas' rich Dreaming lore, many find them to be as impressive and often more mysterious than the better-known Uluru. Certainly, the rocks made a deep impression on the first white visitors at the end of the 19th century and during the first half of the 20th. They described them variously as "a congress of camel-humps", "the temples of an ancient city" and "enormous pink haystacks". It would not require a great leap of imagination to embroider these metaphors to produce non-Aboriginal creation stories equivalent to those of the Dreaming.

As well as evoking specific images, the Olgas emit a raw primordial grandeur. Their stark bulbous forms, straight out of the depths of prehistory, have the power to transport the visitor to the distant past. As Ernest Giles expressed it: "the rounded minarets, giant cupolas and monstrous domes...have stood as huge memorials of the ancient times of earth, for ages, countless aeons of ages, since its creation...."

THE TEMPLE OF KARNAK

"The imagination, which in Europe soars high above our portals, stops short and falls powerless at the foot of the 140 columns…at Karnak."

FRENCH EGYPTOLOGIST JEAN-FRANÇOIS CHAMPOLLION (1790–1832)

To STARE UPWARD INSIDE THE GREAT colonnaded hall of the temple of Amun at Karnak, on the eastern bank of the River Nile, is to feel like a Lilliputian in the land of Gulliver. Gargantuan columns rise like petrified sequoias, their capitals broad enough to support a crowd of 100 people or more huddled together. Elsewhere, other columns, more than 45 feet high, create countless channels of light through this dense rainforest of stone vegetation. The largest religious building ever constructed, the temple was clearly designed to magnify Amun, "king of the gods", and make mere mortals pale into insignificance in his presence.

Karnak is the modern Egyptian name for the temple complex that lay at the heart of Thebes, former capital of the ancient Egyptians, who called it Ipet-isut, "the most select of places". The city rose to prominence during the Middle Kingdom period of Egyptian history (c.1938–1600 B.C.), and the prestige of its local deity Amun, originally a god of the wind, became more widespread.

It was only during the New Kingdom, however, with the coming to national power of Theban nobles, that the city became a grand imperial capital. Now Amun, also known as Amun-Re from his identification with the sun god, became

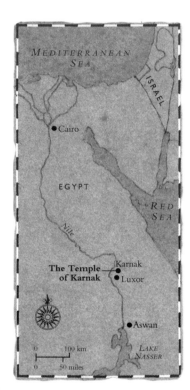

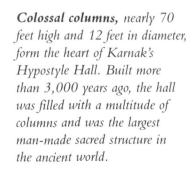

Colossal columns, *nearly 70 feet high and 12 feet in diameter, form the heart of Karnak's Hypostyle Hall. Built more than 3,000 years ago, the hall was filled with a multitude of columns and was the largest man-made sacred structure in the ancient world.*

Ram-headed sphinxes *line one side of the temple's great court. The ram, an aspect of Amun-Re, holds a statue of Ramses II between his hoofs.*

the mightiest of Egyptian gods, and his temple became the grandest in the country. The temple also served as the state's main treasury, with the king, or pharaoh, dedicating to it booty from victorious campaigns abroad. Tribute from foreign provinces and tax revenues also poured in, so that it became the most powerful institution in Egypt.

The temple played an important role in the economic, administrative and social life of the country. It owned vast estates and employed large numbers of administrators, scribes, craftsmen, farmers and gardeners, as well as clergy, musicians and singers. During the reign of Ramses III (1187– 1156 B.C.), the temple controlled at least 7 percent of the population, 81,000 slaves, 421,000 cattle, 433 gardens, 46 building yards and 83 ships.

From the New Kingdom onward, pharaoh after pharaoh built, knocked down, added to, and altered the original core of the temple. As a result, it is now a bewildering agglomeration of gateways, or pylons, courtyards, columns, halls, obelisks and statues. In general, later pharaohs extended the temple westward toward the Nile. Thus Pylon 1, the first gateway the visitor enters, is the last one to have been built. To proceed through pylons and courtyards toward the sanctuary is to walk through lateral strata of Egyptian history.

Although Karnak is often equated only with the temple of Amun, two other distinct precincts form part of the complex.

Taking the form of a ram, and crowned with a solar disc, *Karnak's patron god Amun* (RIGHT) *traverses the heavens in his sacred boat. This finely incised low relief forms part of the shrine of Seti II within the great court.*

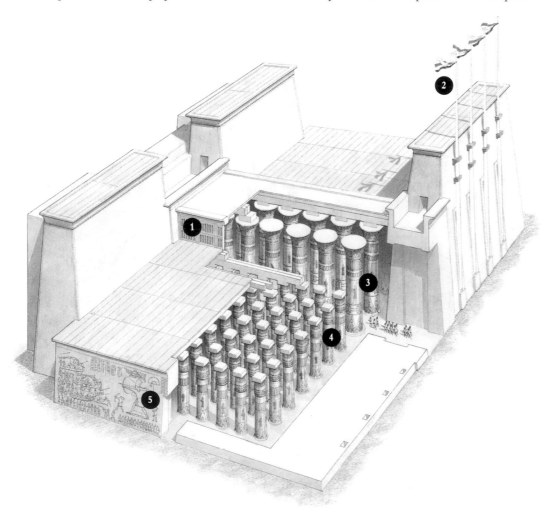

The Great Hypostyle Hall was initiated by Ramses I and completed by Seti I and his son Ramses II. A double row of central columns (**3**) stood higher than the others (**4**), allowing light to filter through clerestory windows (**1**) situated just below the roof. All the walls (**5**) and columns were carved and painted with scenes illustrating cultic acts and heroic deeds of the pharaoh. Priests entered the hall via a massive pylon, which was adorned with flagpoles (**2**).

These belong to the goddess Mut, the wife of Amun, and Montu, who was originally the local god of the city. However, Amun's temple is the best preserved and the greatest in size, covering an area that would accommodate 10 cathedrals.

The approach to Pylon 1 is along an avenue of guardian sphinxes, hybrid creatures with the bodies of lions and the heads of rams. The great sandy-coloured pylon, with its austere double towers, looms ahead, looking like the entrance to a baronial castle. This is clearly what modern Egyptians thought of it since they named the ruins el Karnak – "the fortress".

The first pylon, one of six leading to the sanctuary – the holy of holies – provides temporary shade before the dazzling sunlight of the first courtyard. From here, the second pylon, preceded by huge statues of Ramses II (1279–1213 B.C.), heralds the entrance of the great colonnaded hall. This is officially known as the Hypostyle Hall and was completed by pharaohs Seti I and Ramses II, his successor. It covers an area of about 54,000 square feet and was once roofed and filled with 16 rows containing a total of 134 columns.

The two central rows of columns are higher than those on either side, and this enabled "clerestory" windows to be built

__This grand statue of Ramses II__ in the great court was "usurped" some time after his death by Pinnedjem, a high priest, whose name is inscribed on the statue's kilt.

into the walls that rose above the side aisles. As a result, sharp beams of sunlight shafted through like laser beams. Their light filtered through to other parts of the hall, dimly illuminating columns that were carved and brightly painted with scenes illustrating acts of worship and the pharaoh's heroic deeds. The aim was to create a sense of sombre mystique after the dazzling daylight of the courtyard and before the darkness of the inner sanctum.

With their capitals carved to imitate stylized lotus buds and open papyrus heads, the columns created a sense of luxuriant vegetation. This had a profound symbolic resonance for the ancient Egyptians, since it reminded them of the primordial island of their creation myth. According to one version of this, the earth was once covered with darkness and waters, from which a mud island emerged. On this mound of land grew a reed plant, which became the perch for the falcon god Horus. Sanctified by the presence of the god, the island required divine protection, and so a reed-mat shrine was built around the plant and cordoned off by a reed wall. Later, this structure was expanded into a reed temple with various other rooms added at a level lower than the shrine.

Although there were variations of the myth, it furnished the archetypal model for

Reaching heavenward, *this obelisk is one of two still standing at Karnak. It was cut as a single block from the quarries of Aswan, then polished and inscribed with texts.*

Karnak's crumbling *magnificence before restorations took effect is portrayed in this painting by David Roberts, a 19th-century British artist. The French Egyptologist Georges Legrain began major work on the temple in 1895. Four years later, 11 columns in the Hypostyle Hall fell down after an earthquake. Although restorations had not been completed before Legrain's death in 1917, his work was carried on by Henri Chevrier, Pierre Lacau and other French Egyptologists determined to preserve this greatest of temples.*

all subsequent Egyptian temples, which were seen as the original island of creation. The sanctuary, for example, which housed the shrine containing the cult-statue of the god, always echoed the island's original reed-mat shrine.

Floors were designed to ascend gradually toward the sanctuary before sloping away, imitating the different levels of the island. And columns, with their palm-, lotus- or papyrus-shaped capitals, embodied the lush vegetation of the mythic mound. Thus modern critics who compare Karnak's giant columns unfavourably with the elegant marble ones of ancient Greek monuments miss the point completely: the primary concern of the Egyptian architect was with a mythic truth, not with visual aesthetics.

Beyond the Hypostyle Hall rises the third pylon which, according to an inscription, once had a golden door encrusted with lapis lazuli and other gems, a floor overlaid with silver, and gilt flagstaffs which "shone more than the heavens". The path continues through the fourth and fifth pylons to where the original sanctuary, built by Tuthmosis I (1493–1482 B.C.), stood. However, the one seen today, behind the sixth pylon, was built by Philip Arrhidaeus, the half-brother of Alexander the Great who conquered Egypt in 332 B.C.

The sanctuary was the holy of holies and the focal point of the priests' daily worship. It consisted of a small rectangular chamber within which stood a shrine, inlaid with gold and gems, containing the god's image. The pharaoh, usually deputized for by high

priests, had to attend to the god three times a day. Priests had to shave their heads and bodies, dress in white linen, and wash three times a day to keep ritually pure.

The priest would arrive at the temple carrying a censer billowing with charcoal-burning incense. He then proceeded toward the sanctuary through the pylons, courtyards and Hypostyle Hall. Having reached the shrine within the sanctuary, he broke its clay seal, pulled back the bolts and opened the two doors. Reciting ritual prayers, he saluted the god – believed to be resident in the statue – and prostrated himself. He then chanted hymns, made an offering of honey and walked around the shrine four times.

Next, the priest took the statue out, unclothed it and purified it with incense, water and natron. Having dressed it again, he painted the god's eyebrows with green and black cosmetics and placed on him the royal insignia. He offered the god food and drink before replacing him in the shrine, resealing it with clay. The priest then left the room backward, making sure to sweep away his footprints, thereby removing all trace of mortal presence.

Many of Karnak's columns have bud capitals (BELOW), *imitating in stone the vegetation of the original island in the Egyptian creation myth. For the ancient Egyptians, temples were essentially symbolic re-creations of this island and its shrine.*

The pylons and columns of Karnak loom up behind the temple's sacred lake. This rectangular pool of water symbolized Nun, the eternal ocean. Here, Amun's priests came to purify themselves before carrying out the temple ritual.

For ordinary Egyptians, the sanctuary and, indeed, most of the temple, was out of bounds. Their only chance to see the god was during a festival, when the deity was brought out of his shrine and taken in procession, often to visit another god near by. At Thebes, for example, during the festival of Opet on the 19th of the second month of the year, the gods Amun, Mut and Amun's son Khonsu – known as the Theban Triad – were taken from their respective temples at Karnak to one about a mile south in what is now modern Luxor.

Priests carried each god in ceremonial barques raised on poles on their shoulders to waiting boats on the Nile. As the vessels were towed upriver, with incense wafting from them, an enthusiastic crowd of priests, soldiers, dancers, singers and ordinary townspeople followed their progress on foot and in boats. When the visiting gods had reached the temple at Luxor – where there are still reliefs depicting the festival – they were given offerings of food and drink. Then, at a given point, the gods were taken back to Karnak in the same way they had come.

Unlike other Egyptian temples, that of Amun does not end with the sanctuary. Lying behind it, across a courtyard, is the Festival Hall of Tuthmosis III (1479–1426 B.C.), built to commemorate the pharaoh's military victories abroad. In one room of the building, known as the Botanical Garden, there are reliefs depicting various exotic flora and fauna brought back by Tuthmosis from his foreign ventures, which may have formed the world's first zoological collection.

Next to the hall is the sacred lake, a rectangular pool to which the priests came daily to perform their ritual ablutions. Also it is said that temple lakes were used for certain festival ceremonies. During these, barges carried the image of the god on a symbolic voyage across the lake, whose banks were lined with trees and on whose waters floated blossoms of blue and white lotus plants.

Despite its size, jumbled ruins and tourist invasions, Karnak still preserves its sacred atmosphere, particularly if, at quiet moments, the holy rituals that were performed in the sanctuary or the cavernous twilight world of the Hypostyle Hall can be imagined. Here, above all, the Egyptians created a building fit for the "king of the gods". As the British Egyptologist Margaret Murray expressed it: "In the moonlight…when all is silent, the visitor can imagine the shaven priests…passing through toward the shrine to fall in adoration at the feet of the deity of the greatest temple in the world."

TIMEFRAME

B.C.

c.1938–1600 THE MIDDLE KINGDOM: THEBES AND ITS LOCAL GOD AMUN RISE TO PROMINENCE.

c.1539–1075 THE NEW KINGDOM: THE TEMPLE OF KARNAK BECOMES THE BIGGEST AND MOST IMPORTANT IN EGYPT.

332 ALEXANDER THE GREAT CONQUERS EGYPT.

A.D.

1798 NAPOLEON BONAPARTE LEADS A MILITARY EXPEDITION TO EGYPT; ACCOMPANYING ARTISTS COPY KARNAK'S RELIEFS.

1842 KARNAK IS INCLUDED IN THE PRUSSIAN SCHOLAR RICHARD LEPSIUS'S GREAT STUDY OF EGYPT'S ANCIENT MONUMENTS.

1895 THE FRENCH EGYPTOLOGIST GEORGES LEGRAIN BEGINS TO RESTORE THE TEMPLE.

1899 AN EARTHQUAKE DAMAGES THE HYPOSTYLE HALL.

1903 LEGRAIN DISCOVERS A BURIED HOARD OF 17,000 BRONZE FIGURES AS WELL AS A QUANTITY OF STATUES AND STELAE.

GIFT OF THE NILE

"Food provider, bounty maker", runs an ancient Egyptian hymn describing the River Nile, "who creates all that is good...." To the Egyptians in their desert land, the river was, and still is, their life-giving artery. It made the crops grow, provided fish to eat, and was used for both personal and commercial transportation. In the words of the Greek historian Herodotus, Egypt was the "gift of the Nile".

Until it was regulated by dams, especially the High Dam completed at Aswan in 1970, the Nile rose in late July and from mid-August to late September flooded its valley, nourishing the normally dry land with a layer of silt. Cereals and grain were grown, as were vegetables, herbs, oil-producing crops for cooking and lighting, flax for linen and papyrus, which was made into paper.

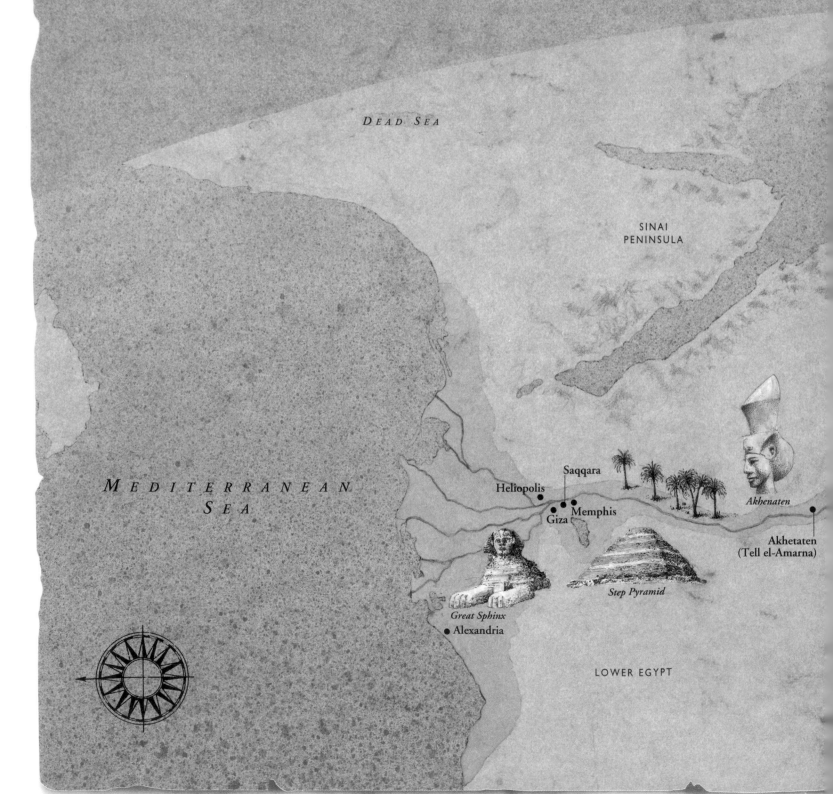

DEAD SEA

SINAI PENINSULA

MEDITERRANEAN SEA

Saqqara

Heliopolis

Akhenaten

Memphis

Giza

Akhetaten
(Tell el-Amarna)

Step Pyramid

Great Sphinx

Alexandria

LOWER EGYPT

Nurtured by the Nile's waters, Egyptian civilization began to mature in about 3100 B.C. It lasted until 323 B.C., when Alexander the Great conquered the country. Now, even after thousands of years, the pyramids, temples and royal tombs still speak of the power and wealth of the pharaohs – the god-kings who ruled the land.

Shown on the map are the fertile Nile Valley, bordered by desert, and some of Egypt's sites and monuments whose remains can still be seen. These include Giza, with its pyramids (pp. 64–71) and Great Sphinx; the Step Pyramid at Saqqara; Tell el-Amarna, where the heretic pharaoh Akhenaten built his capital of Akhetaten; Thebes, with its temples of Karnak and Luxor; the Valley of the Kings and the nearby mortuary temple of Queen Hatshepsut; and Abu Simbel, dominated by the Great Temple of Ramses II.

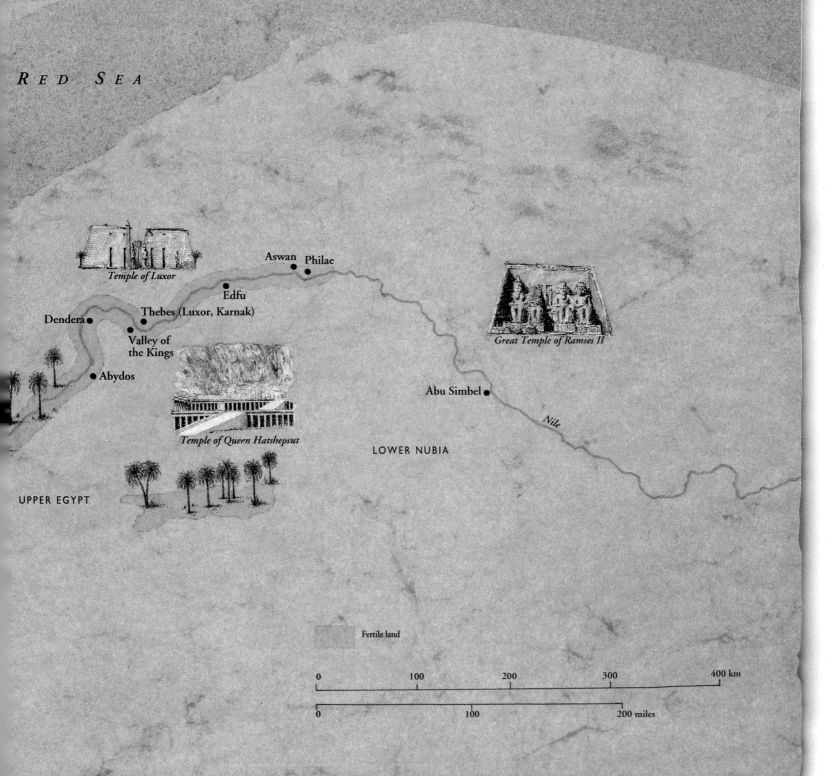

RED SEA

Temple of Luxor

Aswan • Philae •

• Edfu

Dendera • Thebes (Luxor, Karnak)

Valley of the Kings

• Abydos

Great Temple of Ramses II

Temple of Queen Hatshepsut

Abu Simbel •

Nile

LOWER NUBIA

UPPER EGYPT

Fertile land

0   100   200   300   400 km

0   100   200 miles

MEXICO

TEOTIHUACÁN

"Even though it was night...they gathered, the gods convened there in Teotihuacán."

AZTEC CHRONICLE RECORDING TEOTIHUACÁN'S CONNECTION WITH THE GODS

THE AZTECS CALLED IT "THE PLACE OF the gods". And they were by no means the first to be impressed by Teotihuacán's countless temples and the giant pyramids of the Sun and the Moon, which rivalled the pyramids of ancient Egypt in size. From the beginning of the Christian era to about 750, Teotihuacán, with an area greater than that of imperial Rome, was the greatest religious centre in ancient Mexico. Even in the early 14th century, hundreds of years after its eclipse, the Aztecs, who were then the dominant people in the Valley of Mexico, regarded it as a sacred site and buried their rulers there.

The city also occurs in the Aztecs' legends. For they believed that the world had passed through four creations, or "suns", which had been destroyed by jaguars, fire, winds and flood. And, after the end of the fourth sun, it was at Teotihuacán that the gods gathered in darkness to decide which of them should throw themselves into the flames of a ritual fire and become the fifth sun. Eventually, the lowly Nanahuatzin leaped into the flames and became the new sun, renewing the light for humankind.

Nor was Teotihuacán simply a ceremonial centre. At its height in about A.D. 500, it was the largest city in the entire Americas – a grand metropolis of up to 200,000 people. However, since its people left no written documents, scholars have had to rely on the remains of monuments, faded murals, figurines, pots and other material evidence, supplemented by later Aztec legends, for information about this once great civilization.

Teotihuacán's society, it appears, was divided into distinct groups, for example nobles and merchants, and all were governed by a caste of ruler priests. Crafts thrived and artisans included potters and workers in various materials, such as shell, leather, jade, onyx and obsidian, a volcanic glass whose usefulness in making tools and weapons made it the ancient Mexican equivalent of steel. These craftsmen formed their own enclaves within the city, as did resident foreigners.

Monumental stone architecture and an ordered design show that the city's planners were sophisticated architects who had a unity of vision. The buildings were laid out on a geometrical grid in which even a

Monterrey

GULF
OF
MEXICO

MEXICO

Guadalajara

Teotihuacán

Mexico City

0   200 km

0   100 miles

PACIFIC OCEAN

One of the largest structures built in the ancient Americas, the chunky terraced Pyramid of the Sun dominates the site of Teotihuacán, which thrived during the first millennium A.D. as a major religious centre near what is now Mexico City.

river was rerouted to conform to its plan. Its main spine, the Avenue of the Dead, connected the huge marketplace and the so-called Citadel at its southern end with the grand pyramids of the Sun and the Moon to the north. Lining the route were small pyramid-shaped platforms originally topped with temples.

On each side of the avenue stretched palaces and one-storey residential apartment complexes. These were arranged around courtyards in which stood altars – tangible evidence of the importance of religion in Teotihuacán society. The buildings were made of stone and plaster, and many were decorated with murals depicting fish, birds, serpents, coyotes and jaguars, as well as various gods – all executed in vivid blues, greens, reds and yellows. The floors, according to a later chronicler, were made

99

The skill of Teotihuacán craftsmen can be seen in the reconstructed mural of the rain god Tlaloc (ABOVE) *and face mask* (BELOW), *whose nose pendant and ear "spools" were worn by nobles.*

of whitewashed plaster polished with pebbles until it shone "like a silver plate".

Householders channelled rainwater from sloping roofs and pavements into drains that could be plugged and used as reservoirs. And they used circular pits in courtyards and rooms in their dwellings as graves in which the bones of the deceased were usually wrapped in shrouds along with grave goods, such as vases, obsidian objects and textiles.

Teotihuacán first grew to a considerable size toward the end of the first millennium B.C. The reasons are various. For a start, the city lay in a valley that was capable, with intensive irrigation, of producing abundant crops; and it straddled an established trade route from the coastal regions in the east to places farther south. Furthermore, it was a major centre for obsidian, which was quarried nearby. Not least, its status as a traditional hallowed site drew large numbers of pilgrims, for whom it was the Mecca or the Varanasi of its day.

From miles away, visitors saw what looked like a mountain towering up in the city. This was the Pyramid of the Sun –

Teotihuacán was situated in a fertile valley, and its influence reached as far as present-day Guatemala. Its main artery was the Avenue of the Dead (*4*), behind which lay one-storey apartment complexes (*5*). Adjoining the avenue were the pyramids of the Sun (*3*) and Moon (*1*), originally covered in plaster and partially painted, and the Plaza of the Moon (*2*), enclosed by smaller pyramids.

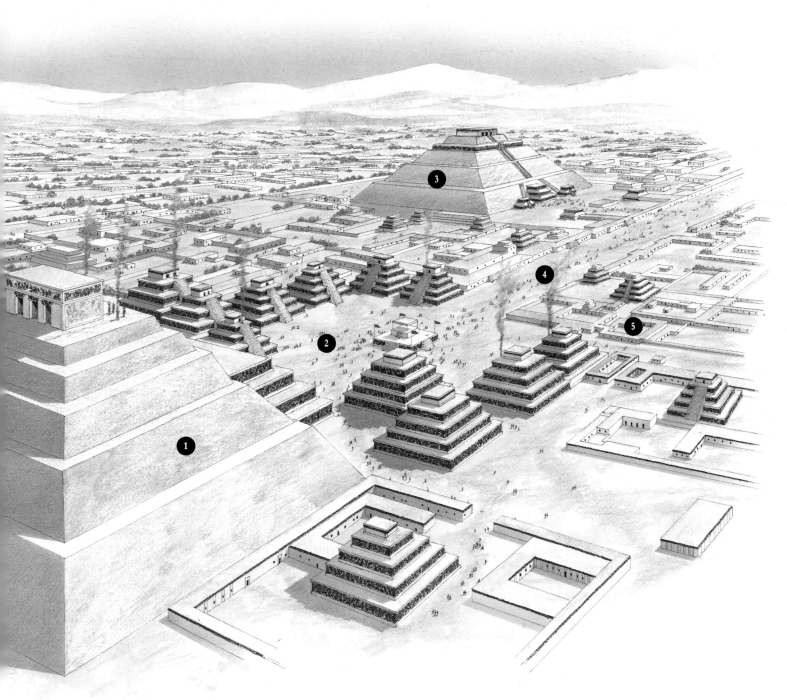

one of the largest structures in the Americas until the 20th century. Rising 230 feet and with sides 738 feet long, the area at its base was about the same size as the Great Pyramid of Khufu at Giza (pp. 64–71).

Its giant superstructure, completed in the first few centuries A.D., was built on a spot already considered holy. For in 1971, archaeologists discovered in the ground below its central point a cave consisting of a long passage with a four-lobed chamber at the end – resembling a four-leaf clover with a long stem. Various pottery shards showed that it had been used as an underground shrine, perhaps for centuries, before it had been built over.

Further corroboration of its sacredness comes from an Aztec legend which held that the Aztec people originally came to their capital of Tenochtitlán (now buried beneath Mexico City) from a place known as the Seven Caves. By analogy, it is possible that the people of Teotihuacán considered their cave to be their original womblike source and then sanctified it by raising their greatest pyramid over it.

Rising in distinct diminishing platforms, the Pyramid of the Sun resembles a Mesopotamian stepped ziggurat rather than a true smooth-sided pyramid. Its massive facade is lined with a monumental staircase leading up to the summit, where a small temple once looked over the grand avenue, plazas and buildings. Here, amid clouds of copal incense billowing up from burners, priests clad in flamboyant feather head-dresses conducted rituals, perhaps to propitiate the sun god – or, during a drought – Tlaloc, the god of rain.

Beyond the Pyramid of the Sun lies the smaller Pyramid of the Moon, a little more than 150 feet high. However, because it occupies higher ground, their summits are about the same height. From the south, the chunky stepped outline of the Pyramid of the Moon, with its broad plaza in front, is framed by the now extinct volcano Cerro Gordo, as if the pyramid's architect had aimed to echo its natural prototype.

In fact, scholars have pointed out various alignments in Teotihuacán that suggest that its buildings were carefully orchestrated. The Avenue of the Dead, for example, runs 15½ degrees east of due north, parallel to the front of the Pyramid of the Sun and along a line that passes through the centre of the Pyramid of the Moon to a depression on top of Cerro Gordo behind it. And from the Pyramid of the Moon, a line runs through the centre of the Pyramid of the Sun to Patlachique Mountain in the distance. In a similar vein, the Pyramid of the Sun and the stemlike passage of its cave seem to have been aligned with the setting point of the constellation known as the Pleiades.

In short, the builders of Teotihuacán appear to have been both astronomers and mathematicians who sought to harmonize their creations with the celestial bodies above and the mountainous landscape all around. As the modern American

The ruins of the temple of Quetzalcoatl lie within the Citadel at the southern end of the Avenue of the Dead. The temple was built in the classic architectural style known as talud-tablero, *in which inward-sloping stone panels* (talud) *alternate with perpendicular ones* (tablero).

Originally covered with lime plaster, the temple's walls were studded with the protruding stone heads (RIGHT) *of Tlaloc, the saucer-eyed rain god, and Quetzalcoatl, the Feathered Serpent – the only occasion that these two deities are seen together in Teotihuacán.*

archaeoastronomer John B. Carlson has written: "Nowhere is the bond between sky and earth more evident than at Teotihuacán...."

Apart from the pyramids of the Sun and Moon, the city's most significant sacred structure was the temple of the god Quetzalcoatl. This lay within the precinct of the Citadel, a vast four-sided complex of temples and palaces, more than 21,000 feet square, which may have been the seat of government. Quetzalcoatl, the Feathered Serpent, had the body of a snake and the feathers of the quetzal bird and was one of the great gods of ancient Mexico. For the people of Teotihuacán, he seems to have been a god of nature; for the Aztecs, however, he was a culture god, inventor of books and the calendar, and identified with the planet Venus.

But Quetzalcoatl and all Teotihuacán's other gods were unable to save the city from its terminal decline. The cause of its end is shrouded in mystery. Perhaps the writing was on the wall in the seventh century, for warrior figures appeared with growing frequency in Teotihuacán art; and this was perhaps an indication of an increased military emphasis by the time of the city's destruction by fire during the mid-eighth century. In the end, there may have been some sort of invasion or civil insurrection. But depletion of natural resources, including severe deforestation, and adverse climatic conditions may also have played a part.

Whatever happened, Teotihuacán became a smoking ruin. Yet the gods did not desert the city. And later, it became a source of spiritual renewal for the Aztecs, for whom the carefully sited pyramids were a living connection between the gods and humankind, between heaven and earth. Its status is evident from the fact that Moctezuma II — the last Aztec ruler before the Spanish conquest in the early 16th century — made pilgrimages on foot to the city's ruins from Tenochtitlán. But after Moctezuma, the city's gods retreated from the brave new world of Christianity, turned from powerful deities into inanimate idols with eyes of stone.

OLYMPIA

"It is possible to see and hear many truly wonderful things in Greece; but there is a uniquely divine character to the mysteries at Eleusis and the games at Olympia."

GREEK TRAVELLER PAUSANIAS (*fl.* A.D. 143–176)

MANY OF THOSE WHO GATHER EVERY four years to watch – or compete in – the Olympic Games may not realize that their origins ultimately go back to a Greek festival first recorded in 776 B.C. This was held at the site of Olympia, northwest Peloponnese, southern Greece, and grew, through the centuries, to become the greatest festival in the Greek world. Here, at the "mother of games", Greeks from the mainland, islands, and colonies in Asia Minor, Italy, and northern Africa competed for the coveted crown of wild olive leaves for themselves and glory for their cities.

The focal point of the Olympic festival was the Altis, or Sacred Grove, a parcel of land measuring 600 by 500 feet and enclosed by walls on three sides and by the hill of Cronus on the fourth. Here, the altar of Zeus – king of the gods – as well as the shrine of the legendary hero Pelops and temples dedicated to Zeus and the moon goddess Hera signified the deep-rooted sacredness of the games, which were conducted in a spirit of religious devotion. Solemn sacrifices and sacred oaths were vital to the proceedings, and the victorious athletes took on the aura of demi-gods.

Olympia is in one of the most scenic, fertile spots in Greece, where the milky waters of the Alpheus River and its small tributary the Cladeus irrigate a broad, lush valley spiked by dark-green cypresses. The drifting scent of resin wafts from pines and in spring, tiny flowers bejewel the revivified grass in dots of colour from the palette of a French impressionist painter. No wonder the Greek traveller Pausanias, who

Two boxers, one bleeding from the nose, fight each other in this detail from a sixth-century Greek vase. Boxing was introduced into the Olympic games in 688 B.C., and contestants wore gloves made of oxhide bindings. Contests were not restricted to a ring, nor were there rounds or weight classification.

visited Olympia in A.D. 174, reckoned that the games were touched with divinity.

Today, there is little left standing of the temples, shrines, statues, and other structures that adorned the site. Earthquakes and the flooding of the Alpheus have taken their toll over the centuries. However, extensive excavations conducted by German archaeologists at the end of the 19th century and during the 20th, have restored the basic shape of the Altis and the foundations of many buildings.

Rows of elegant fluted columns partially mark out the ground plans of the gymnasium where athletes trained and the palaestra, a residence hall and practice ground for wrestlers, both just outside the Altis. Within it, among grey stones scattered like icy fragments left by the retreat of a glacier, the remains of the Prytaneum, a building that housed the sacred hearth with its perpetual fire, can be seen. Here also are the ruins of the temple of Hera and a row of 12 "treasuries." These were small

Olympia's palaestra, *lying just to the west of the Altis, was a practice ground for wrestlers and a residence hall. Dressing rooms looked on to a central courtyard, which was surrounded by elegant colonnades. Here, while spectators sat around chatting and viewing the proceedings, trainers supervised their charges, whose oiled bodies would soon become bespattered with sand.*

105

One of the most venerated shrines in ancient Greece, the temple of Hera was Olympia's oldest sanctuary. Although its remains date from about 600 B.C., an earlier structure probably existed on the site two centuries earlier. The Doric columns were originally made of wood and over time were replaced with stone ones.

templelike structures raised by cities in homage to Zeus or as a thanksgiving for Olympic victories.

In the centre, gigantic column drums, some still embedded fossil-like in the earth, lie in jumbled heaps around the temple of Zeus, whose cult statue was one of the seven wonders of the ancient world. Northeast of the temple rises the hill of Cronus, named for the father of Zeus, at the foot of which was an oracular shrine of Gaia, goddess of the earth. People came to this spot to hear prophecies based on the

interpretation of their dreams. Shrouded in dark green pines, the hill overlooks the elliptical stadium where 40,000 spectators, enjoying the sunshine on the surrounding grassy slopes, cheered on their favourites.

The origins of the Olympic festival are obscure and shrouded in myths and legends. The site is associated with Pelops, son of Tantalus, who won the hand of Hippodameia, the daughter of the local king of Pisa, by beating her father in a chariot race. A cult of Pelops is said to have existed at the site, and according to one

tradition the four-yearly games were held to commemorate his bride-winning race.

Pausanias, however, held that the site was sacred to Cronus before the coming of Pelops; and other legends associate the place with the hero Heracles, famed for his 12 labours, who is said to have measured out the Altis in honor of his father Zeus. But many modern scholars think the games arose from athletic contests performed as part of the funeral rites of a local hero. Such competitions were described by the epic poet Homer (c.800 B.C.) in the *Iliad*, in which they are held in honour of the Greek hero Patroclus after his death at Troy.

The first recorded games took place in 776 B.C., and from then on they were held every four years for about a millennium, until the end of the fourth century A.D. The games cycle was such an important occasion in the Greek calendar that it was used as a chronological reference point for dating other events.

Every four years, special envoys were sent out from the local city of Elis to all parts of Greece to proclaim the sacred truce: any warring had to cease so that Greeks could come to, participate in, and leave the festival in safety. A month before the start of the games, the contestants arrived at Elis, where they were inspected by officials to make sure they had the right qualifications: male, free-born, pure Greek, and free from the pollution of having committed a criminal offence.

By the start of the festival, which took place after the summer solstice during the period of the full moon, Olympia was transformed from a tranquil sanctuary to a thronging tent city. The surrounding fields and woods were filled with campers and their temporary lodgings. An army of hawkers and street entertainers joined ranks with thousands of ordinary visitors.

Poets, politicians, and philosophers came to discuss the issues of the day, press the claims of their respective cities, or simply relive past contests and speculate on those about to take place. For many Greeks, the festival period, when local feuding was sublimated to the higher ideal of national unity and the overriding desire

Competitors entered Olympia's stadium via an arched passageway (BELOW RIGHT) *that resembles the entrance tunnels of modern stadia. Spectators crowded on to the banks surrounding the running track, which was about 210 yards long – the length of a "stade" – and wide enough to accommodate 20 runners.*

Athletes stride out in this detail from a fifth-century vase. Runners competed in races of varying lengths, including ones of 200 yards and 3 miles. All athletes ran naked, a custom initiated, it is said, after a runner's shorts came off in a race in 720.

OLYMPIA

Giant column drums from the temple of Zeus lie next to its foundations. The temple interior was dominated by Pheidias's statue of Zeus, shown in an 18th-century engraving (OPPOSITE). Pheidias's workshop, west of the temple, was later converted into a church; but excavators identified it from sculptor's tools, chips of ivory and bone, and a clay mug with the inscription: "I belong to Pheidias".

This model of Olympia, from the British Museum, shows the temple of Zeus in the centre with the temple of Hera behind, left of the row of templelike treasuries that lie below the hill of Cronus. At top left is the gymnasium – the training ground – and below it, the palaestra. On the right, outside the Altis, is the stadium.

to obey the games' sacred tradition, must have seemed a throwback to the lost golden age of poetic tradition.

The games lasted five days and followed a set procedure. On the first day, white oxen were sacrificed on the altar of Zeus, a two-tiered structure 22 feet high, with the lower stage used for slaughtering animals and the upper for the sacrificial burning. Athletes and judges were then sworn in. Next day, the contests began. In the morning, chariot races were held in the hippodrome (now no longer traceable), followed in the afternoon by the pentathlon – "five contests" – consisting of running, long jump, throwing the discus and javelin, and wrestling.

More sacrifices to Zeus were performed on the third morning, while the afternoon

was devoted to boys' races. For many, the fourth day, featuring such trials of courage and endurance as wrestling, boxing, and racing with armour on, was the climax of the festival. Perhaps the most fascinating – and gruesome – spectacle was the *pancration*, a sort of no-holds-barred wrestling match. Almost everything was permitted – including tripping, kicking, and throttling – except for biting and eye-gouging, and competitors were sometimes killed. The games ended on the fifth day, when prize giving, sacrifices, and feasting were the occasion for merriment.

Victors were not only honoured by receiving an olive wreath ritually cut from a sacred olive tree by a boy with a golden sickle, but were also often commemorated by a statue in the Altis or in a specially commissioned ode. And their cities often gave them more practical rewards such as free meals, money, or theatre tickets. Athenian winners could stay in the city guesthouse free for life; and Spartan victors could join the prestigious royal bodyguard.

Some competitors became the stuff of legend. Pausanias tells of a retired wrestler Timanthes who, discovering he no longer had the strength to bend an enormous bow, threw himself on to a flaming pyre. And there was also the six-times wrestling

champion Milo of Croton, who could hold a pomegranate in such a way that no one could pry it from his hand, and yet his grip did not damage the fruit. Another of his feats was to tie a string around his forehead and then snap it by holding his breath and inflating his veins.

While spectators cheered on the oiled bodies of athletes glistening in the sun and crowds milled around in animated spirits, the temple of Zeus stood out above the proceedings, a solid reminder of the god's presence among mortals. Begun in 468 B.C. and completed in 457, the temple was – at 230 feet long, 95 feet wide, and 68 feet high – one of the largest structures in Greece. It was made of rough local stone covered in a thin layer of white stucco with details picked out in blue, gold, and red.

Inside, behind the facade of Doric columns and bronze doors, the interior was dominated by one of the seven wonders of the ancient world: the sculptor Pheidias's statue of Zeus. Rising 40 feet, it depicted the god garlanded with olive sprigs and sitting on a grand throne made of ivory and gold and encrusted with jewels. With one hand he gripped a sceptre topped by an eagle; in the other he held a winged figure of victory. His sandals and robe, which was inlaid with designs of lilies and animals, were made of gold, his flesh of ivory.

In front of the statue, a pool or tank filled with olive oil moistened the atmosphere

A Corinthian capital evokes *Olympia's Roman period, which began in the latter half of the second century* B.C. *and marked the start of the games' decline. The most famous Roman competitor was Emperor Nero, who entered a chariot race in* A.D. *67. Although he fell from his chariot, the judges tactfully awarded him first prize. Nero celebrated victory by giving a large donation to the games' organizers.*

and prevented the ivory from cracking as well as reflecting the god's somber visage. According to Pausanias, when the statue was finished, Pheidias prayed to Zeus for a sign that he was pleased with his art: the god's approval was given by a flash of lightning that struck the pavement nearby.

The statue impressed all who saw it. The Roman emperor Caligula (A.D. 37–41) liked it so much that he decided to carry it off to Rome. But when his workmen were about break it up, they heard a loud peal of laughter. Then, when their scaffolding suddenly collapsed, they fled in terror. But the statue was too grand a prize to survive being looted forever. In 426, Emperor Theodosius II took it to Constantinople, the capital of the eastern Roman Empire, and there it perished in a fire in 475.

The games themselves had come to an end nearly 100 years before, when the Christian emperor Theodosius I, the Great, ordered them to be closed in about 393. Over the following centuries, earthquakes and floods flattened the buildings and covered them with silt and pebbles. By

medieval times, the local shepherds had no inkling that the place they knew as Andilalo covered the most famous stadium and sanctuary of antiquity.

That Olympia had existed was known to scholars through the writings of Pausanias, but the site was discovered only in 1766 by a Briton named Richard Chandler. In the next century, initial excavations were made by a French team in 1829. However, it has only been as a result of German expeditions from 1875 to 1881, 1936 to 1941, and from 1952 onward that the sacred ruins have fully come to light.

Enough of the site remains to reconstruct in the mind the temple of Zeus gleaming white in the sun, or, walking through the entrance tunnel into the stadium, to hear the roars of the packed terraces. It is possible, too, to imagine, like the poet Pindar (518–538 B.C.), famous for his Olympian odes addressed to triumphant athletes, the boisterous victory celebrations with the evening lit "by the lovely light of the fair-faced moon" and the "holy place...loud with song".

Runners wait for the starting pistol in the Olympic games in Athens in 1896 in this contemporary image (BELOW LEFT). *The games — the first in modern times — were revived after an absence of some 1,500 years through the efforts of a Frenchman named Baron Pierre de Coubertin, who first put forward his proposal for them in 1892. Four years later, de Coubertin's dreams became a reality when the games were opened in Athens by the king of Greece in a stadium specially built for the occasion.*

TIMEFRAME

B.C.	
776	FIRST RECORDED GAMES FESTIVAL AT OLYMPIA.
468–457	BUILDING OF THE TEMPLE OF ZEUS.
c.437	PHEIDIAS BEGINS WORK ON THE STATUE OF ZEUS.
A.D.	
67	THE ROMAN EMPEROR NERO COMPETES AT THE GAMES.
c.393	THE GAMES ARE CLOSED DOWN BY THEODOSIUS I.
426	THEODOSIUS II CARRIES OFF THE STATUE OF ZEUS.
1766	THE SITE OF OLYMPIA IS REDISCOVERED BY RICHARD CHANDLER.
1875	EXTENSIVE GERMAN EXCAVATIONS AT OLYMPIA BEGIN.
1896	FIRST OLYMPIAD OF THE MODERN ERA IS HELD AT ATHENS.
1996	MODERN CENTENARY GAMES ARE HELD AT ATLANTA.

CAHOKIA

"When I examined it in 1811, I was astonished that this stupendous monument of antiquity should have been unnoticed by any traveller...."

HENRY BRACKENRIDGE DESCRIBING CAHOKIA'S MONKS MOUND IN A LETTER TO THOMAS JEFFERSON

WHEN A GROUP OF FRENCH TRAPPIST monks founded a monastery in southern Illinois in 1809, they discovered that their new settlement was blistered with emerald green earth mounds. Everywhere they looked, mounds of different shapes and sizes, overgrown and eroded, bulged from the landscape. One in particular dominated the others, rising up like a small mountain, its mass divided into terraces.

Four years later, however, ground down by malaria and the hardships of daily living, the Trappists decided that their future lay elsewhere. So they departed – unaware that their settlement had been on top of Cahokia, the greatest prehistoric Native American city north of the Rio Grande. Little did they know it, but this rich fertile

Cahokia was the greatest city of the Mississippian people, whose culture is known today through objects such as the shell head with a topknot hairstyle (ABOVE LEFT) *and the shell disc incised with a spider* (LEFT). *The head's stylized weeping eye and the cross on the spider's thorax are symbols which archaeologists connect with a religion known as the Southern Cult, itself associated with the Mississippians.*

112

area had been teeming with thousands of people some 500 years previously.

Yet the Trappists' brief sojourn was not forgotten. Cahokia's great earth mound, on the lowest of whose terraces the Trappists had grown vegetables, was later designated Monks Mound in their honour. That a holy order of another time and culture should be associated with this monument is entirely appropriate, since Monks Mound was the sacred heart of Cahokia. It formed the base of a grand wooden structure that is believed to have combined the functions of both a temple and a palace.

Lying eight miles east of St. Louis, Missouri, Cahokia is named after a Native American people (the name means "Wild Geese"), who inhabited the area in the 17th century. It was the main city and ceremonial centre of a culture known as Mississippian that flourished from c.1050 to 1250.

The Mississippians rose to prominence in the southeast and mid-continent during the ninth century A.D. The most visible characteristic of their civilization was the flat-topped mounds that served as the bases for temples, mortuary houses and royal residences. Prospering on the cultivation of

Dawn light defines the silhouetted summit of Cahokia's Monks Mound, the largest prehistoric earthen work in the Americas. Raised about 1,000 years ago, the mound is composed of an estimated 22 million cubic feet of earth. Its topmost terrace was once crowned by a temple/ palace from where the ruler-priest presided over the city.

corn and other crops along the flood plains of the river valleys, Mississippian towns and villages multiplied. None of them, however, attained the size of Cahokia, which reached its peak in about the middle of the 12th century. At this time, it was the largest settlement in North America, covering an area of about six square miles and with a population of as many as 20,000 people.

The body of the city lay within a long sturdy stockade laid out in the shape of a D. Inside this curtain of wood stretched the broad main plaza, about 40 acres in extent, from which rose a number of earth mounds of different types and sizes. Some were rounded with pointed tops, like cones, while others were elongated, with triangular ends and ridgelike summits. Most common were the temple, or platform, mounds which resembled truncated pyramids. On their flat tops were raised wooden temples and other structures, none of which has survived.

The most imposing structure was Monks Mound, which dominated the city from the northern end of the main plaza. This colossal earthen work – the largest in the pre-Columbian Americas – was started in the 10th century and built and enlarged over 300 years. Its sloping sides rose 100 feet and consisted of four terraces that covered some 14 acres.

On the mound's topmost terrace stood a grand thatched ceremonial building, which was more than 100 feet long and 50 feet high. This was probably the main temple or the ruler's palace – although since the ruler may have combined both religious and political roles, the building probably reflected this duality.

From atop Monks Mound, the ruler and his attendants could gaze over the city with its 120 mounds and the outlying villages. They would have seen the land ruptured with mounds like giant molehills, spacious plazas and small lakes, possibly stocked with

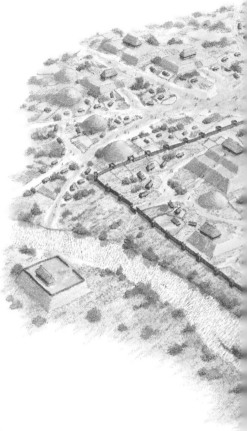

The battered mass of Monks Mound, here seen from the northwest, is the centrepiece of Cahokia Mounds State Historic Site. In 1831, a certain Amos Hill built a house on top of Monks Mound; and he himself is said to have been buried in its northwestern corner. The mound continued to remain in the hands of private landowners until the early 20th century.

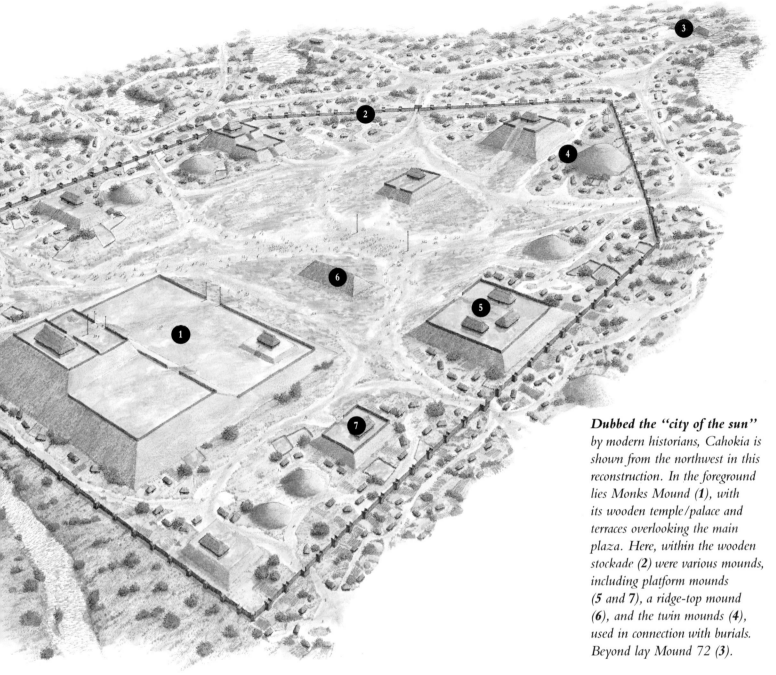

Dubbed the "city of the sun" by modern historians, Cahokia is shown from the northwest in this reconstruction. In the foreground lies Monks Mound (1), with its wooden temple/palace and terraces overlooking the main plaza. Here, within the wooden stockade (2) were various mounds, including platform mounds (5 and 7), a ridge-top mound (6), and the twin mounds (4), used in connection with burials. Beyond lay Mound 72 (3).

fish, where rain had filled pits excavated to provide earth for the mounds.

Surrounding the plazas were small houses made of poles lined with reed mats or intertwined with saplings smeared with clay mixed with grass. In different sectors, craftspeople, such as potters and workers in shell, copper and mica, went about their business. Elsewhere, people dressed in simple loincloths ground corn on large stones, whittled wood into bows, carved stone tobacco pipes or wooden masks, and skinned deer.

Since they were preliterate and so left no written records of their culture and beliefs, most of what is known about the Mississippians comes from material evidence. However, the Native American Natchez people – who were the cultural heirs of the Mississippians – were observed by various French explorers in the lower Mississippi Valley between 1698 and 1731. And scholars believe that Natchez life and customs shed valuable light on those of their Mississippian ancestors.

The Natchez were divided into distinct social classes governed by a ruler-priest known as the Great Sun. He was the representative of the sun on earth and was treated with godlike reverence by his

CAHOKIA

people. For example, wearing a crown of snow-white swan plumes, he was always borne aloft in a litter so that he would not be defiled by contact with the ground.

Only the Great Sun and his priests could enter the main temple, perched on the central mound, where a sacred fire was kept burning and bones of previous rulers were stored. After his death, a lengthy funeral ensued. His wives and retainers were strangled; his house was burned; and his bones, in time, were laid in the temple.

As with the Natchez, the Mississippians had elaborate funeral rituals involving sacrifices. Excavations of Mound 72, a six-foot-high ridge-top mound about half a mile south of Monks Mound, have shown that it enclosed three smaller mounds and burial pits in which almost 300 people were interred. The prize burial was that of a middle-aged man, presumably a chief, whose body had been carefully placed on a bed of 20,000 shell beads.

Surrounding this unknown chief were other grave goods, such as quantities of mica, rolls of sheet copper, hundreds of flint arrowheads and the sacrificed bodies of six of his entourage. Also unearthed, in a pit, were the bones of 53 young women; and below one of the subsidiary mounds lay the skeletons of four men, lying in a row. Their heads and hands had been cut off and their arms overlapped – evidently as part of a ritual act.

Grave offerings feature in other Mississippian burials and include pearls, shell discs used as chest decorations, pots in the shape of stylized heads, and shell vessels. Apart from suggesting an established death ritual, these goods bear motifs which scholars connect with a religion they call the Southern Cult.

These symbols include weeping eyes, crosses, flying winged human figures and sunburst designs; and they appear on clay and shell vessels, copper sheets, stones and textiles. Although much of the cult

Tufted with trees, Monks Mound looks like a natural flat-topped eminence in this drawing made in 1833 by the well-known contemporary artist Karl Bodmer, who also drew sketches of the Twin Mounds. The building on top is the farmhouse erected by Amos Hill two years previously.

A warrior beheading his victim is the favourite interpretation of this soapstone pipe (LEFT) found at the Mississippian site of Spiro in Oklahoma. Elaborate pipes such as this one were used in religious and other ceremonies by the prehistoric Americans.

With its spiky hair and bared teeth, this embossed copper head (LEFT) is thought to portray a warrior of the Mississippian people. It is one of the few objects giving an indication of what these people looked like.

116

remains a mystery, it is believed to have reached its full maturity in about 1250. Elaborate mortuary rituals played a central part, as did an emphasis on aligning buildings with the cardinal directions.

Death rituals were, as Mound 72 shows, important to the Cahokians. Also, the layout of their city indicates that they were fully aware of alignments. Monks Mound, for example, was in the middle of the site, aligned with the four points of the compass. Also, Cahokia's north-south axis ran from Monks Mound's south to Mound 72 via other significantly placed mounds. And other prominent earthen works marked the city's east-west axis.

The discovery in 1961 of the remains of a circle of cedar poles is further proof that the Cahokians used orientations and alignments. Located to the west of Monks Mound and dubbed Woodhenge, the circle was about 1,000 years old and had been enlarged five times (the third circle of 48 posts has been reconstructed on the site). Investigators believe the posts were used for calendrical purposes, perhaps to track the phases of the moon or, more probably, the path of the sun, in order to establish key

seasonal dates, such as the summer and winter solstices. It is also possible that the circle was used to fix the alignments of Cahokia's mounds.

At the spring equinox, when crops had to be sown, an observer standing in Woodhenge at dawn would have seen the sun rise directly over Monks Mound itself. At this key moment in the calendar, the ruler-priest, the servant of the sun, may have emerged from the mound's temple to mark this pivotal event – perhaps by lighting a sacred bonfire.

For some 200 years, Cahokia thrived as the spiritual, cultural and commercial hub of the Mississippians. But toward the end of the 13th century, it began to decline. The reasons remain an enigma. There may have been adverse climatic conditions leading to crop failure, famine and civil unrest. Overexploitation of woodland and other natural resources may also have played a part. Whatever the causes, by the end of the 15th century, Cahokia was a ghost city, its people gone and its mounds overgrown. The city of the sun had been eclipsed; but its great mound has survived, an impressive relic from America's mysterious past.

TIMEFRAME

A.D.

c.800	CAHOKIA STARTS TO EMERGE AS A CENTRE OF MISSISSIPPIAN CULTURE.
c.900	WORK BEGINS ON MONKS MOUND.
c.1150	CAHOKIA REACHES ITS CULTURAL AND POLITICAL ZENITH.
c.1250	THE DECLINE OF CAHOKIA BEGINS.
1809–13	FRENCH TRAPPIST MONKS OCCUPY A MONASTIC SETTLEMENT AT CAHOKIA.
1831	A PRIVATE HOUSE IS BUILT ON TOP OF MONKS MOUND BY AMOS HILL.
1925	CAHOKIA MOUNDS STATE PARK IS CREATED AFTER THE STATE OF ILLINOIS ACQUIRES 144 ACRES OF THE SITE.
1961	EXCAVATIONS UNDER DR. WARREN WITTRY REVEAL THE EXISTENCE OF WOODHENGE CIRCLES.
1982	CAHOKIA IS DESIGNATED A WORLD HERITAGE SITE BY UNESCO.
1989	A NEW MULTIMILLION-DOLLAR INTERPRETIVE CENTRE IS OPENED AT THE SITE.

THE MOUNDS OF ANCIENT NORTH AMERICA

Mainly scattered around the river valleys of the Mississippi and Ohio, the earth mounds of North America are relics of native prehistoric cultures and date from about 1000 B.C. to A.D. 1450. The mounds range from small conical earthen works to large truncated pyramids. The "effigy mounds" are low and, from above, resemble animals, such as a snake or eagle.

Once believed by 18th-century Europeans to be the work of recent invaders, the mounds were created by three indigenous cultures which scholars have termed Adena, Hopewell – both named after find-sites – and the Mississippian, whose great spiritual and political centre was Cahokia (pp. 112–17). Adena people inhabited the eastern woodlands, around the Ohio

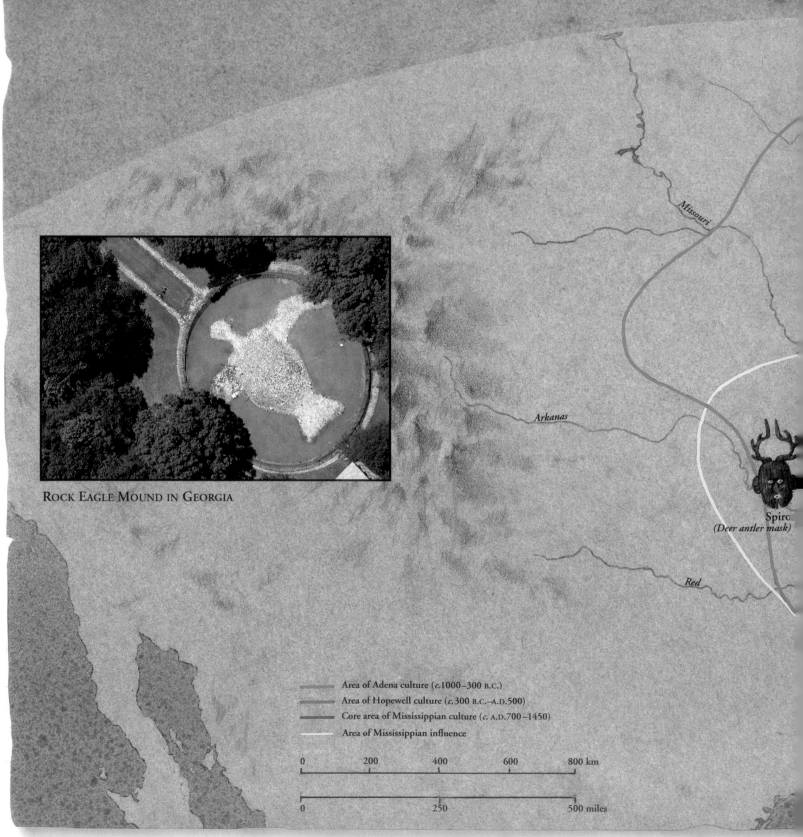

ROCK EAGLE MOUND IN GEORGIA

Missouri

Arkanas

Red

Spiro
(Deer antler mask)

Area of Adena culture (c.1000–300 B.C.)
Area of Hopewell culture (c.300 B.C.–A.D.500)
Core area of Mississippian culture (c. A.D.700–1450)
Area of Mississippian influence

0   200   400   600   800 km

0   250   500 miles

River, and built effigy mounds and circular earthen enclosures – "sacred circles" thought to have had a ceremonial use and which sometimes enclose burial mounds. The Hopewell people – whom most scholars believe developed Adena culture – are known through their mounds as well as their grave goods. These have included conch shells from the Gulf coast and grizzly-bear teeth from the west, which show that the Hopewell were prolific traders. Among the sites in the cultures' core regions shown on the map are Moundville, Alabama, and Spiro, Oklahoma, where a wooden deer antler mask was found; Bird Mound in Wisconsin, and Mound City, Ohio, where a ceramic pot with a spoon-billed duck design was unearthed.

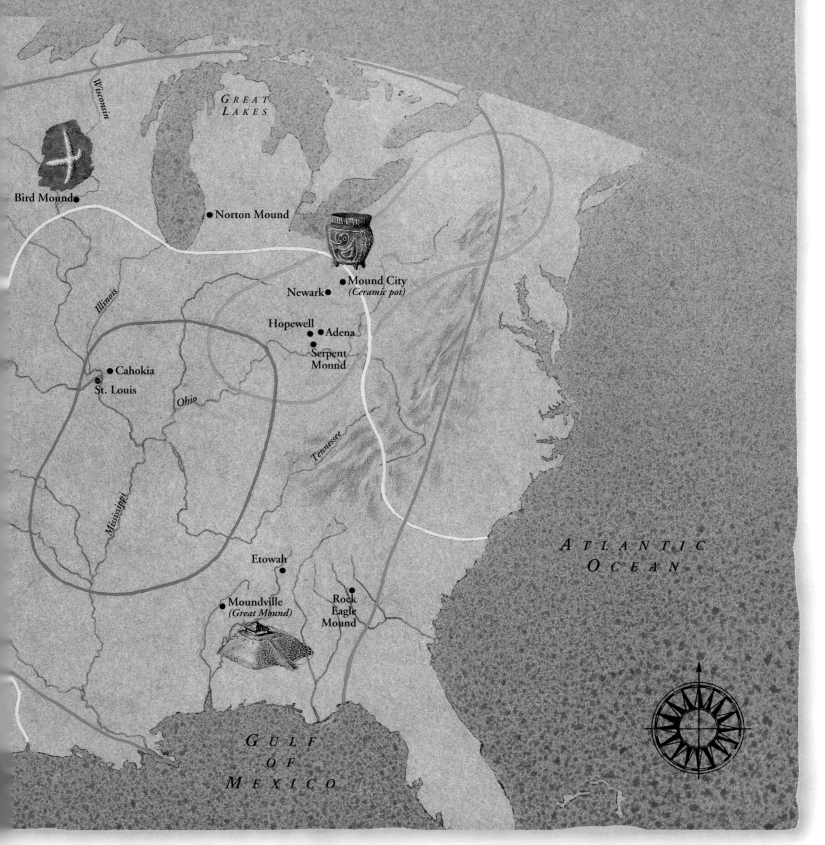

Wisconsin

GREAT LAKES

Bird Mound●

●Norton Mound

●Mound City
Newark● *(Ceramic pot)*

Hopewell
● ●Adena
Serpent
Mound

Illinois

●Cahokia
St. Louis

Ohio

Tennessee

Mississippi

Etowah
●

Moundville
(Great Mound)

Rock
Eagle
Mound

ATLANTIC OCEAN

GULF
OF
MEXICO

PAGAN

"The whole, as seen from the river, might pass for a scene on another planet, so fantastic and unearthly was the architecture."
<small>BRITISH ENGINEER CAPTAIN HENRY YULE ON FIRST SEEING PAGAN IN 1855</small>

ON A HOT, DUSTY PLAIN OF CENTRAL Burma (renamed Myanmar in 1990) more than 2,000 Buddhist pagodas and temples of the ancient city of Pagan form one of the most extraordinary sights in Southeast Asia. Some languages use the expression "as countless as the stars in the sky" in order to convey a huge number; the Burmese, however, say "as countless as the pagodas of Pagan".

As dawn separates the sky from the earth and light ripples over a broad silver coil of the Irrawaddy, Burma's greatest river, a bristling forest of spires, pinnacles, and conical domes spike the air, like giant cacti

and thorns made of stone. As far as the eye can see, sacred shrines, some almost 1,000 years old, stretch away for eight miles along the east bank of the river and for about two miles inland. In some places they cover the ground so densely that it has been said that it is impossible to move without touching something sacred.

Some shrines are dilapidated, their bricks mounds of rubble, their spires toppled. But others, such as the great Dammayangyi, Ananda, and Thatpyinnu temples, tower up like mountains from the flat plain. A few resemble snowy peaks, their white plaster pinnacles rising like stalagmites, their icy facades unmelted by the heat of the sun.

According to tradition, Pagan was founded in 849 by King Pyinbia of the Burmese people, who, during earlier centuries, had migrated to Burma from the region of Tibet. At this time, Burmese power was concentrated in the north of the country, while in the south, a people known as the Mon were supreme.

These power lines changed irrevocably after the accession of Anawrahta to the Pagan throne in 1044. A dashing figure who gained the crown by winning a duel, Anawrahta united Burma for the first time, and with him the country's history properly starts. A strong king, Anawrahta

The temples and pagodas of Pagan *were built between the 11th and 13th centuries A.D. Together they form the greatest assemblage of Buddhist monuments in the world.*

was also a deeply religious man. At the time of his accession, the people of Pagan had mainly believed in spirits known as *nats* and followed forms of Mahayana Buddhism (prevalent in China, Tibet, Japan, and Korea) and Hinduism.

Shortly after his coronation, however, the new king was visited by a certain Shin Arahan, a Buddhist teacher of the Theravada school (prevalent in Southeast Asia and Sri Lanka) and quickly embraced this religion with all the zeal of the convert. Shin Arahan urged the king to obtain one of the 30 copies of the sacred Buddhist Tripitaka scriptures held by the Mon king of Thaton in the south to consolidate the faith.

So Anawrahta duly requested a copy, but was rudely refused. Instead, he took Thaton by force and transported back to Pagan 30,000 Mons – monks, scholars, masons, goldsmiths, carpenters, and artists – as well as the Mon king himself, bound in gold manacles, and his court. The scriptures were borne on the backs of 32 white elephants, and a special library was built to house them.

The influx of Mons was a turning point in Pagan's history. Mon craftsmen passed on their skills to their Burmese counterparts, and Mon scholars taught the Pali language of the scriptures and the Mon alphabet, so that the illiterate Burmese could write down their language. And Shin

A glowing gilt statue of the Buddha stands within one of the four chambers leading off a corridor on each side of the cross-shaped Ananda Temple. Made of teak and rising more than 30 feet, the statue is lit by natural light from an unseen aperture above.

Arahan organized the Mon Theravada monks and sent them out to spread the word.

For the next 200 years, Pagan was the hub of a kingdom roughly the size of modern Burma, or Myanmar, connected to other parts of the country by an extensive network of roads. Rice cultivation improved with the building of irrigation canals, and commerce with Sri Lanka, India, and other countries in the region flourished. Pagan's lacquerware in particular was a prized commodity.

Theravada Buddhism, which is still the dominant religious and social force in the country, prevailed among the people of Pagan, although spirit worship was not completely eradicated. Shin Arahan thought it better to assimilate the *nats* into Buddhism rather than attempt to root them out of the people's affections. Indeed, on the terraces of King Anawrahta's great Shwezigon Pagoda, in the northern part of Pagan, the king placed the wooden images of the 37 traditional *nats* as bait to attract recruits to the new faith.

The Shwezigon, like other pagodas, or stupas, is essentially a reliquary mound. It is said to contain a number of bones of the Buddha, a copy of the Buddha's holy Tooth of Kandy from Sri Lanka, and an emerald Buddha image from Yunnan, in China. Its structure rises on three terraces, studded at the corners with miniature pagodas. Four flights of stairs, aligned with the cardinal

MYANMAR (BURMA)

The Ananda Temple, like other Burmese temples, is primarily a place of meditation rather than congregational worship. Its terraced pyramidal mass, miniature pagodas, dome, and spire are all typical temple elements. On a symbolic level, the structure represents the mythical Indian peak of Mount Meru.

points, run up each side, adding to the sense of vertical thrust. The bulbous bell dome, attenuated by an elegant spire, dominates the centre, exuding a meditative stillness.

After Anawrahta's death in 1077, the next great king of Pagan was his stepson Kyanzittha, who came to the throne in 1084. A just and merciful ruler who presided over an unrivalled period of peace and prosperity in Pagan's history, he improved diplomatic relations with China and stimulated trade and religious ties with Sri Lanka. He also sent a ship full of treasure to India to pay

for the repair of the Mahabodhi Temple at Bodh Gaya (pp. 18–21), where Gautama Buddha had reached his enlightenment.

At Pagan, Kyanzittha erected a host of shrines, none more splendid than the Ananda Temple. According to tradition, he built it in imitation of a cave temple in the Himalayas that had been conjured before his eyes by the artful description of eight visiting Indian monks. Built of brick faced with snow-white stucco, the Ananda resembles a tiered wedding cake. In the centre, six terraces rise above a square-shaped base,

the transition from solidity to the ethereal accomplished by the swelling tower, which is shaped like a beehive or a mitre, and its tapering spire.

From the centre of each side, four projecting vestibules form the plan of a Greek cross, with all four prongs equal in length. Each vestibule leads to a dimly lit corridor and a chamber in which a 31-foot gilded teak Buddha statue greets the visitor with a tranquil expression.

Kyanzittha was succeeded in 1112 by his grandson Alaungsithu, a skilled archer and horseman whose Buddhist piety had been nurtured by Shin Arahan himself. Alaungsithu was famous for his extended journeys abroad to Malaya, Sri Lanka, and Bengal, as well as for the number of shrines that he raised in Pagan. His greatest achievement, however, was the Thatpyinnu Temple, completed in 1144.

Standing about 500 yards southwest of the Ananda, the temple rises more than 200 feet and is the highest shrine in the

city. From a solid base and square-shaped superstructure, a bell dome and spire reach heavenward. From the top, the best views of the city reveal the Irrawaddy sliding south toward Rangoon and the plain of Pagan erupting with shrines, like a moonscape of small extinct volcanoes.

Alaungsithu was murdered by his son Narathu, whose short rule (1167–70) was marked by unrest. To atone for his crimes he built the Dammayangyi Temple, the largest in Pagan, about a mile southeast of the Ananda. The Dammayangyi's fame rests on the quality of its brickwork, perhaps because Narathu threatened to execute the masons if he could poke a needle between two adjoining bricks. But the temple failed to bring the king good fortune: he was assassinated by agents, disguised as priests, sent by an Indian prince whose daughter had become Narathu's wife and had been executed by him.

Pagan's golden age of temple building came to an end during the first part of the

The Gawdawpalin Temple, *shown here with the Irrawaddy River in the background, was founded during the reign of Narapatisithu (1173–1210). The British engineer Captain Henry Yule, who saw it in 1855, described it as "gleaming in its white plaster, with numerous pinnacles and a tall central spire...rising like a dim vision of Milan Cathedral".*

124

13th century. The energy and resources devoted to so many sacred monuments had taken its toll, summed up in the wry Burmese proverb: "The pagoda is finished and the great country is ruined". In the event, it was an external force that eventually finished Pagan.

The death blow came during the reign of Narathihapate, the last of Anawrahta's dynasty, who is remembered for his despotism and his strange boast of being "the swallower of 300 dishes of curry a day". In 1271, he finally sealed Pagan's fate by refusing to pay tribute to Kublai Khan, the great Mongol leader who had made himself emperor of China. War ensued and, in 1283, the khan's Tatar army invaded Burma. Narathihapate, the great curry eater, lost his appetite for the fray and fled from Pagan, earning the sobriquet Tarokpyemin, "the king who ran away from the Chinese".

In 1287, the cowardly monarch was killed by his own son, and in the same year, Kublai Khan's grandson, Prince Ye-su Timur, occupied Pagan, later setting up a puppet government under the rule of one of Narathihapate's sons. Pagan's kingdom quickly dissolved, and the city was never able to regain its former prestige. In the following century, its wooden buildings began to disintegrate, leaving the stone temples and pagodas to litter the terrain like a dinosaurs' graveyard.

In the history of the world, it is doubtful whether any city has expended so much creativity and toil on raising shrines as Pagan did. Perhaps it was a vision of Pagan as a holy metropolis, a city of salvation with its man-made mountains set beside the sinuous Irrawaddy, that lay behind the prayer of King Alaungsithu, inscribed on one of his pagodas: "But I would build a causeway over the river of Samsara [the cycle of birth, death, and rebirth], and would drag the drowning people across it to the City of Eternal Peace...."

Prince Siddhartha Gautama rides out from his palace in this relief (LEFT) from Pagan. Gautama renounced his family and worldly riches and set out to find the ultimate meaning of life. He eventually attained enlightenment, or Nirvana, and became known as the Buddha – the "Awakened One".

Riding a horse and dressed as a prince in imitation of Gautama's renunciation, this young Burmese boy (BELOW LEFT) from Pagan takes part in a Buddhist initiation ceremony.

TIMEFRAME

A.D.

849   PAGAN IS FOUNDED BY THE BURMESE KING PYINBIA.

1044   ANAWRAHTA, BURMA'S FIRST GREAT RULER, SUCCEEDS TO THE PAGAN THRONE.

1084–1112   THE PEOPLE OF PAGAN ENJOY THEIR GREATEST PERIOD OF PEACE AND PROSPERITY.

1144   THE THATPYINNU TEMPLE, THE GREATEST STRUCTURE BUILT BY KING ALAUNGSITHU, IS COMPLETED.

1283   BURMA IS INVADED BY THE FORCES OF KUBLAI KHAN.

1287   NARATHIHAPATE, THE LAST RULER OF ANAWRAHTA'S DYNASTY, DIES. HIS ABANDONMENT OF PAGAN EARNS HIM THE SOBRIQUET: "THE KING WHO RAN AWAY FROM THE CHINESE."

125

THE ROCK OF CASHEL

"Royal and saintly Cashel! I would gaze Upon the wreck of thy departed powers, Not in the dewy light of matin hours, Nor the meridian pomp of summer's blaze, But at the close of dim autumnal days...."

IRISH POET AUBREY DE VERE (1814–1902)

RISING SHEERLY FROM THE EMERALD flatlands of the Golden Vale in Tipperary, southern Ireland, the Rock of Cashel with its serrated skyline of medieval ruins stirs the hearts of the Irish as much as the Parthenon inspires the Greeks or Stonehenge the British. Here, crowning the summit of a grassy 200-foot-high acropolis, the medieval remains of a grand Gothic cathedral, a fortified bishop's palace, a Romanesque chapel, one of Ireland's distinctive round towers, and graves marked by Celtic crosses render in stone the soul of Ireland.

Looming like an operatic backdrop above the small town of Cashel, the Rock is important as the seat of the early kings of

Munster, who ruled more or less of the southern half of Ireland from about A.D. 370 to 1100. And its holiness derives not only from links with Patrick (*c*.390–460), the country's patron saint, but also – after King Murtagh O'Brien granted the Rock to the church in 1101 – from its status as one of Ireland's great ecclesiastical centres.

According to folklore, the Rock was formed when the devil bit a limestone chunk out of the nearby mountains and spat it on to the plain. This demonic association, however, is more than balanced by the holy figure of Saint Patrick, who is said to have visited the Rock in about 450, when he baptized the youthful king Aenghus of the Eoghanacht people.

One tradition says that when the saint reached Cashel he found the people prostrated on the ground worshipping a pagan idol. But on his arrival, the idol and others like it suddenly crashed down. Later, when Patrick was baptizing Aenghus, he unwittingly pierced the king's foot with the spike of his crozier, or staff. When, after the ceremony, he asked Aenghus why he had not yelled with pain, the king replied that he had thought the spiking was part of the baptism!

Aenghus was a devoted Christian, described as a "tree of spreading gold", and a supporter of the monasteries and convents in his domains. By charging a tax on all baptisms carried out, Aenghus was able to secure enough money to supply religious houses with 500 each of sheep, cows, cloaks, and bars of iron every year.

The Rock of Cashel, with its ruined cathedral, round tower, and bishop's palace, is Ireland's most sacred acropolis. The Rock was the seat of the kings of Munster until the Middle Ages, when, in 1101, it was granted to the church.

For the next 650 years, Cashel remained the royal seat of the kings of Munster, even though not all of them resided there. One of the most remarkable monarchs in the later period was Cormac MacCullinan who assumed the crown of Cashel at the start of the 10th century.

Educated in a monastic school, Cormac was a medieval Renaissance man, who was well-versed in Latin and his native Irish language, and combined the roles of poet, historian, philologist, and bishop. At the time of his reign, Ireland was enjoying a

respite from Viking attacks, which had begun at the end of the eighth century. Now, in a general atmosphere of calm, monasteries were being rebuilt and learning once again began to thrive.

Yet for Cormac this idyllic period lasted only until 906. Then Flann Sinna, king of Tara in the northeast, invaded Munster, possibly to avenge an alleged insult to his daughter Gormflaith, who had married Cormac before he had become king. For it seems that Cormac was so devoted to God – he was wont to immerse himself in

Saint Patrick, *shown in this modern illustration, is credited with getting rid of Ireland's snakes, seen here below his feet. Patrick, who systematically converted the pagan Irish to Christianity, visited Cashel in about 450, when he baptized King Aenghus.*

freezing water and chant his Psalter – that he abandoned his bride straight after their marriage and took himself off to a religious house. In any event, the kings of Cashel and Tara and their allies clashed at Ballaghmoon, about 50 miles northeast of Cashel. The battle ended in disaster for Cormac. His horse slipped on a track oozing with mud and blood, and he spilled

from the saddle, breaking his neck. Flann's men then hacked Cormac's head from his body and brought it to their king, who, out of respect for his enemy, kissed the lifeless visage and ordered the head to be buried in a holy place.

Later in the same century, in 976, Cashel was the scene of the crowning of Munster's and Ireland's most famous early king: Brian Boru. Using Cashel as his base, Brian fought against his Irish and Viking enemies, gradually expanding his power until, by the start of the 11th century, he was effectively king of all Ireland. At the same time he set about repairing schools, churches, monasteries, forts, roads, and bridges that had suffered considerable damage during the Viking wars.

In 1014, Brian's victory over the Vikings and the Irish king of Leinster at the battle of Clontarf, north of Dublin, was a decisive moment in Irish history. For although Brian was killed, the battle spelled the end of the Viking threat to Ireland forever.

With the start of the 12th century came the dawning of a new era for Cashel. In 1101, King Murtagh O'Brien donated the Rock to the church, dedicating it to "God, Saint Patrick, and Saint Ailbe". From then on, the strictly religious character of the Rock still seen today took shape. The 92-foot-high rocketlike round tower, which combined the functions of a belfry, a place of refuge from marauders, and a landmark for pilgrims, may already have existed at the time of the donation. But Cormac's Chapel, the earliest remaining house of worship, was built between 1127 and 1134 and named for the contemporary king and bishop of Cashel, Cormac McCarthy.

One of the very finest examples of Romanesque architecture in Ireland, this small steep-roofed building is only 47 feet long and flanked by two square towers that suggest a German influence. This is not as surprising as it sounds, since it is known that the abbot of Regensburg in Germany,

a monastery where Irish monks were resident, sent four craftsmen to help with the building's construction. Both inside and out, masons embellished walls and arches with rich carvings, including human heads, animals, fantastic beasts, and geometric shapes, such as chevrons.

The cathedral of St. Patrick, whose ruins form the greatest part of the Rock, dates from the 13th century. It replaced an earlier structure begun by King Donal Mor O'Brien in 1169, soon after Cashel had been confirmed by papal authority as one of Ireland's four archbishoprics. The proportions of this now roofless edifice are unusual because the building had to fit between the two structures that were already established on the Rock: the round tower and Cormac's Chapel. As a result, the nave, which is usually the largest space in a cathedral, is in this case only half as long as the choir.

Today, the pointed Gothic arches frame vistas of grey stone walls against the open skies. The east wall at the far end of the choir was pierced by three slim lancet windows and flanked on each side by others that would have flooded the building with light. At the other end of the cathedral, the shell of the 15th-century bishop's palace, a sturdy fortified residence 80 feet high, bolsters the west wall.

The cathedral largely survived the ravages of time until the 18th century, but before then, on at least two occasions, it was damaged by fire. In 1494, when Ireland was under the control of the English crown, Gerald FitzGerald, Earl of Kildare, a harsh, brutal man, put the cathedral to the torch. Brought to trial before the English king Henry VII for this sacrilegious act, FitzGerald freely admitted the

Cashel's round tower, probably built around 1100, rises more than 90 feet from the Rock's summit and guards the roofless ruins of St. Patrick's Cathedral.

Cormac's Chapel, shown in this 19th-century engraving, is the architectural jewel of Cashel. Begun in 1127 and consecrated in 1134, it was built in the Romanesque style and shows German and possibly Anglo-Norman stylistic influences. The nave, shown here, was separated from the chancel by a multi-ribbed arch. On the left are flat pilasters bearing arches with moulded starlike chevrons.

crime, saying that he did it because he was convinced his enemy Archbishop David Creagh was inside it.

This outrageous justification, it seems, prompted his accusers to exclaim that all Ireland could not govern FitzGerald. Whereupon Henry, beguiled by the earl's boldness, is said to have replied drily: "Well, then, the earl shall govern all Ireland". There and then, the king made him Lord-Lieutenant over the country.

The second, and greater, disaster occurred about 150 years later in 1647, just after Oliver Cromwell and his parliamentarian forces had defeated Charles I in the English Civil War. In Ireland, Murrough O'Brien, Lord Inchiquin, having been refused the presidency of Munster by his patron Charles I, espoused the Cromwellian cause and was appointed president by parliament. To secure his position, Inchiquin and his troops ravaged the Munster countryside and, in September, besieged Cashel. As Inchiquin's men destroyed the town walls, many townspeople flocked to the Rock and took refuge in the cathedral.

Inchiquin, however, stormed onward, massacring as he went. Finally, having failed to blast his way into the cathedral with his cannon, he piled up mounds of turf against the walls and set fire to them, roasting and suffocating his victims inside. As many as 3,000 people may have died

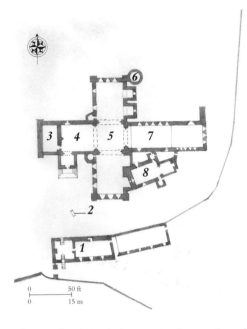

The Rock of Cashel consists of a number of different buildings huddled together into one imposing complex. The main structures are the cruciform cathedral (5), with its nave (4) half the size of its choir (7); the round tower (6); the bishop's palace (3); Cormac's chapel (8); the site of St. Patrick's cross (2), now marked by a replica; and the Hall of the Vicars Choral (1), now a museum and the visitor's entrance.

Irish crosses on the Rock mark a few of its graves, some of them 600 years old. A circle of stone around the intersection of the vertical shaft and the arms distinguishes this type of cross.

in what was Cashel's blackest day. Even children were killed since, as one trooper is said to have commented darkly, "Nits will become lice".

The town, its people, and its cathedral only began to recover from this disaster 40 years later during the reign of James II (1685–88). Sporadic repairs to the cathedral continued throughout the rest of the 17th century, but the building's death-blow came in the next, when in 1749 the Protestant Archbishop Price transferred the status of cathedral from St. Patrick's to St. John's parish church in the town, apparently finding that the situation of the Rock was too "incommodious" for his ceremonial Sunday drive up to it. There is also a tradition that Price stripped St. Patrick's of its roof materials to strengthen the fabric of St. John's.

From this time on, St. Patrick's fell into decay, left to fend for itself against the wind and the rain. However, in the 19th and 20th centuries, restoration programmes have done much to strengthen and preserve the ruins. Whether in summer, when the sun casts sharp shadows on the emerald acropolis, or in winter, when mists wreathe themselves around the rook-haunted stones and Celtic crosses, the Rock casts a spell, recording, like strata, layers of Irish history and legend – sacred and profane – like no other monument in the country.

TIMEFRAME

A.D.
c.450 SAINT PATRICK BAPTIZES AENGHUS, KING OF MUNSTER, AT CASHEL.

976 BRIAN BORU IS CROWNED KING OF MUNSTER AT CASHEL.

1014 BATTLE OF CLONTARF: ALTHOUGH BRIAN BORU IS KILLED, IT SPELLS THE END OF THE VIKING THREAT TO IRELAND FOREVER.

1101 KING MURTAGH O'BRIEN DONATES THE ROCK TO THE CHURCH.

1134 CORMAC'S CHAPEL IS CONSECRATED.

1647 CASHEL IS BESIEGED AND THE CATHEDRAL BURNED BY LORD INCHIQUIN.

1749 ARCHBISHOP PRICE MAKES ST. JOHN'S PARISH CHURCH CASHEL'S CATHEDRAL INSTEAD OF ST. PATRICK'S.

1847 A GREAT STORM BADLY DAMAGES THE BISHOP'S PALACE.

1874–76 THE ROCK'S BUILDINGS ARE REPAIRED BY ORDER OF THE COMMISSIONERS OF PUBLIC WORKS.

1975 RESTORATION OF THE HALL OF THE VICARS CHORAL IS BEGUN.

THE CAVES OF THE THOUSAND BUDDHAS

"The sight disclosed in the dim light of the priest's little oil lamp made my eyes open wide."

SIR AUREL STEIN ON SEEING A HOARD OF ANCIENT MANUSCRIPTS IN THE CAVES IN 1907

IN SANDBLOWN WASTES JUST SOUTHEAST of Dunhuang in northwestern China lies a stretch of cliffs whose man-made caves house an extraordinary collection of sacred objects, including 2,000 statues and 45,000 colourful murals. Ranging from small grottoes to capacious caverns, the Caves of the Thousand Buddhas were hollowed out by Chinese Buddhists from the fourth to the tenth centuries A.D. and contain the world's greatest collection of Chinese Buddhist art.

An oasis town in Gansu province, Dunhuang lies on what was once the ancient silk route. It was the last point before Chinese traders, monks and pilgrims left the boundaries of their country, and the first stopping place for those returning home. There, from A.D. 366, Buddhists began to carve out shrines and temples, as places in which to lodge and to meditate. Within the dimly lit interiors, they would pray for a successful journey across a brutal waterless terrain, or give thanks for a safe return from abroad.

The caves were used and decorated for about 1,000 years until the Yuan period, from which time they began to fall into disuse. But in the late 19th and early 20th centuries, they were visited and made famous by a number of western explorers and scholars, especially the Hungarian-Briton Sir Aurel Stein and the French sinologist Paul Pelliot. These two men, through guile and gifts of money, managed to carry off thousands of manuscripts and silk paintings to the west.

Silken banners rich in subtle colours were taken from the Caves of the Thousand Buddhas in large quantities by the explorer Sir Aurel Stein at the beginning of this century. Known to the Chinese as the Mogao grottoes, the caves were excavated from cliffs (BELOW) by Buddhists, mainly in the course of the first millennium A.D. This banner depicts a bodhisattva – an "enlightenment being" – known as Guanyin, who is associated with mercy.

When Aurel Stein, working for the British Raj in India, reached Dunhuang in 1907 with his faithful Chinese assistant and translator, he found the caves under the protection of a monk named Wang Yuanlu. This pious Buddhist had come to the caves seven years earlier, determined to make it his life's work to restore them to their former splendour.

Stein soon got wind of a rumour that a secret chamber filled with rolls of precious manuscripts had been found in one of the caves. So he and his assistant began to sound out the "shy and nervous" Wang, gently persuading him to let them see the manuscript hoard. Two factors helped Stein: promises of donations to help Wang's renovation work; and the two men's shared enthusiasm for the seventh-century Chinese Buddhist monk and pilgrim Xuan Zhang. Wang had actually commissioned a cave mural depicting Xuan Zhang on horseback carrying a sack of manuscripts; and specimen scrolls in the cave hoard revealed Buddhist texts that had actually been brought from India and translated by Xuan Zhang himself.

This coincidence, and the idea that Stein might be a latter-day Xuan Zhang, finally convinced Wang to allow Stein to see inside the secret chamber. What followed was one of the great moments of central Asian archaeology, akin to Howard Carter's first glimpse inside the tomb of Tutankhamun in Egypt, 15 years later. As the small flame of Wang's oil lamp cast a flickering light

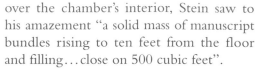

Sacred Buddhist statues emerge from the interior walls of the caves like three-dimensional paintings. Made of terracotta faced with plaster, they provide the caves' focal point. The painters who adorned the caves were either well-known visiting artists paid by the item or local painters paid on a time basis. The pigments used included green malachite and red ochre which were mixed with water.

over the chamber's interior, Stein saw to his amazement "a solid mass of manuscript bundles rising to ten feet from the floor and filling…close on 500 cubic feet".

With the help of some "judiciously administered doses of silver", Stein began to reap the fruits of his carefully nurtured relationship with Wang. Secretly, at night, Stein's assistant brought to his tent sacks containing Buddhist scrolls, written in Chinese, Tibetan, Sanskrit, Sogdian and other tongues, as well as paintings on paper and silken banners. All were destined for New Delhi and the British Museum in London. One of the most valuable items in Stein's haul was a scroll bearing the printed text of the *Diamond Sutra* which, dating back to A.D. 868, is the earliest known printed book in the world.

A year later, in 1908, Paul Pelliot, the French sinologist, visited Dunhuang and also became friendly with Wang. And he, too, was rewarded, coming away with 6,000 manuscripts. But news of his action reached the Chinese authorities, who ordered the remaining manuscripts to be taken to Beijing.

Now, of the 500 caves that have survived, it is possible to visit about 40. Most of them are square in shape, with coffered ceilings and niche-filled walls that are adorned with ancient murals painted with predominantly blue, black, red, green and white colours. Before creating the sacred images, the artists first had to face the stone walls with mud topped by layers of plaster, dung and straw or

A pagodalike structure rises in tiers the full height of the cliff, forming an impressive facade for one of the shrines created during the Tang dynasty, the high point of the caves' art.

animal hair. When this had dried hard, they spread china clay thinly over the surface to make a smooth canvas. More than 10 pigments, including ground gold and silver leaf, were employed. All have retained their freshness except for vermilion red, used in flesh tones, which has oxidized to a dark chocolate colour.

The murals depict a wide variety of Buddhist, secular and natural images and motifs. There are scenes from the life of the Buddha and the *jataka* tales, which tell of his previous lives. Flying Buddhist angels, or *apsaras*, are common, as are depictions of the western paradise of the Buddha Amitabha, with its palaces and pavilions, courtyards and gate-towers. Majestic land-scapes, with mountains soaring above misty clouds, and people making pots, fishing or chopping wood, are also shown. Some

caves show murals from early and late periods since, by the beginning of the 10th century, there was no room left to create more shrines in the saturated cliffs.

The caves' art reached its height during the Tang dynasty, which began at the start of the seventh century. Influenced by Persian and Indian art, Tang figures with their swirling robes and naturalness, some modelled on actual patrons, show a new sense of realism and freshness. And dynamic decorative patterns of plants and leaves in flowering arabesques fill out the spaces between paintings, replacing the static geometric designs favoured before.

To modern visitors, the caves' art is primarily an aesthetic experience. But for the Buddhist pilgrims and travellers of old, it had the spiritual power to inspire devotion. As they returned from wearisome journeys, the sight of the honeycombed cliffs and the welcoming interiors, awash with benevolent figures and lush scenes of paradise, must have banished the memory of hardships and lifted their hearts.

TIMEFRAME

A.D.

1ST CENTURY	BUDDHISM REACHES CHINA, PROBABLY VIA TRADERS FROM CENTRAL ASIA.
366	THE FIRST CAVES ARE CREATED AT DUNHUANG BY CHINESE BUDDHISTS.
618–619	DURING THE TANG ERA, THE CAVES' ART COMES TO FULL MATURITY.
868	THE *DIAMOND SUTRA* IS PRINTED; LATER FOUND BY SIR AUREL STEIN AT DUNHUANG, IT IS THE WORLD'S EARLIEST KNOWN PRINTED BOOK.
1900	WANG YUANLU ARRIVES AT DUNHUANG TO DEVOTE HIS LIFE TO RESTORING THE CAVES.
1907	SIR AUREL STEIN COMES TO DUNHUANG AND TAKES AWAY LARGE NUMBERS OF SCROLLS AND PAINTINGS.
1908	PAUL PELLIOT ARRIVES AT THE CAVES AND LEAVES WITH THOUSANDS OF MANUSCRIPTS.
1961	THE CHINESE GOVERNMENT OFFICIALLY DECLARES THE CAVES A NATIONAL MONUMENT.

THE SPREAD OF BUDDHISM

After the Buddha's death in about 486 B.C., the shock waves of his teaching spread out over the following centuries from the epicentre of the Ganges Valley – as this map shows. According to tradition, Buddhism arrived in Sri Lanka in the mid-third century B.C. By the fifth century A.D., there were reputedly 60,000 monks on the island, supported by the king who had the capacity at his palace to feed 5,000 monks at one sitting. From Sri Lanka, Buddhist teachings later reached Myanmar (Burma) and Thailand. They also spread northwest toward central Asia, reaching Peshawar, in present-day Pakistan, by the first century A.D.

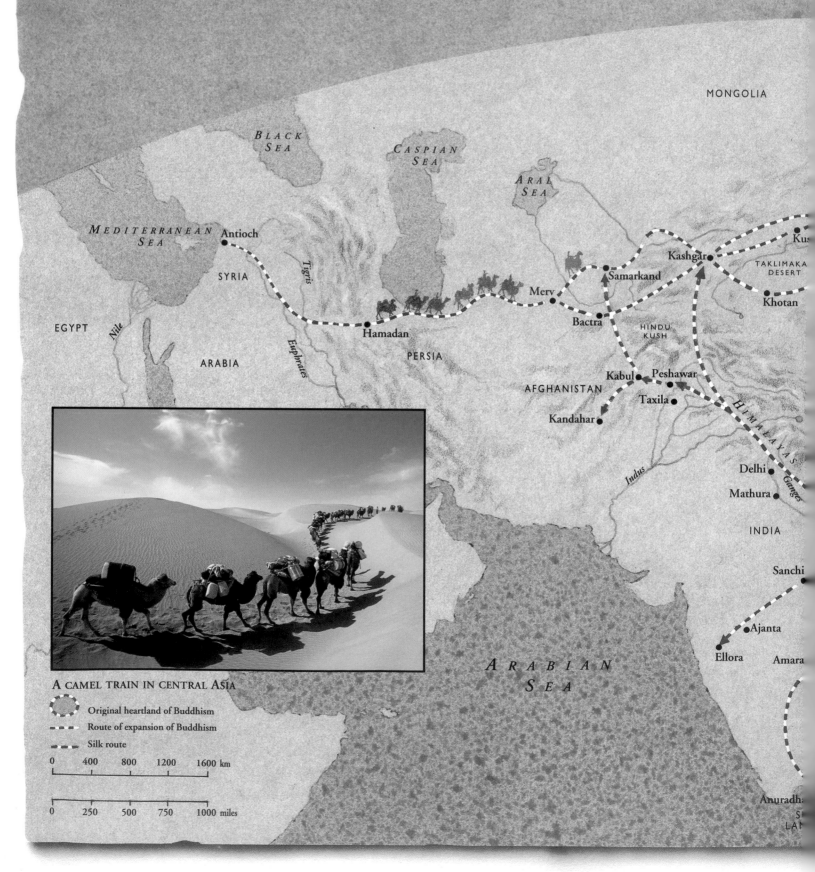

MONGOLIA

BLACK SEA

CASPIAN SEA

ARAL SEA

MEDITERRANEAN SEA

Antioch

SYRIA

Tigris

Kashgar

TAKLIMAKA DESERT

Kus

Samarkand

Merv

Khotan

Bactra

EGYPT

Nile

Hamadan

PERSIA

Euphrates

HINDU KUSH

ARABIA

Kabul

Peshawar

AFGHANISTAN

Taxila

HIMALAYAS

Kandahar

Indus

Delhi

Mathura

Ganges

INDIA

Sanchi

Ajanta

Ellora   Amara

ARABIAN SEA

A CAMEL TRAIN IN CENTRAL ASIA

Original heartland of Buddhism

Route of expansion of Buddhism

Silk route

0	400	800	1200	1600 km

0	250	500	750	1000 miles

Anuradh
S
LA

During the same century, the first Buddhists – probably traders who had converted to the faith – reached China via the silk route. This was in fact a number of ancient routes running from China to the Mediterranean in the west. Camel trains – still used in central Asia, as seen below left – laden with silk trekked westward via Dunhuang (pp. 132–35) and cities such as Kashgar and Samarkand. In the first two centuries A.D., Buddhist monks began to follow traders into China. At first, Buddhism made little impact in the country. However, it eventually became established in the fifth century, and from there it reached Japan via Korea.

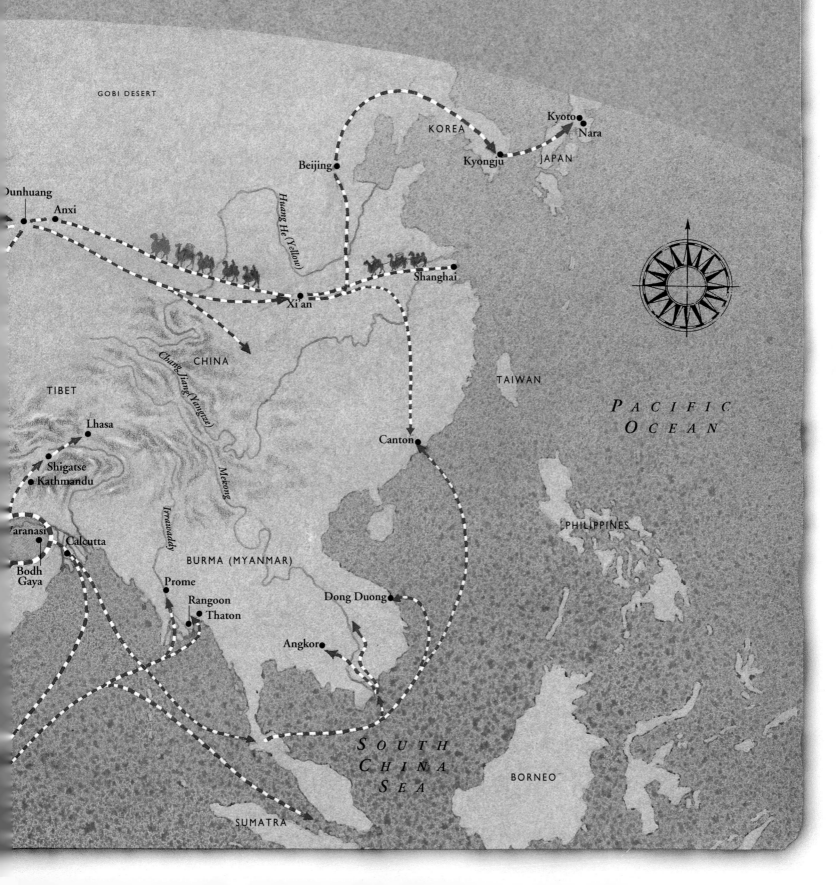

To the
Glory of God

Down the centuries, the religions of the world have inspired millions with their teachings and by the example of their founders. They have also, often allied with nationalism, contributed to some of history's bloodiest wars. But even the most hardened atheist would concede that the belief in God or a transcendent reality has inspired some of the world's greatest works of architecture. Some, such as Germany's spectacular Cologne Cathedral, are breathtaking in size; but, whether large or small, all have been adorned by the finest contemporary craftsmen and artists and sanctified by time-honoured rituals. In Islam, the place of worship is the mosque – a structure that combines an often vast unified space, as in the Süleymaniye in Istanbul or the arch-filled interior of the Great Mosque of Córdoba in Spain, with the intricacies of Islamic art. In this, floral and geometrical patterns dominate – perhaps best shown in the flamboyant Safavid mosques of Isfahan in Iran. In other religious traditions, shrines may be on a smaller scale, but they are equally opulent and encrusted with sacred art. The Buddhist temple of Wat Phra Keo in Bangkok and the Sikh Golden Temple in Amritsar, for example, both glow with golden outer surfaces; while the glories of the Byzantine church of San Vitale in Ravenna lie within, in the form of corruscating mosaics. Less glittering, but equally well crafted, is the Shinto shrine of Ise, whose small unvarnished wooden structures are dismantled and replaced every 20 years, in a ceremony that combines tradition with ritual purity.

Spectacular temples that embody a vision of the divine

Cologne Cathedral's soaring Gothic twin towers are one of the glories of Christian architecture in Europe.

139

ISFAHAN

"The beauty of Isfahan steals on the mind unawares...before you know how, Isfahan has become indelible, has insinuated its image into that gallery of places which everyone privately treasures."

BRITISH TRAVELLER ROBERT BYRON, WHO VISITED ISFAHAN IN 1934

SHIMMERING ABOVE THE HORIZON through the glassy distortions of liquid air, the domes and minarets of Isfahan, which lies on the Zayandeh River about 200 miles south of Teheran, rise heavenward out of a flat, bleak, stony terrain. They proclaim an oasis of flamboyant sacred architecture and Islamic spirituality unmatched in Iran.

Shah Abbas I, the Great (1588–1629), of the Persian Safavid dynasty, made Isfahan one of the most resplendent cities in the world. At its heart he constructed a vast square known as the Maidan, and around this he built the famous Royal and Lutfullah mosques, which epitomize the exuberance of Safavid art. The peacock-blue and creamy brown tiles of their domes, swirling with arabesques and Qur'anic inscriptions, seem to dissolve the structures into insubstantial bodies of glowing colour.

The Safavid dynasty of Persia (modern Iran) was founded in 1501 by a certain Ismail, who after decades of internal disorder in the country reunited it with a series of military victories over his opponents. In 1499, he seized the city of Tabriz in the northwest and, in the following year, he captured Isfahan and Shiraz. In 1501, he proclaimed himself Shah Ismail I, initiating a dynasty that would last for more than 200 years.

The Royal Mosque of Isfahan (RIGHT and BELOW) was built in the early 17th century during the reign of Shah Abbas I and typifies the flamboyant style of Safavid architecture. Its surfaces are sheathed in light-reflecting mosaics and tiles with geometric and flowing floral patterns.

Isfahan lies on the central Iranian plateau surrounded by mountains. In the Safavid era (1501–1732), it became famous for its mosques as well as for its metalwork, textiles, pottery, and carpets.

At the heart of Isfahan was the great square known as the Maidan, constructed by Shah Abbas I. At the far end, a giant portal leads to the Royal Mosque, whose dome blooms like a blue bud. During the Safavid era, the square was bordered with a canal lined by plane trees and enclosed by two-storey arcades that housed coffee and tea houses, taverns, and restaurants.

The open area itself was normally occupied by small tented shops selling, among other things, food, leather and cotton goods, spices, silks, satins, and iron and wooden tools. But it was occasionally cleared for games of polo, at which the shah excelled.

Ismail's son Tahmasp (1524–76) moved the capital from Tabriz southeast to Qazvin to protect it from the ever-present threat of the Ottoman Turks to the west. When Shah Abbas came to the throne, he made his court even safer by transferring it south to Isfahan. He secured his borders from external threat, suppressed rebellions, and embarked on an extensive building programme that included mosques, palaces, a network of paved roads and caravanserais, or rest houses, and irrigation projects. In order to boost the native work force, Abbas brought to Isfahan large numbers of Armenians, as well as master craftsmen from Italy, China, and India.

By Abbas's time, the Safavid court was internationally famous, drawing to it a bevy of European travellers and diplomats eager to savour fabled Persian exotica and develop important trade links. These foreign dignitaries included the Englishman Sir Robert Sherley, who became the shah's personal envoy and helped to reorganize his army; the wealthy Roman aristocrat Pietro della Valle; and, just after Abbas's death, the French traveller and jeweller Jean-Baptiste Tavernier. Also at court were Portuguese, Spaniards, Dutch, and even fair-haired, ruddy-faced Russians,

oiling the wheels of diplomacy with gifts of furs, tusks, and vodka.

Shah Abbas entertained these pale-skinned foreigners with his usual courtesy and curious interest. Physically short, but powerfully built, with a black drooping moustache and small fiery eyes, the shah was one of the towering personalities of his age. Ruthless, energetic, and impatient, he was also an agile thinker and enjoyed the cut and thrust of debate. He loved to hunt and was adept with his hands: he could often be found weaving cloth, or making swords or a saddle for his horse.

The shah's sharp eye for aesthetics was soon translated into bricks, tiles, and mortar. A broad avenue known as the Chahar Bagh was laid out to impress visitors first entering the city. In the middle of this grand 50-yard-wide boulevard ran a water channel, which was built on terraces and punctuated with onyx-edged basins filled with rose heads in the summer months.

On each side of this canal were laid, successively, a row of plane trees, a walk-way, parterres abloom with plants and flowers, and another row of trees. At night, in the tepid scented air, promenaders strolled along the Chahar, perhaps trailing off into the plethora of pleasure gardens

and pavilions that led from the avenue via open archways.

Abbas's most sumptuous monument was the Royal Mosque, which still dominates the southern end of the Maidan. From the mosque protrudes a slightly bulbous pointed dome, electric blue, as if fashioned from the feathers of a bird of paradise. From the dome's gilt finial pointing toward heaven, a whirling pattern of arabesques – white and golden brown tendrils edged with black – cascades down over a sea of turquoise. The dome itself sits on a drum around which runs a band of midnight blue bearing sacred texts in white in the flowing vertical strokes, dots, and squiggles of Arabic calligraphy.

The entrance to the mosque is through an immense portal, nearly 90 feet high, which bursts upon the Maidan like a gaping mouth. Within the frame of a high rectangle, the outline of a pointed arch shapes a deeply recessed semi-dome filled with *muqarnas*, Islamic decorative panels

known as stalactites or honeycomb because of the way they hang down in overlapping layers and are divided into geometrical cells. The *muqarnas* soften the transition from the pointed arch to the horizontal plane of the ground. On a symbolic level, they represent, as the modern Iranian scholar Seyyed Hossein Nasr has explained, the "descent of the heavenly abode toward the earth".

Although the north-facing portal is nearly always shrouded in shadow, the density of blue tiles and the way the cupped surfaces of the *muqarnas* scoop up minimal light makes the whole a crystalline cave echoing with colour. Through the portal doors, which were once encased with silver plate, the path turns to the west so that the mosque's court and prayer hall are aligned toward Mecca (pp. 202–7) in Saudi Arabia, Islam's holiest city and the birthplace of the Prophet Muhammad.

The court itself is checkered with dazzling sunlight and shadows crisply cut

Polo, shown in this Persian miniature, originated in Persia as a cavalry exercise and was played in the Maidan. The game spread to Arabia, Tibet, China, and India, from where the British brought it to the west.

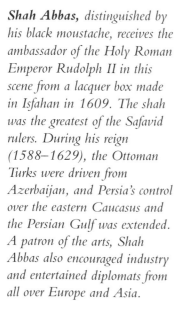

Shah Abbas, distinguished by his black moustache, receives the ambassador of the Holy Roman Emperor Rudolph II in this scene from a lacquer box made in Isfahan in 1609. The shah was the greatest of the Safavid rulers. During his reign (1588–1629), the Ottoman Turks were driven from Azerbaijan, and Persia's control over the eastern Caucasus and the Persian Gulf was extended. A patron of the arts, Shah Abbas also encouraged industry and entertained diplomats from all over Europe and Asia.

The Lutfullah Mosque, like the Royal Mosque, expresses Safavid state religion, which was the form of Islam known as Shiism. Shiites broke away from mainstream Islam in the early seventh century. They hold that only the descendants of Ali, the Prophet's cousin and son-in-law, can be true imams, or religious heads, of the Muslim community.

from the recessed arches of the two-storied arcades and the four *iwans*. These are great vaulted niches or open porches that face the court at the cardinal points and whose arches "move upward like flame toward heaven". In the centre of the court, the water of a square ablutions pool reflects the soft blur of ubiquitous blue tiles and symbolizes the ritual purity that worshippers must take with them into the prayer hall.

The mosque interior is a haven of coolness. Its light-reflecting tiles, with their twirling foliage and stylized blossoms, reflect the Persian love of vegetation and flowers and echo in their fertility the visions of paradise evoked in the Qur'an. The two main focal points are the soaring dome, with its golden sunlike medallion, and the marble *mihrab*, the niche in the southwestern wall which indicates the direction of Mecca and acts as a sound box to magnify the words of the prayer leader.

The Royal Mosque was begun in 1611 and constructed at great speed at the

behest of Abbas, who perhaps feared that he would die before it was completed. That is precisely what happened: the building was eventually finished in 1638, nine years after his death. Several modern critics consider that, as a result of the haste, some of the construction is of less than perfect workmanship.

Time and labour were evidently saved by the use of *haft-rangi* ("seven-colour") tiles. For whereas mosaic tiles were of only one colour and painstakingly cut to fit the requisite space, the *haft-rangi*, by combining several colours on one tile, was cheaper to make and could be used to fill walls more quickly. But its lustre was less brilliant than that of the mosaic tile, and purists bemoan the consequent diminution of colour intensity. Nevertheless, the Royal Mosque's highly charged burst of blue colour remains one of the world's most bewitching sights.

The other great mosque of Shah Abbas's era is located on the lower eastern side of the Maidan and was named for Shaykh Lutfullah, the shah's saintly father-in-law and a renowned preacher. Lacking a courtyard and smaller than the Royal Mosque, the Lutfullah was begun in 1603 and was used by Abbas for private prayer. While blue predominates in the seething mass of minute detail in the tile mosaic sheathing the entrance portal, the principal colour of the dome is a creamy *café-au-lait*,

on which curving, curling arabesques of white and blue intertwine.

Inside the 205-foot-square prayer hall rise eight arches bordered by white calligraphy on a background of cobalt blue. Above, a circular drum pierced with grilled windows forms the base of the dome. This great sacred canopy explodes at its apex in a golden starburst, sending out a shock of lemon-shaped ripples, outlined by buff-coloured bricks, increasing in size from the centre.

The effect is to suggest the descent of the divine, from the one to the many, or perhaps the moment of cosmic creation. At the same time, the cellular ensemble seems to lay bare the structure of the microcosm, highlighting the molecular patterns of the natural world. As such, the dome epitomizes Islamic art, in which symmetry, abstraction and geometry create a unified field of vision, symbolizing the oneness of God.

The French Huguenot Jean Chardin, who visited Isfahan in the mid-17th century, wrote that "when Shah Abbas the Great ceased to breathe, Persia ceased to prosper", and it is true that the end of his reign marked the start of a 100-year decline before the eventual fall of the Safavids. Yet their cultural and religious legacy lives on in Iran, and the mosques of Isfahan, with their magnificent domes, remain one of the country's spiritual highspots.

A cluster of **muqarnas** *fills a recessed niche in this detail from the Lutfullah Mosque. Known as stalactites or honeycomb, muqarnas are characteristic of Islamic architectural decoration. In the words of the Iranian scholar Seyyed Hossein Nasr, they are the "crystallization of the celestial substance or ether in terrestrial forms".*

TIMEFRAME

A.D.

1501	SHAH ISMAIL FOUNDS THE SAFAVID DYNASTY OF PERSIA.
1588	SHAH ABBAS I BECOMES RULER OF PERSIA.
1603	WORK BEGINS ON THE LUTFULLAH MOSQUE.
1611–1638	BUILDING OF THE ROYAL MOSQUE.
1629	SHAH ABBAS I DIES.
1666	SHAH ABBAS II DIES; FROM THIS TIME ONWARD THE DECLINE OF THE SAFAVIDS BECOMES MORE EVIDENT.
1732	SAFAVID RULE ENDS.

WAT PHRA KEO

"Angels in every place and every part of this realm join in praise and rejoicing at the completion of this eminent work of merit according to our desire!"

KING RAMA V AFTER THE FINAL COMPLETION OF THE WAT PHRA KEO IN 1882, THE CENTENARY OF ITS CONSECRATION

THE COMPOUND OF THE ROYAL PALACE in Bangkok encloses a cornucopia of golden and tile-encrusted sacred buildings that form the spiritual heart of the country. Consecrated in 1782 and known as the Wat Phra Keo, Temple of the Emerald Buddha, this holy complex boasts shrines and gilded spires, towers and cloisters. The shrines are studded with deep red, green and blue tiles and mirrored glass; and the whole has been described as a sacred fairytale world of pavilions and pinnacles and compared to the fantastical creations of the modern Spanish architect Antoni Gaudí.

Entering the temple enclosure is like stepping into an enchanted forest, whose trees, shrubs, bushes and log cabins have been turned into solid monuments with hard, light-reflecting surfaces. As tiny metal chimes dangling from eaves tinkle in the wind, mythical figures, as if transformed into statues, emerge from their surrounds.

On guard at entrances are *yakshas*, pop-eyed, pug-nosed giants whose snarling fanged mouths are directed at potential demon assailants. Elsewhere *kinnaris* – half-woman, half-bird creatures – and *nagas*, or mythological serpents, loom into view. And there is also the *garuda*: a winged beast with the head and legs of a bird and torso of a man that is Thailand's national emblem.

In contrast to these strange hybrids of folk tradition, the most sacred object in the temple – and the country – is a small statue of green jade. This is the famous Emerald Buddha, which sits cross-legged in the meditation pose atop an altar within the principal sanctuary, or *bot*, in the south of the compound. Commanding the devotion

The Emerald Buddha *sits enthroned on top of an ornate altar in the central shrine of the Wat Phra Keo temple complex in Bangkok, the capital of Thailand. The jade statue is only about two and a half feet high, but its preservation is considered crucial for Thailand's protection and welfare.*

Sunlight gleams *off the gilded surfaces of the Wat Phra Keo, Thailand's holiest temple. In the centre can be seen the spire of the Golden Chedi and, to the left, the library and the Royal Pantheon.*

of the Thai people, of whom 90 percent are Buddhists of the Theravada tradition, the statue is also the country's talisman.

The Emerald Buddha first came to light, it seems, in 1436. It was found inside a *chedi* (a domed reliquary monument) in the northern Thai town of Chiang Rai after the *chedi* had been cracked open by a lightning bolt. The statue was covered in plaster and gilt. But after its solid green emerald body was revealed, it attracted the attention of the king of nearby Chiang Mai, who ordered the statue to be brought to his capital.

The elephant entrusted with the sacred object, however, refused to return to Chiang Mai and made its way to the city of Muang Lampang, farther south. Interpreting this as an omen, the king left the statue there and built a temple around it. In later years, the Buddha was transferred to Chiang Mai and then stolen by invaders from Laos, which borders Thailand to the east. There it remained for 200 years before the Thai general Chakkri recaptured it during the reign of King Taksin in 1778.

General Chakkri succeeded Taksin as Rama I and founded the Chakkri dynasty that still presides in Thailand. He also began the building of Bangkok, with the Royal Palace and the Wat Phra Keo at its heart. In 1784, in a grand procession, the small, much-travelled statue was brought into the sanctuary. Here it was placed on a canopied throne on the top of a gleaming

altar rising as a tiered pyramid some 40 feet above the floor.

Today, a tangible reverence pervades the blue-tiled *bot*, which stands on a marble platform whose base is adorned with golden *garudas* clutching *naga* serpents. Buddhist pilgrims arrive at the entrance door, which is inlaid with mother-of-pearl and flanked by guardian statues, with offerings of cut flowers, incense and gold leaf (to press on gilt statues as an act of merit).

After taking off their shoes, the pilgrims quietly proceed into the cavernous 60-foot-high interior, whose shuttered natural light makes the deep red and old gold of the ceiling glow. They sit down on the marble floor and meditate, light joss sticks, lay bunches of flowers, or prostrate themselves before altars. The atmosphere of devotion is intensified by the heady fragrance of sandalwood and jasmine and the *sotto voce* intonations of private prayers.

Most visitors contemplate the tiny Buddha, a mysterious green figure clothed, according to the season, in one of three

Thai pilgrims light joss sticks and make offerings of cut flowers within the compound of the Wat Phra Keo. Most proceed to the main sanctuary, where vivid murals glow out of the incense-smoky light. The paintings include scenes from the jataka tales, which relate incidents from the Buddha's previous lives.

Like a giant cartoon strip, murals (LEFT) stretch around the cloisters surrounding the Wat's buildings. They depict the epic Ramakien, *which tells of the adventures of King Rama and his wife Sita, who was abducted by the evil king Ravana of Sri Lanka. Rama, however, rescued her with the aid of the monkey god Hanuman.*

Guardian **yakshas** *within the temple compound fulfil the role of spiritual bodyguards – their fearsome fanged faces are designed to scare away devils.* Yakshas *and other folkloric creatures such as* kinnaris *were gradually assimilated by Buddhism, which was officially recognized in Thailand in its Theravada form under the medieval king Rama Khameng. His grandson later invited Sri Lankan monks to come and strengthen the Buddhist community, or sangha.*

golden robes and protected by a series of diminishing umbrellas above his head. Despite the glut of ornate objects – golden Buddha statues, gold candlesticks, cups, incense burners on lacquered tables, lamps and tiered umbrellas – that compete for the attention, the green figure eclipses all.

Outside the sanctuary the main group of buildings to catch the eye is the Golden Chedi, the Mondop, or library, and the Royal Pantheon, all standing in a line on a raised marble platform. The Chedi is a beacon of golden light, its great curving bell-like dome with its ringed base and cone-shaped spire scooping up the sun's rays. Built during the reign of Rama IV (1851–68), it is said to house part of the Buddha's breastbone. Beside it stands the Mondop, in which Buddha statues and miniature white elephants stand on a silver floor. A cabinet inlaid with mother-of-pearl contains the Tripitaka, sacred Buddhist scriptures.

Next to the Mondop on the marble platform rises the Royal Pantheon, which

has the plan of a Greek cross and is encased in red and blue tiles. The building is topped by a *prang* – a richly carved, cigar-shaped tower whose design owes much to the Khmer style of architecture, a style that reached its height in the medieval city of Angkor Wat in Cambodia.

Apart from these elegant monuments of devotion, Buddhist pilgrims are drawn to the series of 178 continuous murals painted around the Wat's cloisters. First created in the time of Rama I and later restored, the murals depict the *Ramakien*, a Thai version of the *Ramayana*, a 48,000-line Indian Hindu epic written about 2,000 years ago.

The Wat Phra Keo, with its Golden Chedi conducive to meditation, its sacred scriptures and murals, and its Royal Pantheon, satisfies the spiritual and patriotic aspirations of the Thai people. And underlying all is the Emerald Buddha, its green body, eerily lit and encased in glass, as magical as a hologram. It radiates a meditative stillness, bringing unity to the chaotic mixture of forms.

TIMEFRAME

A.D.

c.1275–1317	THE REIGN OF THE THAI KING RAMA KHAMENG DURING WHICH THERAVADA BUDDHISM IS MADE THE COUNTRY'S OFFICIAL RELIGION.
1436	THE EMERALD BUDDHA IS DISCOVERED WITHIN A *CHEDI* IN CHIANG RAI.
1778	GENERAL CHAKKRI RECAPTURES THE EMERALD BUDDHA FROM THE LAOTIANS.
1782	ACCESSION OF CHAKKRI TO THE THAI THRONE AS RAMA I; THE WAT PHRA KEO IS CONSECRATED.
1784	THE EMERALD BUDDHA IS INSTALLED WITHIN THE WAT PHRA KEO'S MAIN SANCTUARY.
1882	THE WAT PHRA KEO IS FINALLY COMPLETED 100 YEARS AFTER ITS CONSECRATION.

GREAT MOSQUE OF CÓRDOBA

"Córdoba, with her ancient houses, has her mosque where the eye is lost in marvels."

FRENCH WRITER VICTOR HUGO (1802–85)

IN THE 10TH CENTURY A.D., CÓRDOBA, in Andalusia, southern Spain, was the most civilized city in the western world. At a time when the rest of Europe was barely emerging from its Dark Age, Córdoba was the capital of the Spanish Muslim dynasty of the Umayyads (756–1031), whose empire covered most of Spain. And of the number of resplendent palaces, mosques, mansions and gardens that were built during this era, none surpassed Córdoba's Great Mosque – La Mezquita. Founded in the late eighth century, this jewel of western Muslim architecture grew to

become the third-largest sacred structure in the Islamic world.

Hemmed in by the milky brown-green waters of the Guadalquivir River to the south, and elsewhere by the densely packed buildings of the old town, the Great Mosque from the outside resembles a broad rectangular fortress. Its honey-coloured walls, buttressed and crenelated like the teeth of a saw, rise up in places to a height of 65 feet. Yet behind these forbidding ramparts a world of great delicacy is concealed: a courtyard of trees and fountains; and a prayer hall with walls adorned

A Christian cathedral erupts from the middle of the Great Mosque's prayer hall. Built in the 16th century, the cathedral was – and is – seen by many as a violation of the Moorish structure.

150

by mosaics and calligraphic inscriptions and filled with hundreds of slender columns and striped arches.

The Great Mosque stands on ground that has been sacred to three different religions. The first temple built on the site, at a time when Córdoba was a provincial capital in the Roman Empire, was dedicated to Janus, the double-faced Roman god of gates and doorways. With the breakup of the western Roman Empire in about the middle of the first millennium A.D., Córdoba eventually came under the control of the Visigoths, a barbarian people of the north, who espoused the Christian faith. As a result, the Roman temple was turned into the Christian church of St. Vincent.

Candy-striped horseshoe arches *fill the interior of the Great* *Mosque. Founded in the eighth* *century, the mosque was added to* *over the next 200 years so that it* *became one of the largest sacred* *structures in the Islamic world.*

In 711, however, a Muslim force from northern Africa invaded Spain. Within a short time, the Moors, as these Arabs and northern African Berbers became known, had taken control of most of the country. In Córdoba, the Moorish rulers turned half the church of St. Vincent into a mosque, allowing Christians to worship in the other half. But the arrangement ended during the time of the Umayyad Abd ar-Rahman I (756–788), who had fled to Spain from Damascus, where his dynasty had been deposed as caliphs, or spiritual leaders, of the Muslim world.

In 784, Abd ar-Rahman began work on the Great Mosque, incorporating parts of the old church into it. Over the next two centuries, the mosque was enlarged and adorned by his successors. However, the building's sacred orientation again changed

direction in 1236, when Córdoba was captured by Ferdinand III, the Christian Spanish king of Castile, and the mosque reverted to a Christian sanctuary.

For nearly three centuries, the structure was little modified. But in 1523, against the wishes of the city council, the local clergy, backed by Emperor Charles V, authorized the building of a cruciform cathedral in the middle of the mosque. Pillars, arches and part of the wooden ceiling were torn down in order to make way for this new, anomalous structure that rose above the mosque's roof like a Spanish galleon on a Moorish sea.

The emperor later confessed: "Had I known this, I would never have allowed the ancient building to be touched: you have put what can be seen anywhere in the place of what was unique." And during the

Abd ar-Rahman I, *who began the building of the Great Mosque, holds court in this romanticized 19th-century Spanish painting. Abd ar-Rahman was the founder of the Umayyad dynasty that ruled most of Spain from 756 until 1031, when the country dissolved into separate kingdoms. During this period, Córdoba became famous for its culture, particularly during the reign of Abd ar-Rahman III in the 10th century, when the arts and sciences flourished.*

19th century, the influential French writer Théophile Gautier wrote in the strongest terms of "this parasite of a church…an architectural wart breaking out on the back of the Arab structure".

Yet despite the aesthetic disruption of the original edifice, there is something spiritually harmonious in the close proximity of different religious traditions within a confined area. Old Roman and Visigothic pillars bear the weight of Moorish arches; carved mahogany choir stalls contrast with the empty spaces of the Muslim prayer hall; and graphic crucifixes and other figurative Christian icons are offset by the abstract, geometrical and floral patterns of Islamic art.

The main entrance to the mosque compound is through the Christian-built Door of Forgiveness in the northern wall, from which rises a tiered Christian bell tower built on the foundations of the mosque's minaret. This leads into the Court of the Orange Trees, a peaceful prelude to the mosque interior. Orange trees set out in rows, swaying palms – trees loved by the Moors, nostalgic for their desert homelands – and the brimming pools of fountains proclaim an oasis of spiritual refreshment.

From the court, access to the vast mosque interior is via the Door of Palms, which is flanked by two Roman columns, a reminder of the mosque's ancient heritage. As the first vista of the interior opens up, outdoor heat gives way to a still coolness, soothing shadowy light replaces the dazzling glare of the sun.

The eye is then filled with a forest of marble arches sprouting from the marble floor, as if a palm grove had been encased in stone and planted in regular rows. Aisle upon aisle stretches away, each spanned by double red-and-white striped arches, one above the other, their curving lines lit and

The mosque's **mihrab** *is a small chamber that indicates the direction of Mecca. Its horseshoe arch is alive with mosaic arabesques and foliage. They were created, it is said, by a Christian craftsman who had come to Córdoba from Constantinople. The dome of the* mihrab's *antechamber (*BELOW LEFT*) shows Islam's emphasis on abstract and geometric art.*

This detail from a medieval Moorish manuscript tells the story of the lovers Bayad and Riyad. It is one of the few illuminated manuscripts to have survived from the Moorish period. With its fecund trees and people dressed in rich flowing gowns, the image conjures up the sophistication and sensuality of Moorish life, in which poetry, wine, music and affairs of the heart played an important part.

half lit in the splashes of light filtering through the windows in the roof.

Together, these aisles constituted the mosque's prayer hall. Every Friday, the faithful would fill the vast area and perform their ritual prayers – standing, kneeling and bowing down to touch the carpet-swathed floor with their foreheads. Above them, like the starry canopy of heaven, hundreds of chandeliers and silver, golden and brass lamps hanging from silver chains shed a glittering light on the marble surfaces. Behind them, the arches of the northern wall were open to the Court of the Orange Trees, from which the scent of blossom would waft into the interior, mingling with the scent of aromatic lamp oil.

The aisles lead visually to the southern *qibla* wall, which is oriented toward Mecca (pp. 202–7), and the *mihrab*, a niche or recess built into the *qibla* wall, from which the imam conducts prayers. The *mihrab* in the Great Mosque is a small octagonal chamber entered by a horseshoe arch that looks like a giant keyhole. Flanked by two dark green and red-flecked columns, the arch erupts like a sunrise, its surface a lacework of glittering mosaic.

The Great Mosque, *with its cathedral dominating the Córdoban skyline, is the city's major attraction for visitors. Since its fall to the Castilian king Ferdinand III in the 13th century, Córdoba has never recaptured the eminence it enjoyed during its Moorish era. Once famed for its silks, brocades, leather goods and jewellery, its industries now consist principally of tourism, textiles and brewing.*

The mosque grew over some 200 years. Abd ar-Rahman I's building, a small simple structure with 11 aisles, was lengthened southward toward the river by Abd ar-Rahman II (822–852), who added eight bays. In the next century, the pious caliph al-Hakam II, who almost destroyed every vine in Spain because of a Qur'anic injunction against wine-drinking, again enlarged the mosque southward, nearly doubling its size.

The final structural changes to the mosque were made in 987 by al-Mansur, the powerful vizier who ruled during the reign of al-Hakam's weak son Hisham II. Al-Mansur extended the mosque to the east by adding eight more aisles. Before the work began, the architects had to buy the house and garden of a widow which stood on the development site. However, the woman refused to move unless she was relocated in a place whose garden had a palm tree as beautiful as the one she already possessed. Al-Mansur, whose customary ruthlessness was leavened by a streak of generosity, agreed, sent officials to comb Córdoba for such a garden, and bought it at great cost.

By the late 10th century, the mosque had reached its high point, both in size and splendour, enjoying more than 200 years of Muslim worship before Córdoba fell to a Spanish Christian army in 1236. Although sacred space can be altered, it is not so easily destroyed. Despite the later intrusion of the Christian cathedral, with its Gothic arches and Baroque mahogany pulpit, the prayer hall preserves its identity and the sanctity established in Roman times. And perhaps, as Théophile Gautier wrote, "the ancient mosque…may yet last long enough to see a fourth creed established beneath the shadow of its arches, celebrating with other forms and other hymns the new god, or rather the new prophet, for God is always the same."

TIMEFRAME

A.D.

711	A MUSLIM ARMY INVADES SPAIN.
756–788	REIGN OF ABD AR-RAHMAN I, FOUNDER OF THE SPANISH UMAYYAD DYNASTY.
784	WORK BEGINS ON THE GREAT MOSQUE.
987	THE LAST ALTERATIONS TO THE MOSQUE ARE MADE BY THE VIZIER AL-MANSUR.
1236	CÓRDOBA IS CAPTURED BY FERDINAND III.
1492	THE CITY OF GRANADA, THE LAST MOORISH STRONGHOLD IN SPAIN, FALLS TO A SPANISH CHRISTIAN ARMY.
1523	A CATHEDRAL IS BUILT IN THE MIDDLE OF THE MOSQUE DURING THE REIGN OF EMPEROR CHARLES V.

THE SÜLEYMANIYE

*"I have built thee, O Padishah, a mosque which will
remain on the face of the earth till the day of judgment…"*

WORDS ATTRIBUTED TO THE SÜLEYMANIYE'S ARCHITECT SINAN
ADDRESSING SÜLEYMAN I

ONE OF THE GRANDEST MOSQUES EVER conceived, the Süleymaniye was built during the reign of the Ottoman sultan Süleyman I, the Magnificent (1520–66). The mosque's cascade of domes and minarets dominates the Istanbul skyline from its position on the city's third hill, and its overwhelming sense of internal space has struck awe in worshippers and visitors for more than 400 years.

The Turkish traveller Evliya Çelebi Efendi, for example, wrote in the 17th century that he once followed 10 European visitors – "Frankish infidels" – into the mosque and watched them throw back their heads to take in the yawning interior. As their mouths fell open agog with amazement, they "tossed up their hats and cried out…'Mother of God!'"

The long reign of Süleyman I, the greatest of the Ottoman sultans, marked the high-water mark of Ottoman civilization. New territories, including parts of what are now Hungary, Iraq and Libya, were added to the empire, and the imperial fleet, especially under the Greek-born admiral Barbarossa, maintained a dominance over Mediterranean shipping that ended only in 1571 with the Ottoman defeat at the Battle of Lepanto.

On the home front, Süleyman continued to transform Istanbul – formerly the Byzantine capital of Constantinople,

Muslims congregate inside the vast interior of the Süleymaniye, one of the largest mosques in the world. Built by the Ottoman architect Sinan during the 16th century, the mosque overlooks the Golden Horn (BELOW), an inlet of water that divides old Istanbul from the modern city.

captured by the Turks in 1453 – into a city that was worthy of imperial pretensions. Fountains, palaces, bathhouses, schools, theological colleges, or *madrasahs*, hospitals and mosques were just some of the structures created in Istanbul and other parts of the empire.

In 1550, the sultan's greatest architect, Sinan, began work on the Süleymaniye, arguably his greatest achievement. On the third of Istanbul's seven hills, a large workforce, consisting mainly of Greeks and Armenians, laid the foundations and brought limestone blocks and marble from quarries on the coastal islands of the Sea of Marmara. Taking the great Christian church of Hagia Sophia (built some 1,000 years before) as an inspiration, Sinan began to translate his blueprint into solid masonry, using a basic geometric ground plan of a square enclosing a circle.

That Sinan took a personal interest in the nuts and bolts of the construction is clearly attested by another story related by Evliya Çelebi Efendi. Süleyman, apparently, wanting to see for himself the progress that his favourite architect was making, arrived at the building site unannounced and with a small bodyguard. The sultan picked his way through loose

The turban-topped cenotaph of Süleyman I, seen here in the centre, lies inside a small mausoleum, or türbe, *within the mosque complex. It is flanked by the cenotaphs of his daughter and two later sultans.*

Süleyman (LEFT) *was an astute statesman and brilliant general who guided the Ottoman Empire to its zenith. He was devoted to his alluring and strong-willed wife Roxelana* (FAR LEFT)*, whose influence over her husband seemed excessive to some contemporaries.*

chippings and scaffolding in search of Sinan. But instead of finding the architect poring over plans or imperiously giving orders, he heard his voice booming from the top of some scaffolding berating a luckless stonemason for imperfect workmanship and telling him to watch how it should be done.

Completed in 1557, the Süleymaniye was the largest mosque in the Ottoman Empire. Its giant bulk, overlooking the inlet of water known as the Golden Horn, is approached from the northeast via a winding narrow street, choked with traffic and pedestrians. As the road bends round, the mosque suddenly looms into view like a sea-going liner. Its dove-grey dome seems to spawn smaller domes that soften the descent from the generous curves of the cupola to the vertical uplift of the walls.

And the sense of downward pressure from the domes is offset by the four pencil-thin, needle-pointed minarets that soar upward, spiking the blue air.

A stone wall, punctuated by iron-grilled windows, surrounds the mosque, its courtyard and the royal graveyard. Within this compound, a path leads to the stone steps of the main entrance. Between two columns of verd antique, a predominantly dark green marble, a heavy green padded curtain separates the inside from the outside, the sacred from the profane. A gold calligraphic inscription set within a rectangular panel adorns the curtain. Set in the wall to the right of the entrance is a row of steps and seats at which the faithful must perform ritual ablutions – washing their feet, hands and faces – before entering the holy space.

The mosque's domes rise above elegant rows of arches that form a colonnade along the four sides of its courtyard. The arches rest on 24 columns that were taken by Sinan's builders from ruined buildings in and around Istanbul.

For non-Muslim visitors, however, the mosque's entrance is through the court-yard, adjoining its western facade. An elegant, spacious quadrangle, the courtyard is lined on three sides with porticoes, whose arches stem from granite, marble and beet-red porphyry columns and are topped by small domes. In the centre, a rectangular ablutions fountain, made of marble with grilles of iron latticework, provides the focal point.

Although the courtyard offers shade and quietude, it also functions as an overspill area if the mosque becomes too full. Thus, the side adjoining the mosque has two *mihrabs*, niches that indicate the direction of Mecca (pp. 202–7), which Muslims must face when they pray.

Through the western doorway of the mosque, the first impression is of a vast cavern and a sea of red carpets stretching away. The sense of an engulfing unified space is much greater than in a cathedral, where the nave, transepts, choir and chapels chop the enclosed area into formal divisions. From above, hundreds of black

Muslims perform their ablutions outside the Süleymaniye before proceeding inside. The ritual purity required before entering a mosque entails the washing of feet, hands and face.

This plan of the Süleymaniye (BELOW RIGHT) *shows the mosque itself (10) standing between the courtyard (9) and the graveyard (4). Other buildings that made up the mosque complex included the law colleges (1, 2, 5 and 6); the baths (3); the hospital (7); and the public kitchens (8).*

metal chains pour down from the ceiling bearing the weight of a horizontal web of chandeliers, whose hundreds of lights fan out just above the head, like illuminated lilies lying over a lake of carpets.

All around, sweeping arches, chequered with grey and russet marble, and massive load-bearing columns and piers elevate domes and semi-domes toward heaven. The sober — almost severe — chiefly grey decor is enriched by circular and lancet stained-glass windows that shine out from the *qibla* wall, that is, the one facing Mecca.

The main dome is pierced by 32 windows. At its centre, a circle of tight-knit golden arabesques sends out sparking shoots of swirling Arabic calligraphy like a spinning firework. The whole is a bursting sun around which the mosque is harmoniously aligned.

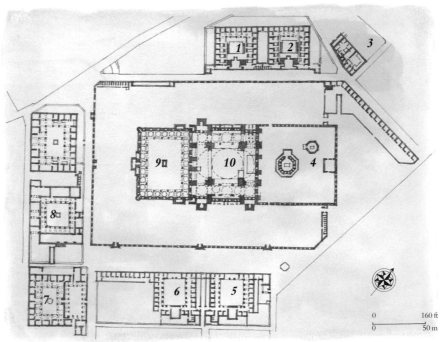

The grandeur of Süleyman's mosque is captured in this English illustration painted in 1588, 22 years after the sultan's death. The mosque is enclosed by a domed wall, and in the foreground the royal mausoleum can be seen.

The Süleymaniye was undoubtedly impressive to western Europeans. According to the 17th-century Turkish traveller Evliya Çelebi Efendi, for example, one visitor said of the mosque: "Nowhere is there so much beauty, external and internal, to be found united."

Unlike Hagia Sophia, which is now a museum, the Süleymaniye has remained a religious building. At sundown, as the tangerine light casts a glow over its western walls and lights begin to twinkle across the Golden Horn, the muezzin's magnetic call draws the faithful to the mosque. Worshippers enter holding their shoes; the men proceed to the front, to sit in a line near the *mihrab*, while the women gather at the back of the building in specially set-aside enclosures.

The white-turbaned imam, the local spiritual leader, stands in the mihrab, its curved recess acting as a natural amplifier for his hypnotic chanting, which seems to trigger sudden responses of bowing, kneeling and prostration, as each person falls into the rhythm of devotion.

In the past, however, the Süleymaniye was much more than just a place of worship. For outside the compound's perimeter wall, Sinan built a complex of buildings, known as a *külliye*. This housed four *madrasahs*; a school where muezzin learned the Qur'an, the holy book of Islam; a hospital for the infirm of body and mind; a kitchen that prepared food for the poor; and a guest-house for important visitors. In effect, the Süleymaniye was a microcosm within Istanbul, a place of sanctity and devotion which also catered for scholarship and the human needs of ordinary people.

The Süleymaniye also encloses in its compound a graveyard. Prominent are the two royal mausolea, or *türbes*, of Süleyman and his queen Haseki Hürrem, who is better known in the west as Roxelana, "the Russian". Süleyman's *türbe*, which is larger than that of his queen, is a small domed octagonal building. Inside, in muted light, the sultan's long triangular cenotaph, draped in green cloth and surmounted by the royal turban, stands in the centre. On each side are smaller cenotaphs belonging to his daughter, Princess Mihrimah, and two later sultans, Süleyman II (1687–91) and Ahmet II (1691–95).

Süleyman fell in love with Roxelana early in his reign and, forsaking the other women in his harem, he made her his queen. His devotion to her was so evident that many contemporaries felt this beautiful, powerful woman had cast a spell on him, which explains her nickname: the *Cadi,* or Witch. It is even said she persuaded her husband that his eldest son, Mustapha, was plotting against him and had to be dealt with. Mustapha was duly executed, and this paved the way for Roxelana's own son Selim (who was later known as "the Sot") to succeed to the Ottoman throne.

Of all the various buildings of the Süleymaniye complex, perhaps the least noticeable and least visited is the small tomb of Sinan himself, which lies outside the main compound to the northwest, facing the Golden Horn. This modest white marble tomb, set into the garden wall of the house where he once lived, has a grille through which can be seen the marble sarcophagus with its turbaned tombstone.

Sinan was born of Greek Christian parents in Anatolia in 1489. His childhood was relatively conventional, and he learned the skills of a stonemason and carpenter from his father. In 1512, however, his life took a dramatic turn. A party of imperial officials, conducting the annual levy of Christian youths for service in the Ottoman army's crack Janissary corps, picked out the young Sinan. He was taken to Istanbul to

The silhouette of the Süleymaniye *seen from the Golden Horn is one of Istanbul's most famous skylines. The mosque's position on one of the city's hills gives it a prominence worthy of the Ottomans' greatest ruler.*

one of the palace schools and converted to Islam. Then, after a period of rigorous training, he served in the army as a military engineer, eventually rising to the rank of chief of the artillery.

In 1538, having cut his teeth on military projects, such as building bridges and fortifications, Sinan began his first civilian work – a mosque – as chief of the imperial architects. Over the next 50 years, Sinan undertook an enormous number of projects – 79 mosques, 34 palaces, 33 public baths, 19 tombs, 55 schools, 16 poor houses, 7 *madrasahs* and 12 caravanserais.

Sinan died in 1588, at the grand age of 99. His memory, however, lives on – not only through his portrait, which adorns modern Turkish lira bills, but also, particularly for the people of Istanbul, in the domes and minarets of the Süleymaniye, its interior a sacred space melting away the passage of time to the golden age of Süleyman's empire.

TIMEFRAME

A.D.

1489	SINAN, ARCHITECT OF THE SÜLEYMANIYE, IS BORN.
1520–66	REIGN OF SÜLEYMAN I, DURING WHICH THE OTTOMAN EMPIRE REACHES ITS APOGEE.
1538	SINAN BUILDS HIS FIRST MOSQUE.
1550	WORK BEGINS ON THE SÜLEYMANIYE.
1557	THE MOSQUE IS COMPLETED.
1566	SÜLEYMAN I DIES.
1571	THE OTTOMANS ARE DEFEATED BY A CHRISTIAN FLEET AT THE BATTLE OF LEPANTO.

THE EMPIRE OF SÜLEYMAN THE MAGNIFICENT

For more than 450 years, the Ottoman Turks presided over an empire that ranks among the world's greatest. Beginning in 1453, it reached its peak during the reign of Süleyman the Magnificent (1520–66), who ruled most of the Middle East, northern Africa, western Asia, the Balkans and Hungary. As sultan, Süleyman was both the spiritual and political head of the empire and controller of all the holy places in his domains. These included the Great Mosque of Kairouan; the Mosque of Ibn Tulun in Cairo; the Great Mosque of Damascus; and the Shehzade Mosque in Istanbul, all of which are illustrated here.

Süleyman was champion of Islamic law – the *shari'a* – and introduced the Qur'an as the basis of education. He encouraged the use of Arabic script in

HOLY ROMAN EMPIRE

Paris

Danube

Vienna

Buda

Pest

Mohacs

Buch

Belgrade

Venice

Sofia

Rome

IONIAN ISLANDS

At

Madrid

MALTA

M E D I T E R

Tunis

Kairouan
(Great Mosque)

Tripoli

AFRICA

| 0 | 200 | 400 | 600 | 800 km |

| 0 | 200 | 400 miles |

Turkey and supported calligraphers and textile workers. His rule was generally tolerant by the standards of the time. Non-Muslims, who formed more than half of the population of the empire, were exempt from military service. They were also given a form of indirect rule known as the millet system, which meant they could administer their own spiritual, educational and judicial affairs.

After Süleyman's death during a siege in Hungary in 1566, the Ottoman Empire began its slow decline. The government was severely hampered by nepotism, endemic corruption and the inability to modernize and compete with European states such as Spain, Portugal and England. Dubbed the Sick Man of Europe during the 19th century, the empire was eventually formally dismantled in 1924.

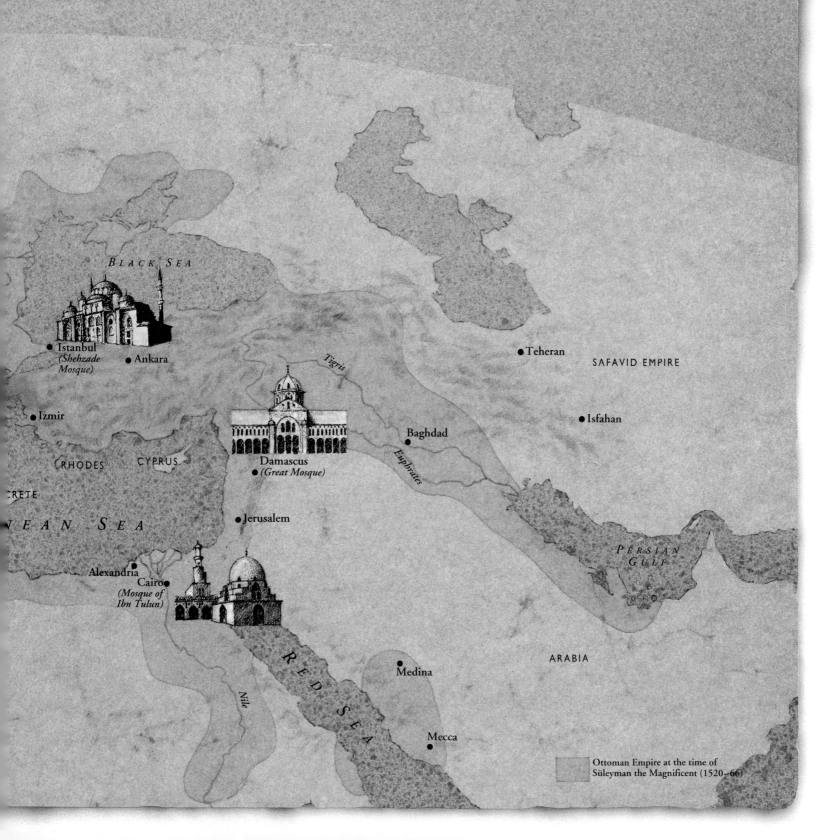

BLACK SEA

Istanbul
(Shehzade Mosque)

Ankara

Teheran

SAFAVID EMPIRE

Izmir

Tigris

Isfahan

Baghdad

Damascus
(Great Mosque)

Euphrates

RHODES   CYPRUS

CRETE

Jerusalem

NEAN SEA

PERSIAN GULF

Alexandria

Cairo
(Mosque of Ibn Tulun)

RED SEA

ARABIA

Medina

Nile

Mecca

Ottoman Empire at the time of Süleyman the Magnificent (1520–66)

INDIA

THE GOLDEN TEMPLE

"The one God pervades every place. He alone dwells in every soul."

FROM THE *ADI GRANTH*

RISING LIKE A GILDED LOTUS FROM AN artificial lake in the city of Amritsar, northwestern India, the Golden Temple is the holiest shrine in the Sikh religion. Originally founded in about 1589, the Golden Temple, or Harimandir, in its present form dates from the late 18th and early 19th centuries. Its golden boxlike structure, as if crafted by Fabergé, is testimony to the brilliance of art executed in the service of God.

Connected to its surrounding complex by a marble causeway, the temple consists of two storeys. The lower one is fashioned from pale marble inlaid with delicate floral patterns in mother-of-pearl, onyx, lapis lazuli, cornelian, and other gemstones. Its four sides face the cardinal points and are punctuated by the dark frames of four open doorways. Above this marble sheathing rise walls of sheet copper covered in gold. Inscriptions from the Sikh holy scriptures, written in the flowing Gurmukhi script of the Punjabi language, add a brocaded texture to the golden facades.

On top, the roof is clustered with small gilded kiosks with fluted, pumpkinlike domes and spires. In the centre, the larger dome of a pavilion known as the Shish Mahal, or Mirror Room, a sanctuary used for meditation, gathers sunlight and flashes it out like a beacon.

Inside the temple, its spiritual heart is expressed not in the form of a god-image, but by the Sikh holy book, known as the *Adi Granth* or *Guru Granth Sahib*. This is laid out on a divan below a gilded and

jewelled canopy. Every day, in the early hours of the morning, the book is carried in procession to the temple from the Akal Takht, a domed building that lies opposite the causeway. Once it has been installed, designated Sikhs declaim holy verses from it continuously throughout the day. At night, it is returned to the Akal Takht.

The Sikh religion was founded by Guru Nanak (1469–1539), a spiritual teacher

Casting its gilded reflection on Amrita Sarovar, the Pool of Nectar, the Golden Temple lies at the spiritual heart of the Sikh community.

166

A marble causeway more than 200 feet long and lined with gilded lamps connects the Harimandir to the mainland. Opposite the causeway entrance stands the Akal Takht, which serves as the seat of the Sikhs' supreme religious council.

who lived in the Punjab. He taught that there is only one God and one humanity and that those who earnestly seek God will discover the divinity within themselves.

After Guru Nanak died, his teaching was carried on by nine successive Gurus, all of whom are revered by Sikhs. Guru Gobind Singh, the 10th and last Guru who died in 1708, declared that after him there would be no more human Gurus. Instead, he conferred Guruship on the sacred scriptures – the *Guru Granth Sahib* – and on the Sikh community or *Panth*.

It was the Fifth Guru, Arjan, who created the first temple at Amritsar. With money donated by the Sikh community, he built it on land that had been given by the Emperor Akbar (1556–1605), the most religiously tolerant of the Muslim Mughal rulers of India. This shrine, expressive of the new Sikh religion, differed from Hindu temples in important structural and symbolic ways.

An attitude of spiritual openness was shown by the fact that the foundation stone was laid by a Muslim mystic from Lahore named Mian Mir. Also, whereas Hindu temples are raised on plinths, this Sikh shrine was built in a slight depression so that worshippers would have to walk down to it in a spirit of humility. Furthermore, it was given four doors, instead of one, to show that it was open to all four castes of Hinduism. And inside, the focal point was the holy scriptures, not an image of Vishnu, Shiva or another Hindu god.

For the next 150 years, the temple remained at the heart of Sikh worship. Then, in the 18th century, Mughal power began to wane, and this encouraged the armies of the Afghan king Ahmad Shah Durrani to make frequent incursions into northwestern India. In 1757, in reprisal for Sikh guerrilla attacks on Afghan troops and materiel, Durrani raided Amritsar, destroyed the temple and filled the sacred lake with slaughtered cattle. Further attacks followed over the next seven years. However, in 1765, the temple was finally rebuilt in essentially the form it has today.

The structure was later refurbished at the start of the 19th century by one of the most famous Sikh rulers, Maharaja Ranjit Singh. Rendered blind in one eye from smallpox, illiterate and fond of jewels and

Guru Nanak sits with the other nine Gurus, who are haloed, in this Sikh painting. Also shown are a Hindu, sitting beside Guru Nanak with a peacock fan, and a Muslim musician.

beautiful women, the charismatic Ranjit Singh carved out an empire that stretched from Peshawar, in present-day Pakistan, and the Himalayas south to the Sutlej River, one of the tributaries of the Indus. He turned Amritsar into a prosperous trading centre and donated some half a million rupees for the temple to be refashioned in marble and gold leaf by the best craftsmen of the time. From this time, the shrine became known as the Golden Temple.

In fact, the temple consists of more than just one glittering building. An entire complex surrounds the shrine and includes guesthouses, offices, a kitchen and refectory and watchtowers. An inlaid marble pavement, backed by colonnades, borders the sacred pool so that pilgrims can circumambulate the shrine itself. Just south of the Harimandir is the Guraka Bagh, the

Garden of the Guru, in which a pool, fruit trees and pavilions stand next to a 130-foot domed tower.

Built in 1798, the tower was named after Baba Atal, the seven-year-old son of Guru Hargobind Singh. According to Sikh tradition, Baba Atal had brought back to life a young friend who had died from a snake bite. But he was then reprimanded by his father for expressing his spiritual power through miracle working rather than by teaching and upright living. Repentant for his deed, Baba Atal decided to give up his life for the one he had saved, so he lay down next to the pool and died.

It is, however, the golden shrine itself that burns brightest in the Sikh soul. Thousands come to visit it every year, both from the Punjab and abroad, viewing it as the Darbar Sahib, the Court of the Lord. Here, in Amritsar, the heart of the Sikh community, they can cross the elegant causeway and, as if passing into a celestial realm, hear the incantations of God's word echoing around the temple walls.

TIMEFRAME

A.D.

1539   GURU NANAK, FOUNDER OF THE SIKH RELIGION, DIES.

c.1589   THE FIRST TEMPLE IS BUILT AT AMRITSAR BY GURU ARJAN, REPUTEDLY ON A SPOT WHERE GURU NANAK USED TO MEDITATE.

1757   AHMAD SHAH DURRANI ATTACKS AMRITSAR, DESTROYS THE TEMPLE, AND POLLUTES THE SACRED LAKE.

1765   THE TEMPLE IS RECONSTRUCTED AFTER THE AFGHAN ATTACK.

1801–39   RULE OF MAHARAJA RANJIT SINGH, WHO HAS THE TEMPLE REFURBISHED WITH GOLD LEAF AND MARBLE.

1984   INDIAN ARMY TROOPS ATTACK SIKH SEPARATISTS INSTALLED IN THE GOLDEN TEMPLE.

SAN VITALE

"There is no other church in Italy that can compare...."

NINTH-CENTURY RAVENNA CHRONICLER
ANDREA AGNELLO ON SAN VITALE

THE CHURCH OF SAN VITALE IN Ravenna in northeastern Italy seems a small and humble edifice compared with the great cathedrals of northern Europe, with their spires and acres of stained glass. Yet its plain brick walls conceal within one of the great glories of western spiritual art: a cavernous interior whose surfaces are aglow with sacred mosaics.

On walls and ceilings, thousands of tiny coloured glass cubes form glittering tableaux of biblical scenes. Cast in gold and all of the shades of the rainbow, Jesus Christ, Abraham, Moses and various saints and angels shine out of these crystalline tapestries that become incandescent under the flaming buds of candlelight.

Some 15 centuries ago, Ravenna was one of the great cities of the west. In the early fifth century, at a time when Roman Italy was under threat from advancing barbarian tribes, Emperor Honorius elevated Ravenna to capital of the Western Roman Empire because of its natural defences of marsh and sea. Later, in 540, it came under the control of the Byzantine

A relic of the golden age of Byzantine rule in Italy, San Vitale was founded about 1,500 years ago and contains some of the most important sacred mosaics in Europe. The view here is from the central part of the church below the dome, looking toward the apse with its grand mosaic of Jesus Christ (ABOVE RIGHT).

The chief jewel of San Vitale's apse is this mosaic of Jesus Christ enthroned. Standing on either side of him are winged angels. They present the figures of Ecclesius – the local bishop under whom San Vitale was begun in about 526 and who holds a model of the church – and Saint Vitalis, the third-century Italian martyr after whom the church is named.

emperors of Constantinople (modern Istanbul), who ruled it through governors, or exarchates, for about 150 years.

During this golden age, the city was adorned with churches, baptisteries and mausolea whose interior decoration became the wonder of the western world. Of all Ravenna's holy monuments, none surpassed San Vitale, which was consecrated in 547 during the reign of Justinian I, one of the great Byzantine rulers.

The church's austere, compact exterior leaves the visitor unprepared for the opulence within. Inside, light from arch-shaped

windows illuminates galleries, where women sat during services, and reflects off marble columns that frame oblique vistas into shadowy aisles. From the centre, below the dome, the eye is drawn to the triumphal arch through which the chancel and apse – San Vitale's chief glories – beckon. Here, in a glowing cave of sparkling light, the figures of Christ, the four Gospel writers – Matthew, Mark, Luke and John – and other holy figures loom from the walls in coruscating jigsaws.

From a distance, the mosaics look like a seamless whole. Only on closer inspection

does it become evident that their magic lies in tiny *tesserae* – small glass cubes in a plethora of colours from rich blues through violets, greys and greens to reds and browns. Particularly eye-catching are the golden cubes, used to fill haloes or background space, which were made by pressing gold leaf on to a glass base and securing it with a thin layer of glass. The *tesserae* were set into damp plaster at slightly different angles to break up the light and create a sparkling effect.

The rich complex patterns of the mosaics are perhaps best appreciated in the centre of the chancel ceiling. Here, the Lamb of God shines out against a starry blue sky within a circular wreath supported by four angels standing on blue spheres.

Below this radiant presence, on the left-hand wall, the apostles John and Luke sit on either side of a triple-arched opening against a rocky landscape. Their respective symbols, the eagle and the ox, stand above

them like heraldic devices; and they hold open their books, looking upward for divine inspiration. In the space between the scenes is a riot of verdant foliage, vines laden with white and red grapes growing out of urns, and peacocks and doves.

On the opposite wall, the apostles Matthew and Mark echo John and Luke. Below them, a semicircular panel, or lunette, features Abel, the second son of Adam, offering a sacrificial lamb and the priest-king Melchizedek presenting bread. These two Old Testament characters were depicted as a thematic prelude to the figure of Christ in the apse, since their offerings foreshadow, respectively, the sacrifice of Christ for humankind and the bread of the Eucharist, or Mass.

The apse – the visual climax of the church – adjoins the chancel and cups and reflects light around its semicircular structure. In its centre, staring out across the church and flanked by angels, is the

Countless tiny bricks *make up the exterior of San Vitale, which belies the colourful light-reflecting walls within. The structure is surmounted by a conical dome, which was composed of clay pots that slotted into each other and were topped by layers of timbers and tiles. As a result, the dome was so light that it did not need supporting buttresses.*

majestic figure of Christ, sitting on a blue globe signifying heaven. With his purple robes, short hair and clean-shaven face, he has the look of a Roman emperor, but on a cosmic scale. For the faithful, the seated Christ is the most sacred of the mosaics. However, the most sumptuous are those depicting Justinian and his wife Theodora, which dominate the apse walls on each side of Christ.

The son of a peasant, Justinian rose to become one of the greatest Byzantine rulers. A man of vision and great energy, he is most famous for his codification of Roman law in his *Codex Justinianus*, a work that has had enormous influence in the west. In the mosaic, his imposing figure in a deep purple robe stands out from his cortege of white-clad attendants. A few wisps of hair escape from under his crown, and his large oval eyes suggest dignity and sternness in equal measure. His golden halo is a visual link with the one behind Christ – a reminder of his status as Christ's representative on earth. By the same token, his attendants are depicted as earthly equivalents to Christ's angels and saints.

Gazing out from the opposite wall is his flamboyant wife, Theodora, the daughter of a circus bear keeper, who gained notoriety as a low-life dancer and actress. Festooned with pearls and other jewels, the empress wears a purple robe, on which the three Magi are embroidered in gold, and holds a gold chalice. Her eyes, said by one contemporary historian to be "always grim and tense", convey more the sense of wistful preoccupation, as if the mosaicist had captured a premonition of her imminent death from cancer in 548.

Adorned with well-known sacred – and secular – figures, San Vitale remained the jewel of Byzantine-administered Ravenna until the eighth century, when the city was taken first by the Lombards and then by the Franks. From then on, Ravenna went into gradual decline, eventually becoming a medieval backwater.

However, the city's mosaic-encrusted churches, and in particular San Vitale, are like sacred furnaces, keeping the fires of religious art burning. As one contemporary inscription put it: "Either light was born here or reigns imprisoned."

TIMEFRAME
A.D.
404 EMPEROR HONORIUS MAKES RAVENNA THE CAPITAL OF THE WESTERN ROMAN EMPIRE.
493 RAVENNA IS CAPTURED BY THEODORIC, KING OF THE OSTROGOTHS.
521–532 ECCLESIUS PRESIDES AS BISHOP OF RAVENNA AND DURING THIS TIME SAN VITALE IS FOUNDED.
527 JUSTINIAN I BECOMES THE NEW BYZANTINE EMPEROR IN CONSTANTINOPLE.
540 BYZANTINE FORCES UNDER BELISARIUS CAPTURE RAVENNA FROM THE OSTROGOTHS.
547 SAN VITALE IS CONSECRATED.
548 EMPRESS THEODORA DIES.
751 THE LOMBARDS OCCUPY RAVENNA.

The mystic Lamb of God, Agnus Dei, *is the dominant figure in the mosaic in the ceiling of the chancel. Surrounding it are four angels, who rest on globes.*

San Vitale was built as a centralized church with two concentric octagons forming its basic structure. Its main features are its entrance (1), the central space (2) below the dome, the chancel (3) and the apse (4) with its mosaics of Jesus Christ and Justinian and Theodora.

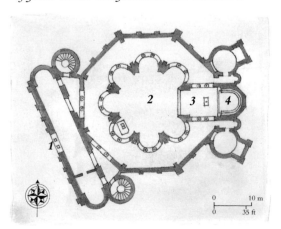

ISE

*"I know not what is within, but I am
in tears with gratitude."*

<small>JAPANESE PRIEST SAIGYO DESCRIBING ISE IN THE 12TH CENTURY</small>

THE GRAND SHRINE OF ISE, SITUATED within a forest on the southwestern side of Ise Bay, southern Honshu, is one of the oldest Shinto shrines in Japan. However, its thatched wooden buildings are, paradoxically, among the newest. For, every 20 years, at vast expense, they are dismantled and replaced with identical structures on an adjacent plot.

This periodical, phoenixlike rebirth, which began back in the seventh century A.D., gives Ise a fascinating sense of both freshness and continuous tradition. And its mystique is also heightened by the fact that

its compounds are closed to everyone except priests and members of the Japanese imperial household. The ordinary visitor must peer through the gateway's white silken curtain for a tantalizing glimpse of the pristine structures that are hedged in by evergreens and cloaked in mystery.

Unlike the soaring cathedrals of Europe – lit with stained-glass light – or gilded Buddhist temples, or tile-encased mosques, Ise's buildings are of the utmost simplicity. Set within two rectangular compounds, the cabinlike shrines are built of the pale wood of *honiki*, Japanese cypress, which is left

Amaterasu, the sun goddess, *is the patron* kami, *or deity, of Ise's Inner Shrine. In this 19th-century print by the Japanese artist Kunisada, she emerges from a cave amid dazzling streams of light. According to Japanese myth, she had hidden herself in the cave because of her brother's riotous behaviour. However, she was lured out of her hiding place by other deities and again brought light to the world.*

174

Weathered with moss and lichen, the wooden gateway to Ise's Inner Shrine marks the threshold beyond which ordinary visitors must not pass. Every 20 years, Ise's buildings are renewed in a ceremony thought to date back some 1,500 years.

unpainted and unvarnished. The steep roofs are made of a deep, highly manicured brown reed thatch. And this combination of well-wrought raw materials, surrounded by groves of towering cryptomeria trees and exposed to the wind, the sun, and the stars, creates a sense of the divine appropriate to Japan's native religion.

For Shinto, "the way of the gods", is based on reverence for the *kami*, the innumerable deities that inhabit natural phenomena such as trees, rocks, waterfalls, or indeed anything that has qualities out of the ordinary, such as an echo, thunder, or even a particularly gifted person. Thus, in Japan, there are literally thousands of shrines dedicated to *kami*, particularly in places of natural beauty. And this mystic sense of nature, which elevates the mind of the worshipper from the level of the mundane to that of the spiritual, has characterized Ise since its beginnings.

175

The holiest part of Ise is Naiku, the Inner Shrine, dedicated to the *kami* Amaterasu Omikami, the sun goddess, from whom the Japanese imperial family traces its descent. Geku, the Outer Shrine, which lies about four miles from the Inner and is only slightly less revered, is dedicated to Toyouke no Omikami, the ancient goddess of farming, food, and harvest. Its layout and the structure of its buildings are similar to those of Naiku.

To reach the Inner Shrine, visitors must cross the Isuzu River via an arched footbridge and a *torii*. This distinctive Shinto gateway consists of two upright posts joined at the top by two horizontal ones and marks the transition from the profane to the sacred. The devout then proceed upstream to an area of the river bank where they can wash their hands and

rinse out their mouths with water in an act of purification.

The main, gravel-lined approach road winds through huge cryptomerias and eventually leads to the thatched-roof gateway of the shrine. Here, only priests and members of the imperial household can pass through the shrine's four surrounding fences, again made of unvarnished wood, that mark out the sacred ground around the principal sanctuary and the smaller subsidiary buildings.

The main structure, constructed in the *shinmei* ("divine brightness") style, is set about seven feet above the pebble-covered ground on stout poles. Some scholars believe this follows the example of ancient granaries or storehouses that were raised to prevent rats and other vermin from gaining entry; others point to primitive Japanese

Ise's structures are made of unvarnished cypress wood and incorporate traditional features of Japanese architecture. The roofs, for example, have distinctive X-shaped end rafters, or chigi; and a series of cigar-shaped logs, or katsuogi, lies at right angles to the roof ridge.

Pilgrims trek to Ise in this 19th-century print. For many, the pilgrimage was literally the journey of a lifetime. At the shrine, street performers such as jugglers and musicians thronged outside the numerous inns and restaurants, enlivening the festive atmosphere.

JAPAN

houses, raised on piles like ancient lake dwellings, as a precedent.

It is said that the sanctuary houses the sacred mirror, which, along with the sword and jewel kept elsewhere, comprise the Japanese imperial regalia that legitimize the emperor's authority. According to tradition, the mirror is the same one that was used to lure Amaterasu from her hiding place in a well-known Japanese myth.

The story goes that the goddess, upset by the unruly behavior of her brother Susanoo, the storm god, retreated into a cave, casting the world into darkness. Eventually, she was lured out by the sound of gods and goddesses making merry and cheering as they watched the goddess Uzume perform a sexy dance. Piqued with curiosity, Amaterasu emerged from the cave and saw herself reflected in a mirror that had been hung by the gods on a tree opposite the cave. As she stared at her own face, she was quickly grabbed by a god, and her light once again illuminated the world.

Amaterasu then gave the sacred mirror to her grandson Ninigi no Mikoto, who brought it down from heaven to earth, with instructions that it should be housed in the palace of Emperor Sujin, who, according to tradition, lived in the first century A.D. Eventually, in later years, it was moved to Ise.

Ise was originally barred to the common people and preserved for the emperor only. However, when imperial funds for the shrine dried up in medieval times, the Ise priests sent agents all over the country to encourage people to make the pilgrimage there and set up fund-raising associations. Apart from its religious aspect, the pilgrimage involved much merriment and festivity, since Ise had a good number of eating houses, taverns, and brothels.

The atmosphere now is more sober. But the magical alliance of Ise's natural setting with the mysterious, partially seen sanctuary that houses the sacred mirror remains. This, and the healing balm of tranquillity, oozing like sap from the protective trees, continues to draw thousands of visitors, as impressed by what they *cannot* see as by what they can.

TIMEFRAME

A.D.

C.7TH CENTURY	FIRST REBUILDING OF THE ISE SHRINES.
1600– 1868	BEGINNING OF THE EDO PERIOD DURING WHICH, ON THREE OCCASIONS, MILLIONS OF PILGRIMS CONVERGE ON ISE.
1868	RESTORATION OF IMPERIAL RULE IN JAPAN; SHINTO IS INJECTED WITH ELEMENTS OF NATIONALISM.
1945	THE EMPEROR OF JAPAN DISCLAIMS HIS STATUS AS A *KAMI*.
1947	THE JAPANESE CONSTITUTION GUARANTEES SEPARATION OF STATE AND RELIGION.
1993	THE ISE SHRINES ARE REBUILT IN OCTOBER.

177

SHINTO SHRINES OF JAPAN

The indigenous religion of Japan, Shinto began in the mists of prehistory as a cult of the *kami* – the countless gods that are believed to inhabit natural phenomena, but which can also be personified. For example, the *kami* Inari was originally a guardian deity of agriculture but is now petitioned for prosperity by businessmen. There are about 80,000 Shinto shrines in Japan. Some are large, others more intimate. Almost all have a *torii,* a gateway of two columns crossed by two beams. Typical shrine structures include a *haiden,* a raised, roofed platform where offerings and prayers to the *kami* can be made;

SOUTH KOREA

SEA O.

Izumo
(Izumo)

J   A   P

Fukuoka
(Dazaifu Tenmangu)

MIYAJIMA
(Itsukushima)

● Hiroshima

Nagasaki ●

KYUSHU

Kyoto *(Kami Kamo,*
Kitano, Fushimi Inari)

▲ Mt. Aso

SHIKOKU

Osaka   Nara
(Sumiyoshi)   *(Kasuga)*

Mt. Miwa ▲   ● Ise
(Omiwa)   *(Grand)*

Mt. Kirishima

PACIFI

● *(Kasuga)* Important Shinto shrine
▲ Mountain sacred in Shinto

and a *honden,* the central building which houses a sacred object in which the *kami* are believed to reside. Most of Japan's shrines are located on Honshu in areas of great natural beauty. Some of the more important ones depicted on the map are Izumo; the Grand Shrine at Ise (pp. 174–77); the mountain shrine of Aso; Itsukushima, with its *torii* standing in the sea; and Sumiyoshi in Osaka. Japan's most sacred mountain is Fuji, shown below in a painting by Katsushika Hokusai. This distinctive peak rises 12,500 feet and is holy to Shintoists and Buddhists alike. More than 300,000 pilgrims climb it every year.

MOUNT FUJI BY KATSUSHIKA HOKUSAI (1769–1849)

COLOGNE CATHEDRAL

"I saw the cathedral in the middle of the city...
They call it, not unjustly, the finest in the world."

ITALIAN POET PETRARCH, WHO VISITED COLOGNE IN 1331

THE TWO GREAT TOWERS OF COLOGNE Cathedral, standing side by side like giant chess pieces, burst upward more than 500 feet, their lacy, conical spires reflected in the Rhine River that sweeps past to the east. This, the largest Gothic cathedral in northern Europe and one of the most imposing in the world, was described by the 19th-century Swiss historian Jacob Burckhardt as "the revelation of an unparalleled and divine genius".

The entire edifice – with its mass of flying buttresses and pinnacles, as if frozen on like stalagmites – gives an overwhelming sense of vertical thrust. Its gravity-defying

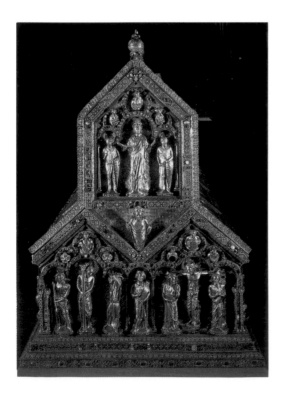

structure embodies the medieval architect's vision of a temple that would lift hearts and minds heavenward.

The unbridled height of the cathedral, or Dom, is even more apparent from inside. Those who enter through the main western portal inevitably throw their heads back to gaze at the soaring vaulted ceiling, which seems to float above the 56 elegant clustered pillars that raise it more than 140 feet above the floor. The eye is then drawn to the eastern end, where light, tinted by stained glass, filters through into seven cell-like radiating chapels. The light also diffuses into the semicircular walkway that gives access to the chapels and into the choir, where 104 oak seats, carved with grotesque figures, foliage and animals, form the largest one in Germany.

Begun in the 13th century and built over a period of 600 years, including a 300-year hiatus, the cathedral is a cultural colossus dominating one of Germany's most historic cities. For Cologne's origins go back 2,000 years to when its site was first settled by the Romans in about 38 B.C. Eighty-eight years later, Emperor Claudius granted it the status of a Roman *colonia*, or colony – from which its name derives.

When Constantine the Great, who became the first Christian Roman emperor, built a bridge and castle there in 310,

The jewel of Cologne Cathedral, *the shrine of the Magi contains relics reputedly of the three wise men. It was begun by Nicholas of Verdun in 1182 and finished in about 1220.*

A Gothic wonder *soaring above the rooftops of Cologne, the Dom is Germany's most celebrated cathedral. Work on the building began in the Middle Ages, but stopped in the 16th century owing to a lack of funds. As a result, the structure was completed only in 1880.*

Cologne already had a Christian community. Later, during the course of the eighth century, Charlemagne, who would be crowned Holy Roman Emperor in 800, appointed the city's first archbishop.

Although there had been a Christian place of worship on the site of the Dom since Roman times, the first cathedral was built in the ninth century under the guidance of Archbishop Hildebold, Charlemagne's friend and spiritual mentor. Consecrated in 870, the Old or Hildebold's Cathedral became known as the "mother and master of all churches in Germany".

Lifting the spirit heavenward, the Dom's pillars raise the roof of the nave nearly 150 feet above the ground. The view here looks toward the high altar and the choir, the oldest part of the building.

One of the largest crucifixes in the western world, the late 10th-century Gero Crucifix (BELOW RIGHT) is six feet high and made of oak. It now hangs near the Chapel of the Sacrament. The letters INRI above Jesus' head stand for the Latin words meaning Jesus of Nazareth, King of the Jews.

The gaping structure of the cathedral is shown in this 18th-century engraving. The view is from the southeast, with the choir and its cluster of spires rising on the right. To the left, a crane protrudes from the stump of the southern tower. The cathedral's unfinished state became such a familiar sight within the city that a local saying was coined: "When the cathedral is completed, the world will end."

However, even this great structure would eventually be superseded.

The inspiration for a bigger building came about 300 years later when holy relics were taken to Cologne from Milan. These sacred objects, originally brought back from the Holy Land to Constantinople in the fourth century, were reputedly of the Magi, the three wise men or kings who, according to Saint Matthew's Gospel, came from the east to attend the birth of Jesus.

Installed in a sumptuous golden shrine, the remains of the Magi put Cologne on the pilgrim's map at a time when Europe's highways were alive with pious travellers making their way to similar shrines all over the continent. The city was now the largest in Germany – with 40,000 citizens and 150 churches – and a major cultural and trading centre. And before long, its newfound spiritual prestige and increasing numbers of visitors provided the impetus to create a building worthy of housing the relics.

Begun in 1248, the cathedral was built in the Gothic style under the guidance of its architect, Master Gerhard, who was influenced by the great French cathedrals

of the time, especially Amiens, which he had seen and possibly worked on. The bulk of the building was made from stone quarried from nearby mountains. The slabs were roughly hewn, dragged to the Rhine, then ferried down to Cologne. There, they were taken to a workshop where about 25 stone masons began to finish them.

The cathedral's eastern part – the choir – gradually rose like a great crown next to the Rhine and was consecrated in 1322. Work continued slowly on the rest of the structure. But by 1560, with the cathedral's massive skeleton still unfinished – it was described by one later visitor as a "broken promise to God" – funds had run out: building ground to a halt.

By this time, Cologne had lost its medieval prosperity, and the necessary money and will to reactivate construction did not

People milling around in front of the Gothic portals of the Dom's west façade give an indication of the scale. The Portal of Peter on the right is the only one of the cathedral's nine portals to be finished in the Middle Ages. Its bronze door, however, was installed in 1889.

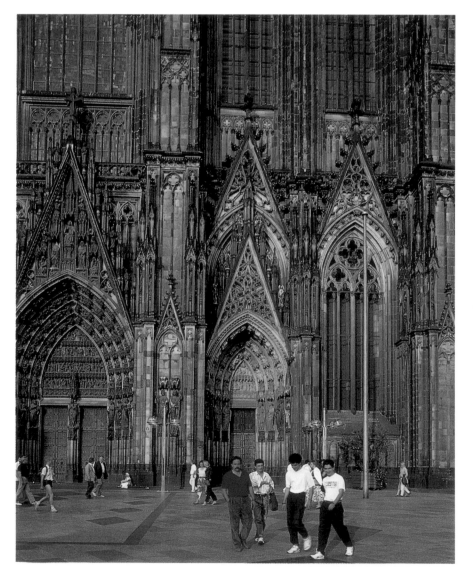

materialize until the 19th century. Instead, the cathedral's half-finished carcass became one of Europe's more curious sights. The ever-present but stationary crane fixed to the south tower seemed almost to be part of the building's fabric, a familiar landmark to the people of Cologne.

The great German writer J.W. von Goethe, who visited the Dom in 1774, summed up both the pride and frustration felt by visitors: "In company with others I did indeed admire its wonderful chapels and columns, but when alone I always lost myself in gloom in contemplation of this vast edifice, thus checked in its creation while far from complete. Here, again, was another great idea not realized!" And the 19th-century British Romantic poet William Wordsworth was moved to write after a visit: "O for the help of Angels to complete/This Temple…."

Twenty years after Goethe's visit, the cathedral's fortunes seemed to reach a nadir when Cologne was occupied by French forces from 1794 to 1815. During this time, the cathedral was used for storing straw; lead was stripped from its roof; and wood furnishings were ripped out for firewood.

Goethe's enthusiasm for Gothic architecture, however, helped to inspire the first German Gothic revivalists, including Friedrich von Schlegel, Joseph Görres and Sulpiz Boisserée. And they began to campaign for the resumption of work on the Dom. Eventually, amid a new mood of enthusiasm and optimism, work again started on the cathedral in 1842 by order of King Frederick William IV of Prussia. In 1880, some 600 years after its inception, the building was finally finished.

For the next 60 years the cathedral stood resplendent beside the Rhine, the very embodiment of the Gothic spirit in Germany. But during World War II, its future hung in the balance as the Allies bombed Cologne, destroying 90 percent of the city centre. The fabric of the cathedral was badly damaged when it was hit 14 times by incendiary bombs. However, restoration work began soon after the war, and by 1956 the cathedral was in use again.

Thousands of visitors now come to the Dom every day, drawn by its sheer size and the sacred treasures it houses. Chief among these are the Gero Crucifix, the triptych, or three-panelled painting, of the *Adoration of the Magi*, and the golden shrine housing the relics of the Magi.

Fashioned from oak in about 975 and named after a local archbishop, the Gero Crucifix hangs near the Chapel of the

***The* Adoration of the Magi**
*by the artist Stefan Lochner is
one of the highlights inside the
cathedral. Formally called the
Altarpiece of the City Patrons,
it was commissioned in the mid-
15th century for the Council
Chapel. During the French
occupation, the painting was at
first hidden in a cellar, but was
later, in 1809, brought into the
cathedral. The central panel* (LEFT)
*depicts the Magi presenting their
gifts to the Virgin Mary and the
Christ Child.*

Sacrament just beyond the northern transept. It is six feet high and, although it has been repainted several times over the centuries, it depicts Christ crucified with powerful realism: the Lord's black hair flows on to his taut shoulders, and the creases of flesh on his chest evoke the sagging lifeless-ness of a corpse.

Opposite the cross, in the Chapel of Our Lady, stands the *Adoration of the Magi*, painted in about 1450 by local artist Stefan Lochner. The central panel shows the enthroned figure of the Blessed Virgin, clad in deep purple and wearing a golden crown. She holds on her knee the Christ Child, whose halo gleams like a golden

coin. Around them, in fur-lined and brocaded coats of red and green, the Magi offer their gifts.

The most important of all the Dom's treasures, however, is the shrine of the Magi. Situated behind the high altar in a glass case, the shrine is a large basilica-shaped oak chest encased in gold and silver, studded with jewels, and embossed with various biblical scenes, including the baptism of Jesus and the Virgin Mary holding the Christ Child with the Magi in attendance. For all the cathedral's awesome size, its sacred heart and spiritual *raison d'être* is this small shrine, a glorious relic of an age of faith and miracles.

TIMEFRAME

B.C.
c.38   THE ROMANS FIRST SETTLE THE SITE OF COLOGNE.

A.D.
50   EMPEROR CLAUDIUS GRANTS THE SETTLEMENT THE STATUS OF A *COLONIA*.

310   CONSTANTINE THE GREAT FORTIFIES COLOGNE.

800   CHARLEMAGNE BECOMES HOLY ROMAN EMPEROR.

870   THE OLD CATHEDRAL IS CONSECRATED.

1164   FREDERICK BARBAROSSA TAKES THE RELICS OF THE MAGI FROM MILAN; THEY ARE LATER INSTALLED IN COLOGNE CATHEDRAL.

1248   THE BUILDING OF THE GOTHIC CATHEDRAL BEGINS.

1322   THE CHOIR IS CONSECRATED.

1560   DUE TO A LACK OF FUNDS, WORK ON THE CATHEDRAL STOPS.

1842   FREDERICK WILLIAM IV ORDERS WORK ON THE DOM TO RESUME.

1880   THE CATHEDRAL IS COMPLETED.

At the Journey's End

THE ROLE OF THE PILGRIMAGE, BOTH IN practice and in its symbolic resonance, has had a profound significance in all religions. Intrinsic to pilgrimage is the idea of a journey – at a material level this might be to a temple, a city, a shrine or a holy relic. On the spiritual plane, however, the pilgrimage represents the journey toward ultimate truth, a higher consciousness or God; and the actual – often arduous – trek involved, with its travails and time for reflection, serves to promote spiritual ardour and self-knowledge. Yet for many pilgrims, the journey's end brings, first and foremost, tangible benefits. For Hindus, for example, to die on the banks of the River Ganges in VARANASI is to escape the constant round of life, death and rebirth. In the ancient world, pilgrims made their way to the Greek oracular shrine of DELPHI to ask the priestess of the god Apollo questions

Spiritual magnets drawing pilgrims to their sacred precincts

concerning their everyday lives – for instance their business ventures and marriages. During the Middle Ages, Christian Europe was crisscrossed with a network of pilgrimage trails leading to sacred shrines – one of the most important being that of Saint Thomas Becket in CANTERBURY CATHEDRAL in southern England. And Christian pilgrimage continues to thrive, particularly at LOURDES in France – the most frequently visited healing sanctuary in the world.

The holiest place in the Islamic world is MECCA in Saudi Arabia, and thousands of Muslims make their way there every year on the *hajj*, a pilgrimage that includes various holy sites in and around the city. Nor does the pilgrimage always end with a temple or shrine: MOUNT KAILAS in Tibet, for example, still has the power to draw devotees to the 32-mile pilgrimage path that girdles its snowcapped summit.

Tibetan pilgrims trek around Mount Kailas, a peak considered sacred by both Buddhists and Hindus.

VARANASI

"Benares [Varanasi] is older than history, older than tradition, older even than legend, and looks twice as old as all of them put together!"

MARK TWAIN

THE BUILDINGS OF VARANASI, THE holiest Hindu city in India, loom like an operatic set over a coil of the River Ganges. Thousands come to the city every year to visit temples, walk along pilgrimage routes, and purify themselves in the Ganges. And thousands never leave. For to die within the sacred precincts of Varanasi is to gain liberation from the relentless cycle of birth, death and rebirth which Hindus call *samsara*.

Also known as Benares, Banaras and Kashi – the City of Light – Varanasi has the most spectacular river frontage in the country. For three miles, spires, tiered towers, tiny shrines, multistoried buildings, pavilions and temples explode from steep banks of broad steps, or *ghats*, that lead down into the water. At dawn, as the sun god Surya burns off the milky mist from the river, the sandstone facades are revealed in all their gilded glory, like a sheer cliff face that has been sculpted into curved niches, spiky cones, arches and columns.

At the river's edge, crowds of people plunge into the water, pour it over their heads, or, on the steps bristling with umbrellas, practise yoga or meditation. For Hindus, no river is more sacred than the Ganges, which, according to legend, fell from heaven. To imbibe a few drops of Mother Ganga's water is enough to be cleansed of the sins of a lifetime. And although the river daily receives thousands of tons of sewage, not to mention the ashes and even corpses of the deceased, its ritual

With legs crossed and in deep meditation, this Hindu sadhu, or holy man, withdraws into a private interior space away from Varanasi's ceaseless bustle. Many sadhus and sannyasins, or those who have renounced the world, can be seen among the ordinary pilgrims who make their way to this sacred city.

Leading down from densely packed towers and buildings, the steps, or ghats, of Varanasi are constantly crowded with people making their way to the Ganges to bathe in its waters. Countless Hindu pilgrims pour into Varanasi every year – many with the intention of dying there and thus escaping from the cycle of birth, death and rebirth.

purity is undimmed. Bottles of Ganges water are prized possessions, and drops from them are administered to the lips of the dying.

As the *ghats* begin to seethe with men and women, young and old, the fringes of the river are ribboned with the rainbows of brilliant silk saris, as if the water had reached a state of crystalline purity and was refracting light into spectral colours. The river front is punctuated with more than 70 *ghats*, each with its own history and legends. Most sacred is Manikarnika, one of the city's two burning *ghats*, where corpses are cremated and their ashes cast on to Mother Ganga's watery back.

The Manikarnika cremation ground is run by a caste of "untouchables" known as the Doms. Corpses dressed in white or red cloth and bound to ladderlike bamboo stretchers are brought here around the clock. During the day, the sacred funereal fires shed plumes of smoke after the morning mists have dispersed. At night, glowing charcoal and sputtering flames cast eerie shadows on to the stone facades of the adjacent buildings.

Although Varanasi's innumerable temples and shrines are dedicated to a variety of Hindu gods, it is Shiva who is revered more than any other. Shiva, one of the three deities of the Hindu trinity (along with Brahma and Vishnu), appears in many forms. He rides a bull and wields a trident of destruction, but also carries a drum of creation. He is often portrayed as an ascetic

yogi, his body smeared with ashes. When not appearing naked, he is sometimes depicted wearing a tiger or elephant skin, or with snakes draped around his neck. Yet he is also the suave silken-robed bridegroom sitting with his wife Parvati.

Shiva's emblem is his *lingam*, a stylized phallic symbol resembling a stubby conical shaft set in a circular base and which represents his creative and erotic aspects. It also appears in the form of a blazing pillar of light in a Hindu myth connected with Varanasi. According to this legend, Brahma and Vishnu were debating which of them was the supreme god when a great fiery shaft of light suddenly burst up from the ground between them and shot upward into the heavens.

Astonished by this dazzling column, the two gods set about investigating it. Vishnu, in the form of a boar, clawed his way down into the depths of the earth; while Brahma, mounted on a goose, soared high into the heavens. But both failed to reach the shaft's ends. Then, when they returned, they found to their amazement Shiva emerging from the pillar of light. Vishnu was duly respectful toward this divine figure, but Brahma snubbed him. So, as a punishment, Shiva hacked off one of Brahma's five heads. However, the god's skull adhered to Shiva's hand. Try as he might, he could not shake it off until, after wandering around India, he came to Varanasi where it fell off, releasing Shiva from his sinful action.

Its spires rising like gilded metal flames, the Vishvanatha temple is dedicated to the god Shiva. Inside its inner sanctum, worshippers may obtain darshana – the holy sight – of Shiva in the form of a black stone lingam *set into a solid silver altar in the floor.*

In addition to being imbued with mythical resonance, Varanasi is also one of India's most historic cities. Its origins go back at least 3,000 years to when the Ganges valley was first settled by the descendants of the Aryan people who invaded the northwest of India in about 1500 B.C. By the sixth century B.C., the city was the capital of the kingdom of Kashi and was visited by Gautama the Buddha, the founder of the Buddhist religion, who preached his first sermon at Sarnath, now one of the city's suburbs.

In subsequent centuries, Varanasi passed into the political orbits of various northern Indian kingdoms. In the seventh century A.D., the Chinese traveller Xuan Zhang described it as an oasis of shady trees, sparkling streams, temples and shrines. His words recall the epithet "Forest of Bliss", accorded to Varanasi in traditional Hindu scriptures.

Varanasi reached the height of its prosperity in the Middle Ages, when it became the power base of the Gahadavala kings, whose liberal reign fostered Hindu religion and scholarship. This changed dramatically with the invasion of northern India by Muslim forces under Muhammad Ghuri in the late 12th century. Varanasi's sacredness proved to be no barrier to Muslim aggression: its buildings were sacked and its temples destroyed. Nearly 1,500 camels, it is said, were needed to carry off the plunder.

In the centuries that followed, the Ganges valley was ruled by Muslims, notably the Mughal emperors (1526–1857). During this time, Varanasi's fortunes fluctuated between times of harsh repression and of revival. From the start of the British rule of India at the end of the 18th century, the city maintained its sacred character and its reputation as a major seat of Hindu learning, especially later with the building of the Banaras Hindu University in 1916. It also retained its pre-eminent position as a place of pilgrimage – a status it still holds today.

One of the most popular pilgrimages around the city itself is known as the Panchakroshi. Pilgrims set out before dawn and bathe in the Ganges at the Mani-karnika *ghat* before proceeding clockwise around the outskirts of the city along the part-paved, part-dirt, main road. Four resthouses provide accommodation along the way for this 50-mile trek, which takes

In a riot of swirling colours, *crowds of people gather on one of Varanasi's many ghats, which border the Ganges for a distance of about three miles. Among the throng are priests, who set up straw umbrellas on the steps. Sheltered from the sun, they make their living by giving blessings for a fee.*

Those who venture into the river bathe in its water, drink it, or pour it over their heads. Some, such as this woman (RIGHT), make an offering of a small lamp.

Children brandish sparklers during the celebration at Varanasi of Divali, the Hindu festival of lights, held during the month of Karttika (October/November). This life-affirming event, as well as other festivals such as Holi – when people playfully splash each other with coloured water – is a counterbalance to the sombreness of the burning ghats of Varanasi.

five days and involves stopping at a total of 108 shrines.

An even more popular pilgrimage is the Panchatirthi, which runs along the Ganges starting from the banks of the Asi *ghat* in the south. Pilgrims must stop and bathe at five designated *tirthas*, or fords. *Tirthas* refer not only to literal crossing places, but also to spiritual fords where people can "cross over" from the world of *samsara* to a transcendent realm of spiritual liberation.

At each stop, pilgrims must recite the *samkalpa* – a vow of intent to worship – or hear it recited for them by a priest. One of the highlights of the route is the fourth

tirtha at the Panchaganga *ghat*, whose imposing frontage rises from small, boxlike shrines at the water's edge up tiers of stone steps to a stately domed mosque of the Mughal period.

It was on the steps of this *ghat* that Kabir, one of India's great medieval saints, succeeded in procuring the blessing of the Hindu guru Ramananda. As a low-caste Muslim weaver, Kabir had to obtain this by guile: he lay across the steps in the dim light of dawn so that Ramananda would trip over him on his way to the river. The ruse worked, and Ramananda, stumbling in surprise, uttered the words "Ram!

Smoke rises from the fires *and embers of one of Varanasi's* cremation *ghats. The dead are brought here at all hours of the day and night, and their ashes are cast into the Ganges. Hindus believe that at death only the body dies, while the spirit or soul (atman)* lives *many times in different bodies until* moksha *– the liberation from the cycle of birth, death and rebirth – is achieved.*

Ram!" – thus unintentionally blessing Kabir with the name of the god.

In addition to these specific sacred routes and *tirthas*, there are countless temples where pilgrims can worship the many gods of the Hindu pantheon. The Vishvanatha ("Lord of All"), one of Shiva's names, is one of the most spectacular, its gleaming gilded spires leaping heavenward like buds of flame. Built in 1776, the temple is set back from the river and open only to Hindus.

To the south of the city stands the temple of Durga, with its sacred tank of water and multitiered golden spire, or *sikhara*, rising above its compound walls. Durga's role as a protector deity is shown in a mural next to the temple door, where, dressed in a red sari, she rides a tiger and brandishes a sword, trident and mace. Inside, visitors must run the gauntlet of the resident monkeys, which scamper around snarling and baring their teeth. Devotees bring offerings of coconuts, sweet things or garlands of flowers to Durga's image, which takes the form of a silver mask fringed with glittering red cloth and is believed to have suddenly manifested itself magically some time in the past.

Although every part of Varanasi is sacred at all times, certain festivals intensify the sense of holiness. One of the most attractive is Divali, the festival of lights, held during the month of Karttika (October/November). In preparation for this, houses and streets are decked out with tiny electric fairy lights, candles and oil lamps.

As night-time approaches, the darkness is dispelled by myriad points of light. The streets blaze with artificial illumination and Mother Ganga is afire with the tiny flames of floating lamps, as if a swarm of fireflies had settled on the dark folds of her mantle. At this time, Varanasi takes on the glory of a heavenly city, the deathly fires of the burning *ghats* outshone as it truly becomes Kashi, the City of Light.

TIMEFRAME

B.C.

c.1500	THE ARYAN PEOPLE INVADE INDIA FROM THE NORTHWEST; IN SUBSEQUENT CENTURIES, THEY MOVE INTO THE GANGES VALLEY.
c.531	GAUTAMA THE BUDDHA PREACHES HIS FIRST SERMON AT SARNATH, A SUBURB OF VARANASI.

A.D.

c.635	THE CHINESE PILGRIM XUAN ZHANG VISITS VARANASI.
1194	MUSLIM FORCES ATTACK AND DEVASTATE THE CITY.
1440	KABIR IS BORN; INFLUENCED BY ISLAM AND HINDUISM, HE BECOMES ONE OF VARANASI'S MOST FAMOUS HOLY MEN.
1526	THE RULE OF THE MUGHAL EMPERORS OF INDIA BEGINS.
1707	THE MUGHAL EMPEROR AURANGZEB, RESPONSIBLE FOR REPLACING SEVERAL OF VARANASI'S HINDU TEMPLES WITH MOSQUES, DIES.
1916	BANARAS HINDU UNIVERSITY IS BUILT; IT WILL BECOME, IN THE 1990S, ONE OF THE LARGEST RESIDENTIAL UNIVERSITIES IN ASIA.
1948	INDIA GAINS INDEPENDENCE FROM GREAT BRITAIN.

GREECE

DELPHI

"I know the number of the sands, and the measure of the sea;
I understand the dumb and hear him who does not speak."

THE DELPHIC ORACLE IN REPLY TO QUESTIONERS SENT BY KING CROESUS OF LYDIA

L YING JUST NORTH OF THE GULF OF
Corinth, which cuts a blue gash out of
the Greek mainland, Delphi was the seat
of the most famous oracle in the ancient
world and the holiest place in Greece.
From its central location and spiritual
preeminence, Delphi was thought to be the
omphalos, or navel, of the world, a belief
supported by the myth of Zeus releasing
two eagles from opposite ends of the earth
– the spot below where they met, Delphi,
was deemed to be the centre and was
marked by a conical stone.

For about 1,000 years until the oracle's
demise in the fourth century A.D., people
would come from all over Greece and farther abroad on foot, by ship, or in chariots
to question the oracle of Apollo about their
businesses, marriages, farming, colonial
enterprises, and other concerns. Apollo
responded to these petitions through his
priestess, the Pythia, a local peasant woman
who had to be more than 50 years old and
lead a blameless life. In Apollo's temple, she
would go into a trance and utter a stream
of apparently incoherent speech. This was
then interpreted by a priest, who translated
it into verse and conveyed the answer to
the questioner.

There were other oracles in ancient
Greece, for example at Dodona in the
northwest. This oracle was associated with
Zeus, who was believed to have communicated answers to questions through rustling
the leaves of a sacred oak tree. But Delphi
was by far the most famous, counting
among its petitioners kings and emperors

Delphi was the home *of the*
most famous oracle in ancient
times and was held to be the
centre of the world. Standing
apart from the main temenos,
or holy area, is the sanctuary
of Athena Pronaia (RIGHT).
Here, three elegant Doric
columns are all that remain of
the tholos, *a circular building*
of the fourth century B.C. *whose*
function is unknown.

194

An Ionic capital stands next to the sacred way, which snakes its way up through the sanctuary. Visible in the background is the Treasury of the Athenians, presented by them to Apollo soon after their victory over the Persians at the Battle of Marathon in 490 B.C.

such as Croesus of Lydia (in modern Turkey), the Macedonian conqueror Alexander the Great, and the notorious Roman emperor Nero.

One reason for its prestige was undoubtedly due to its setting. No other place in Greece can parade such raw elements of natural beauty. The *temenos*, or holy area, of Apollo, where the oracle was located, was built on a slope cupped by towering 900-foot-high cliffs that are known as the Phaedriades, the Shining Ones, because

at dawn and twilight they glow with incandescent light, as if they were the translucent crust of some volcanic furnace. From a deep cleft in the cliffs run the pellucid waters of the Castalian spring, famous since ancient times for inspiring poets. Below the sanctuary, a deep broad gorge filled with the thousand swaying heads of silvery-green olive trees sweeps down to the waters of the gulf.

The whole area, dominated by the craggy peaks of the Mount Parnassus range, is prone to sudden electric storms, when Zeus "hurls his thunderbolts with sparking hand", as well as earthquakes and landslides. Buzzards and vultures soar upon thermals above the cliff tops, and innumerable bees and cicadas make the landscape buzz and whirr with life.

Delphi is the sort of place that makes the modern Gaia theory – that the earth is a living organism – so plausible. No wonder, then, that before the site became dedicated to Apollo, Delphi was sacred to Ge – also known as Gaea – the earth goddess. According to legend, her oracular shrine, originally called Pytho, was guarded by a giant serpent, the Python, a creature commonly associated with the chthonic, or earthly, power of nature. Apollo, god of

The polygonal wall, a detail of which is shown here, lies below the temple of Apollo and is covered in inscriptions, many of which tell of slaves being set free by their masters.

light, reason, and civilized arts such as music, medicine, and archery, came to the shrine, slew the Python and installed there his own priestess, the Pythia.

In historical times, Apollo's oracle grew in prestige and, by the end of the seventh century B.C., this was reflected in the opulence of the buildings of the sanctuary, the remains of which can still be seen. Kings and city states, wishing to honour or show their gratitude to Apollo, as well as demonstrate their wealth, set up a number

of statues, monuments, and small temple-like "treasuries" that housed precious offerings. King Croesus, for example, sent to Delphi a gold lion, weighing a quarter of a ton, standing on a 117-brick pyramid of white gold.

The statues and treasuries bordered the sacred way that zigzagged up the slope of the *temenos*, to the grand Doric temple of Apollo, in which the oracles were given. Today, the temple is shorn of all but a few of its columns, which are weathering back

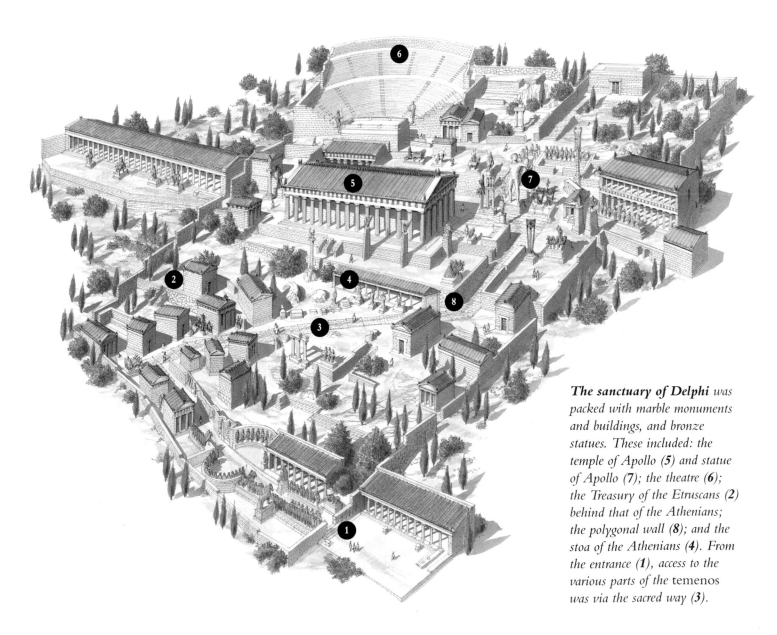

The sanctuary of Delphi was packed with marble monuments and buildings, and bronze statues. These included: the temple of Apollo (5) and statue of Apollo (7); the theatre (6); the Treasury of the Etruscans (2) behind that of the Athenians; the polygonal wall (8); and the stoa of the Athenians (4). From the entrance (1), access to the various parts of the temenos was via the sacred way (3).

to their natural state, and its ground plan is laid bare. But its size and position, commanding sweeping views over the Pleistos Gorge, are awesome.

According to the Greek traveller and writer Pausanias, who visited Delphi in the late second century A.D., several temples were built on this site. They had been made, successively, of laurel branches; beeswax and feathers; bronze; and, finally, stone. This stone temple burned down in 548 B.C. It was immediately rebuilt but collapsed in an earthquake in 373 B.C. Its successor is the one whose remains can be seen today.

Above the temple there is a well-preserved theatre and, at the top of the site, a stadium. This was used for the Pythian games festival, which, after 582 B.C., was held every four years. The entire sacred area, which measures about 200 by 140

yards, must have been a glittering array of marble and bronze. Nero is reported to have stolen more than 500 bronze statues, but still at least another 3,000 remained.

Despite such impressive displays of city wealth, the living pulse of the sanctuary was the oracle. This affected the fate of men and women and the destinies of city states. Pilgrims who came here, already moved by the natural grandeur and dazzled by the material wealth, were likely to be further impressed by their encounter with the Pythia. For when she spoke, it was the god Apollo himself speaking through her, like a ventriloquist.

Such a dramatic spiritual encounter required elaborate preparatory rituals. Although the sources give an inconsistent, patchwork picture of the procedure, it seems that the Pythia, the priests, and the questioners all had to purify themselves in

The Pythia was Apollo's priestess through whom the god communicated replies to questions. In the decoration from this fifth-century Greek vase (BELOW), she sits coolly on a tripod and holds a laurel sprig and a bowl, possibly filled with holy water. She is being questioned by King Aegeus of Athens.

A 19th-century engraving shows the Pythia in a trance. No evidence exists for the snakes, but these creatures represent the earthly power of nature and the Pytho, killed by Apollo.

The temple of Apollo still dominates the temenos *of Delphi, even though only a few of its Doric columns are standing. Inside the temple, the main part, or* cella*, led to the* adyton – *the inner sanctuary where the Pythia sat, screened from the questioners and priests.*

the waters of the Castalian spring. Then, to test whether it was propitious for the god to enter the Pythia and give a consultation, a sacrificial goat was sprinkled with cold water. If it shivered, perhaps symbolizing the Pythia's trance state, then the omen was good for an oracle session.

Questioners had to buy a sacred cake and offer it on the altar outside the temple. Then, one by one, they were taken inside to sacrifice a goat or sheep on the inner hearth within the *cella*, or main part of the temple. They then proceeded to the *adyton*, or inner sanctuary, and sat there in expectant silence with the priests.

The Pythia sat on a tripod – a bronze bowl mounted on three legs – hidden from their view, probably by a curtain. By this time, she was already in a trance, possibly helped by chewing laurel leaves and drinking sacred water. One source suggests that her tripod was placed over a fissure in the bedrock from which emanated an intoxicating vapour. However, archaeologists have found no evidence of any such crack.

One of the priests then conveyed to her the questioner's inquiry and, after she had uttered the mysterious answer, he gave the reply to the inquirer in verse.

Many of the oracles seem to have been cryptic or equivocal. Croesus, for example, was told that if he attacked the Persians he would destroy a great empire. He did – but it turned out to be his own empire. Nero was warned to fear "three and seventy years", but did not realize that it referred not to his old age but to his successor Galba. Despite such ambiguities and the potential for the Delphic priests to influence the Pythia's responses for political ends, the oracle retained its prestige until the first century B.C. when Greece was under the sway of Rome.

By the first century A.D., however, the site was in serious decline. The Greek writer Plutarch (c. A.D. 46–120), himself once a priest at Delphi, wrote a treatise called *On the Failure of Oracles*, a phenomenon he attributed to a general decrease in population. And when Pausanias visited

The Bronze Charioteer, *excavated at Delphi, advertises an international festival of Greek drama at Delphi in 1990, a theatrical tradition begun here by Angelos and Eva Sikelianos. Countries represented included Germany, Denmark, Italy, England, Holland, Spain, and France.*

In the 1990s, the British writer Tony Harrison's Trackers of Oxyrhynchus *was performed in Delphi's stadium. The comic play, which featured a chorus of satyrs (*BELOW*), was based on a fragment of a play by the classical dramatist Sophocles.*

Delphi in the next century, he found it neglected and deserted.

The last recorded oracle was given in about A.D. 362, in response to an enquiry by the Roman emperor Julian the Apostate. The oracle stated poignantly: "Tell the king this: the glorious temple has fallen into ruin; Apollo has no roof over his head; the bay leaves are silent, the prophetic springs and fountains are dead." In 393, the Christian emperor Theodosius officially closed the oracle down: Apollo, the god of light, who had conquered the earth goddess, had now himself succumbed to a new god, of a different, but more powerful, spiritual light.

During the succeeding centuries, the sanctuary fell into ruin and, by the Middle Ages, the village of Castri had grown up over it. Although the site was identified as Delphi in the 17th century by two scholars,

the Frenchman Jacques Spon and the Briton George Wheler, it was only in 1892 that a French archaeological team succeeded in gaining permission from the Greek government to dig there. To do this they had to shift the existing village, stone by stone, half a mile to the west, against the will of the inhabitants.

The excavations once again made Delphi famous. Nor had Delphi lost its sacred aura. Even without the Pythia, the shrine still proved an inspiring place for visitors, who came from all over the world to see it. In particular, Apollo's breath entered the soul of a Greek poet named Angelos Sikelianos (1884–1951), who, with his American-born wife Eva, believed that Delphi could once again be a powerful international spiritual centre.

To this end, they aimed to stage a Delphic festival featuring a production of the classical playwright Aeschylus's play

Delphi's **omphalos,** *or navel, stone was thought to mark the centre of the world. This Roman copy of an original is made of marble and housed in Delphi's museum.*

Prometheus Bound. The daughter of a millionaire, Eva made sure that money was no object in capturing, down to the minutest detail, the authenticity of ancient Greek drama as she saw it.

On May 9 and 10, 1927, the festival took place, despite the fact that the Greek tourist department discouraged visitors – many of them distinguished – from attending, since they feared that Delphi was ill-prepared to receive a sudden influx of people, who might be put off the place for good. However, the play – the principal event – was a sensation, with the actors' words unexpectedly magnified to dramatic effect by the echoing Phaedriades cliffs.

Although the festival was held again in 1930, it was less successful, and the new Delphic dream faltered. Angelos died in 1951, estranged from his wife. Eva returned from the U.S. for the funeral and stayed on in Greece, shortly to die there herself. At her burial at Delphi, the local women who had appeared in *Prometheus* back in 1927 spontaneously sang part of the lines that they had learned for the play under Eva's direction.

Yet the creative seeds sown by Angelos and Eva did not fall on stony ground. In the late 1960s, the idea for an international drama festival was mooted by the Greek government and later came to fruition. The festival is now a regular event, with troupes coming from Europe and beyond to stage classical drama in the summer.

Even in the winter, a time when it was said Apollo used to leave the sanctuary for three months to go to the "land of the Hyperboreans" somewhere in the north, thousands of modern pilgrims come to Delphi. They come not on foot or in chariots but by bus; not to question but to admire the mountains and valley, the ancient temple, stadium and theatre, even the local Christian monasteries: to admire the presiding spirits of Gaia, Apollo, and Christ in reciprocal harmony.

TIMEFRAME

B.C.

c.600 — DELPHI IS ESTABLISHED AS AN IMPORTANT ORACLE CENTRE.

582 — THE PYTHIAN GAMES ARE REORGANIZED.

548 — TEMPLE OF APOLLO IS BURNED DOWN; IT IS SOON REBUILT.

373 — THE SECOND STONE TEMPLE IS DESTROYED BY AN EARTHQUAKE, BUT IS REBUILT.

A.D.

362 — THE ORACLE GIVES THE LAST RECORDED ANSWER TO A QUESTION BY EMPEROR JULIAN THE APOSTATE.

393 — EMPEROR THEODOSIUS CLOSES THE ORACLE DOWN.

1892 — FRENCH ARCHAEOLOGISTS BEGIN THEIR EXCAVATION OF THE SITE.

1927 — PRODUCTION OF AESCHYLUS'S *PROMETHEUS BOUND* IS PUT ON AT DELPHI BY ANGELOS AND EVA SIKELIANOS.

MECCA

"The first sanctuary appointed for mankind was that at Bakkah [Mecca], a blessed place, a guidance for the peoples."
THE QUR'AN 3:96

WHEN MUSLIM TUAREGS PRAY IN THE middle of the desert, they dismount from their camels and draw the outline of a mosquelike structure in the sand. These nomadic Berber people of the Sahel regions of Africa then enter this "enclosure" and, using the sun as a guide, face Mecca, a small city in Saudi Arabia. And in mosques all over the world, from the United States to China, Britain to the Sudan, worshippers bow down to pray five times a day facing special niches, or *mihrabs*, that show them the direction of Mecca.

Known to the Muslim faithful as Umm al-Qura – the Mother of Cities – Mecca is the holiest place in the Islamic world. Here, the Prophet Muhammad (*c.* A.D. 570–632), the messenger of God and founder of the Muslim faith, was born. Here, too, within the city's Great Mosque, is the most sacred Muslim shrine: the Ka'aba.

According to tradition, this cube-shaped building, draped in black cloth embroidered with a band of sacred verses in gold and silver thread, was originally built as a replica of a heavenly prototype. It was

Muslims fill Mecca's Great Mosque, in whose courtyard stands the Ka'aba, the holiest shrine in Islam – reputedly founded by Adam. Pilgrims, such as those below, must process around the Ka'aba seven times. The shrine itself is covered with an embroidered cloth, or kiswah, which is renewed every year.

sacred to the Meccans before the time of the Prophet. And since the birth of Islam in the seventh century, it has been the focal point of the *hajj*, now the world's largest annual pilgrimage. One of the "five pillars" of Islam, the *hajj* lasts several days, during which pilgrims must carry out certain rituals in Mecca and at sacred sites nearby.

Hemmed in by the Sirat Mountains, Mecca is set in a sun-bleached arid landscape about 45 miles east of the Red Sea port of Jedda. In many respects, it resembles a typical Middle Eastern city, with its highrise apartments and hotels and cosmopolitan populace. During the *hajj*, however, around a million visitors from all over the world pour into the city. Streets teem with people. Pedlars do a brisk trade selling anything from dates and prayer beads to carpets and shawls. Muslims of different colour and social background mingle together, filling the air with a hubbub of exotic languages and dialects.

For all *hajjis* – as the pilgrims are called – the Great Mosque, with its huge marble courtyard enclosed by two-storey colonnaded galleries, provides the "still point of the turning world". The building seems to be bolted down by a pair of minarets at each of its four corners. And at its centre,

the Ka'aba is the hub around which not only Mecca, but also the entire Muslim world, revolves.

Up to the time of the Prophet, during the "age of ignorance", Mecca was an oasis town on the caravan trade route linking the Mediterranean lands to the north with southern Arabia, eastern Africa and southern Asia. The local Arab tribes worshipped natural phenomena, such as trees and rocks, and numerous gods, including al-Uzza, the Mighty One, and al'Lat, the great Mother Goddess. The Ka'aba, which housed and was surrounded by pagan idols, was *the* pilgrimage centre of the area.

The fate of the city changed with the birth of Muhammad in about A.D. 570. The Prophet was born into a well-to-do family, but had no formal education. At the age of 25, he married a woman named Khadija, whose caravans he managed. The turning point in his life came 15 years later when he

Many Muslims commemorate their pilgrimage to Mecca by painting murals on their houses. On the one below in Luxor, Egypt, the hajji *has depicted the Ka'aba and a ship – his means of transport to Mecca.*

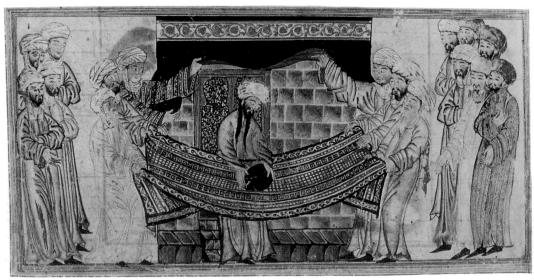

The Prophet Muhammad handles the sacred Black Stone in this early 14th-century illustration from the Universal History *of Rashid al-Din. About 11 inches wide and 15 inches high, and mounted in silver, the stone is set in the southeastern corner of the Ka'aba, here shown behind the Prophet.*

Hajjis *must go back and forth between the hills of al-Safwa and al-Marwa along a covered walkway. The rite commemorates the time when Abraham, revered by Muslims as a prophet, was ordered by God to leave his wife Hagar and son Ishmael in the desert. In her frantic search for water, Hagar ran up and down the two hills until she discovered the well of Zamzam (which is now enclosed within the confines of the Great Mosque).*

was 40. While visiting a cave on nearby Mount Hira in order to meditate, he had a vision of the angel Gabriel, who told him to "Recite: In the Name of thy Lord who created Man of a blood-clot."

It was the first of many revelations Muhammad received until his death in A.D. 632. They were later collected into the sacred book known as the Qur'an, which forms the basis of Islam ("submission to God"). But Muhammad's message, which stressed the oneness of God and attacked vices such as pride and avarice, aroused the hostility of his fellow Meccans. In 622, he left Mecca for the town of Yathrib (later renamed Medina, City of the Prophet).

But in 630, after continual warfare between the Meccans and Muhammad and his followers, or Muslims, the Prophet entered Mecca with an army. Meeting little resistance, he cleansed the Ka'aba of idols and dedicated it to Allah, the One God. From then on, Mecca was to be the focal point of Muslim, not pagan, pilgrimage.

Two years later, Muhammad again left Medina for Mecca, this time to make what was to be his last pilgrimage. At the plain of Arafat, about 15 miles east of Mecca, Muhammad preached to an assembled host of some 30,000 followers. Afterward, he raised his eyes heavenward and cried: "My Lord! Have I delivered aright the Message I

was charged with and fulfilled my calling?" The answer was given by the rapt crowd, who shouted: "Yes, by God you have!"

The Prophet died at Medina about two months later. But the Islamic faith spread like wildfire by force and treaty under the Muslim caliphs, or "successors". Within 100 years, Muslim authority stretched from Spain to India.

Islam is now one of the world's largest religions, with Mecca at its hub. Muslims consider the city and an area several miles around it to be *haram* ("restricted", "sacred") and off-limits to non-Muslims. Thus the number of westerners who have risked their lives to make the *hajj* has been few. Two notable adventurers who did were the Swiss Johann Burckhardt, in 1814, and the Briton Sir Richard Burton, in 1853. Both men succeeded by speaking

fluent Arabic or Persian and being heavily disguised and steeped in Islamic culture.

Taking place during the Muslim month of Dhu-al-Hijjah, the *hajj* must be performed once in a lifetime by all Muslims who have sufficient means and are sane. Before entering the sacred area around Mecca, pilgrims have to enter a state of ritual purity, or *ihram* ("consecration"); and men must put on special dress consisting of two seamless white sheets.

Some pilgrims put on the *ihram* dress at mosques on the boundaries of the sacred area. Others don it at Jedda, the most common place of arrival, or at departure points in their native countries. But once in *ihram*, pilgrims must not cut their hair or nails, have sexual relations, or kill animals, except those that are harmful, such as poisonous snakes and scorpions.

Pilgrims (ABOVE LEFT) *rest on the plain of Arafat. Most stay here from noon until after sunset in prayer and meditation, frequently repeating the talbiyah. This is the central invocation of the* hajj *beginning with the words "Labbayka-Llahumma labbayk" – "Here am I God! Here I am!" On the next day, at Mina, pilgrims throw stones at three pillars, one of which is shown above.*

A Muslim noble travels in style to Mecca in this illustration (OPPOSITE) *from Sir Richard Burton's book,* Pilgrimage to Al-Madinah & Meccah *(1855).*

The hajj *begins with the* tawaf *around the Ka'aba (1), then a run seven times between al-Safwa and al-Marwa along a causeway (2). After proceeding to Mina (3) and Arafat (4), the pilgrim returns to Muzdalifah (5) and from there walks the five miles back to Mecca.*

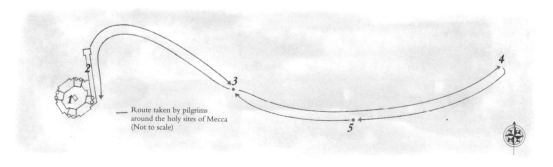

Route taken by pilgrims around the holy sites of Mecca (Not to scale)

On the first day of the pilgrimage, the 8th Dhu-al-Hijjah, pilgrims perform the *tawaf*, the ritual procession seven times around the Ka'aba. If possible, they kiss the Black Stone in the southeastern corner. In practice, however, the swirling mass of humanity prevents many from kissing the stone, so a gesture toward it suffices.

Next, pilgrims run seven times between two small hills, al-Safwa and al-Marwa, which adjoin the mosque courtyard and are enclosed and connected by a walkway. The next destination is the town of Mina, about 5 miles away, followed by the plain of Arafat, 10 miles farther to the east. The day is spent in prayer and meditation, after which the pilgrims head back toward Mecca via Muzdalifah and, again, Mina. Here, they throw small stones at three stone pillars. These represent the three occasions on which Abraham threw stones at the devil, who was tempting him to disobey God's command to sacrifice his son Ishmael.

The *hajj* enters its final stage with the "festival of the sacrifice", when a sheep, goat, cow or camel is sacrificed to commemorate Abraham's sacrifice of a ram

instead of his son. The pilgrimage ends in Mecca with a final *tawaf* around the Ka'aba.

The days spent in and around Mecca are the spiritual high-point of a Muslim's life, especially before modern transportation, when many pilgrims came from as far away as western Africa and India by foot, sometimes taking two years to complete their journey. Many would travel in huge caravans. In 1324, for example, the African king Mansa Musa stopped at Cairo en route for Mecca with a retinue of 60,000.

The *hajjis* now arrive by plane, ship and bus, the poorer among them sometimes spending their life savings on the trip. For all, the first glimpse of the holy city is an awesome moment, a unique frisson such as that described by Sir Richard Burton. As he approached Mecca at night, his Muslim companions suddenly cried out: "'Meccah! Meccah!'...'The Sanctuary! O the Sanctuary!' exclaimed others; and all burst into loud 'Labbayk', not unfrequently broken by sobs. I looked out from my litter, and saw by the light of the Southern stars the dim outlines of a large city, a shade darker than the surrounding plain."

TIMEFRAME

A.D.

c.570	MUHAMMAD, THE PROPHET OF ISLAM, IS BORN.
622	MUHAMMAD LEAVES MECCA FOR THE TOWN OF YATHRIB (MEDINA) – AN EVENT KNOWN AS THE *HIJRA*, OR "EMIGRATION".
630	MECCA IS TAKEN BY THE MUSLIMS, AND THE KA'ABA IS CLEANSED OF IDOLS.
632	MUHAMMAD'S LAST PILGRIMAGE TO MECCA BEFORE HIS DEATH THE SAME YEAR.
1324	THE AFRICAN RULER MANSA MUSA MAKES THE PILGRIMAGE TO MECCA WITH 60,000 FOLLOWERS.
1814	JOHANN BURCKHARDT GOES TO MECCA IN DISGUISE.
1853	SIR RICHARD BURTON, POSING AS A PERSIAN DOCTOR, PERFORMS THE *HAJJ*.
1987	SHIITE IRANIAN PILGRIMS DEMONSTRATE AT MECCA AND A RIOT ENSUES; SOME IRANIANS ARE SHOT BY SAUDI POLICE.
1991	ABOUT TWO MILLION PILGRIMS CONVERGE ON MECCA FOR THE *HAJJ* – ABOUT 720,000 OF THEM FROM OUTSIDE SAUDI ARABIA. THESE INCLUDE 130,000 IRANIANS, THE FIRST TIME THEY HAVE COME SINCE 1987.

At the Time of the Prophet

The world into which the Prophet Muhammad was born in A.D. 570 was dominated by two regional superpowers. To the north and west of the Arabian peninsula lay the lands of the Christian Byzantine empire; to the east stretched the empire of the Persian Sasanian kings, who made the monotheistic religion of Zoroastrianism their state creed.

The Arabian peninsula itself was crisscrossed by trade routes and formed an important commercial link between Europe and the Mediterranean world and India and the Far East. Camel trains, laden with silks, spices, perfumes, precious metals and other commodities, would follow tracks across a hot, inhospitable terrain, stopping for rest, food and water at oases. And Mecca (pp. 202–7), the birthplace of Muhammad, was a major stopping point on routes linking southern Arabia with the Mediterranean and eastern Africa, and the Red Sea with the Persian Gulf.

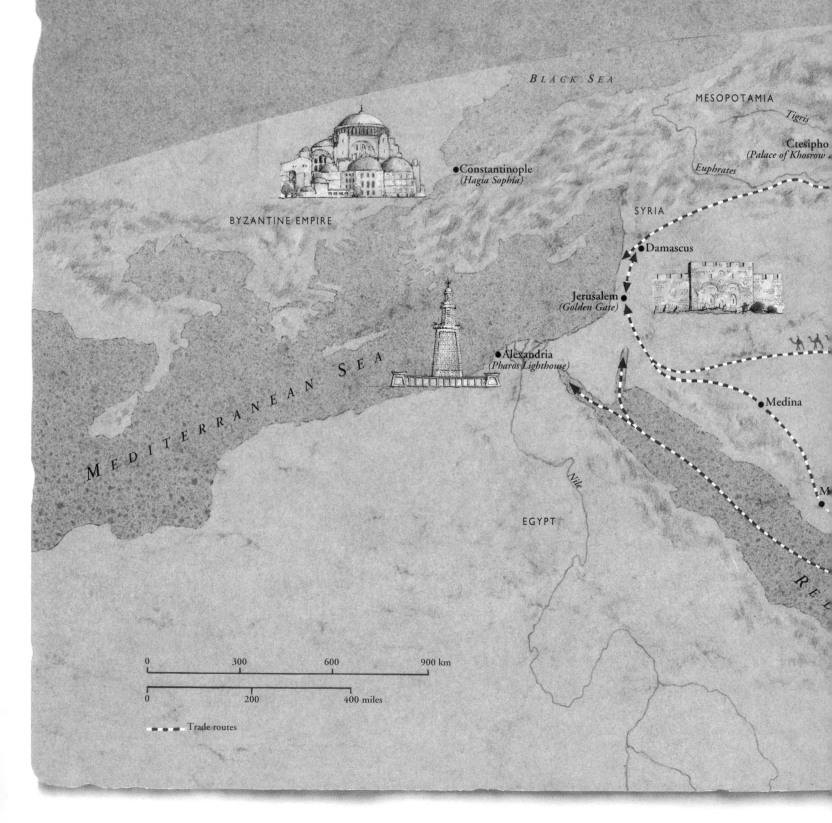

BLACK SEA

MESOPOTAMIA

Tigris

Ctesipho
(Palace of Khosrow

Euphrates

SYRIA

• Constantinople
(*Hagia Sophia*)

BYZANTINE EMPIRE

• Damascus

Jerusalem
(*Golden Gate*)

M E D I T E R R A N E A N   S E A

• Alexandria
(*Pharos Lighthouse*)

• Medina

Nile

EGYPT

M

R E D

| 0 | 300 | 600 | 900 km |

| 0 | 200 | 400 miles |

- - - Trade routes

The map shows the heart of Muhammad's world – the major trade routes and the important cities of the time. These included the Byzantine capital of Constantinople (modern Istanbul) with its magnificent church of Hagia Sophia; Ctesiphon, capital of the Sasanians, dominated by the palace of King Khosrow I; Alexandria, whose lighthouse was one of the wonders of the ancient world; Jerusalem, whose Golden Gate was built in early Byzantine times; Damascus; and Aden.

One of the Prophet's most significant achievements was to unite the feuding nomadic tribes of Arabia and weld them into a well-disciplined, hard-fighting force. And, following his death in 632, the old imperial powers began to lose ground on all fronts. Between 634 and 650, Muslim forces succeeded in routing Byzantine and Persian armies and took control of Libya, Egypt, Palestine, Syria, Iraq and most of Persia (modern Iran).

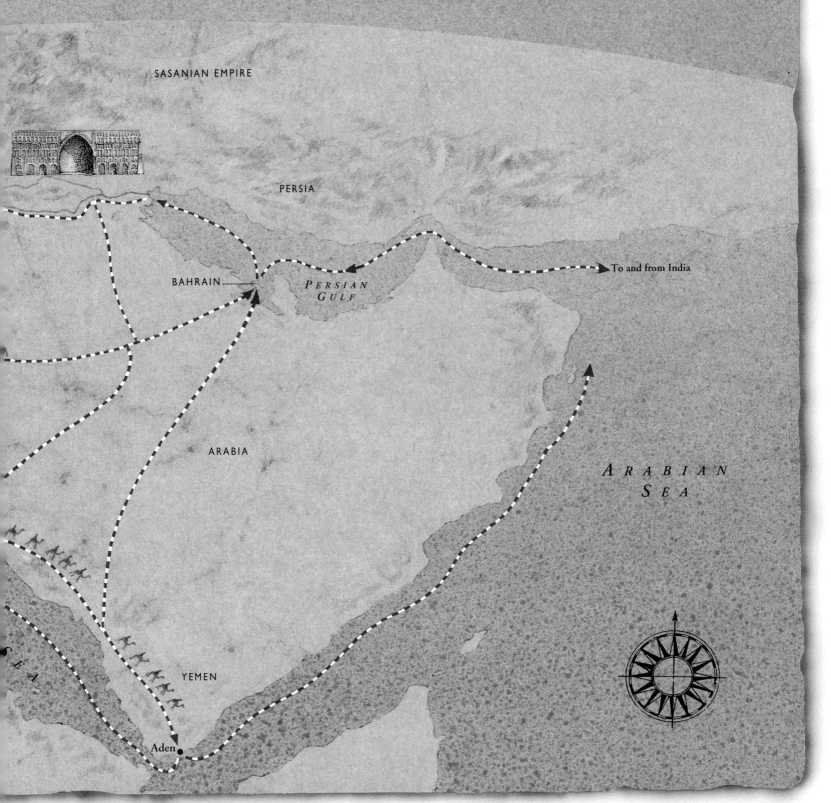

SASANIAN EMPIRE

PERSIA

To and from India

BAHRAIN

PERSIAN GULF

ARABIA

ARABIAN SEA

SEA

YEMEN

Aden

MOUNT KAILAS

"There is no mountain like Himalchal, for in it are Kailas and Manasarovar. As the dew is dried up by the morning sun, so are the sins of mankind at the sight of Himalchal."

FROM THE HINDU SCRIPTURE THE *RAMAYANA*

IN A REGION OF BARREN PLAINS SWEPT by icy winds, in southwestern Tibet, Mount Kailas rises above a girdle of rocky peaks like a full moon above the horizon. Its distinctive cone of ice is a crystalline canvas on which the rising or setting sun paints in violet or gold; or, in the rarefied air 15,000 feet above sea level, makes it shine "brighter than the light of a thousand suns" against the cobalt vault of heaven.

Part of the mountain's sacred aura is due simply to its appearance. Its four distinct facades, cut like the facets of a diamond, are directed toward the cardinal points. On its southern side, a vertical gash intersects a horizontal striation, creating an image that resembles a swastika, an ancient Indian

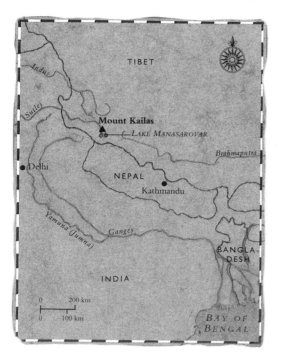

symbol of power. And its symmetrical northern face, with its unalloyed white dome, justifies its title Kang Rinpoche, Jewel of the Snows.

Kailas is sacred to Buddhists, Hindus, Jains and Bon-po, adherents of Tibet's pre-Buddhist Bon religion. Pilgrims of these faiths trek to the mountain to perform the ritual circumambulation, or *parikrama*, around its girth. This takes place along a 32-mile circuit dotted with cairns, prayer flags streaming in the wind, small square-shaped domed monuments, or *chortens*, and monasteries that provide welcome shelter.

The arduous journey, over rough terrain and up and down steep inclines, usually lasts from one to four days on foot. Yet, a few devoted pilgrims traverse the route by prostration: lying flat on their stomachs with arms outstretched, they stand up at the point reached by their hands and then repeat the process. This tortuous method can take up to a month to complete.

For Buddhists, performing the *parikrama* once atones for the sins of a lifetime, while completing 108 circuits enables them to reach Nirvana, or enlightenment. Pilgrims also perform the *parikrama* around the holy lake of Manasarovar, which lies a few miles south of Kailas, like a pool of rippled silk shot through with changing shades of deepest blue. Separated from Lake Rakshal Tal, its western neighbour, by a narrow strip

Sacred shrines, such as this domed chorten, *dot the pilgrimage route around Mount Kailas, which is revered in four religions.*

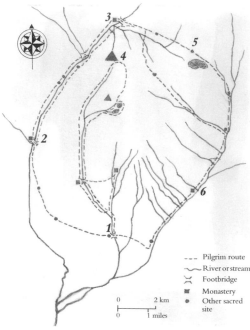

For Hindus, as for Buddhists, Kailas is the abode of the god Shiva, shown here with his wife Parvati and their children. Hindus also identify the peak with the mythical Mount Meru. This cosmic mountain lies at the centre of the universe and around it revolve the sun, moon and stars. Girdled by concentric rings of seven continents alternating with seven oceans, Meru's four faces are aligned with the cardinal points and are made of gold, crystal, lapis lazuli and ruby.

of land, Manasarovar is 15 miles wide and was once ringed by eight Buddhist monasteries. Hindus believe the lake was created from the mind of the god Brahma, and that the god Shiva, incarnated as a swan, glides across the surface. In more recent times, some of the ashes of Mahatma Gandhi, India's great spiritual leader and political reformer, were scattered into Manasarovar's waters soon after his death in 1948.

Most pilgrims who come to Kailas are Tibetan Buddhists, for whom the mountain is the abode of Demchog, a *yidam,* or deity, who has four faces, coloured red, blue, green and white, and wears a tiger skin and a crown of human skulls. His consort is the red-skinned Durje Phangmo, who dwells on a small peak to the west of Kailas and

with whom Demchog is usually depicted in a sexual embrace.

Hindus, by contrast, revere the mountain as the home of the god Shiva, the destroyer and regenerator, often shown as a great ascetic yogi deep in meditation on Kailas's summit. There he is joined by his wife Parvati, revered as the daughter and personification of the Himalayas.

For Jains, whose religion, with its emphasis on asceticism and non-violence originated in India in the sixth century B.C., Kailas is known as Astapada. Here, Rishabha, the first saint in their tradition, gained his enlightenment.

The native Tibetan Bon-po regarded Kailas as a holy place well before the advent of Buddhism. A famous legend involving Kailas records the contest of magic between the 11th-century Buddhist poet and ascetic Milarepa and the Bon priest Naro-Bonchung. The story symbolizes the power struggle between the two religions.

The contest reached its climax when the two contestants decided to race each other to the top of Kailas. At the race's appointed time, Milarepa's followers were aghast to

TIBET

The pilgrimage route around Kailas, shown in this diagram (LEFT), *covers more than 30 miles and is dotted with shrines and monasteries, or gompas. Pilgrims usually start at the town of Tarchen (1) and walk clockwise to Chukku Gompa (2) and Dirapuk Gompa (3), directly north of Kailas (4). The Dolma La pass (5), the highest point of the route at 18,600 feet, marks the homeward run via Zutulpuk Gompa (6).*

Pilgrims at the Dolma La pass bow in worship beside a huge stone draped in prayer flags and inscribed with mantras.

see Naro-Bonchung soaring toward the summit perched on his drum, while their master seemed blissfully unconcerned. Then Milarepa suddenly stirred himself and flew off, beating his opponent to the top: Buddhism had triumphed. However, Naro-Bonchung was allowed to inhabit a peak nearby, suggesting a reconciliation between the two faiths.

Few westerners have seen or performed the pilgrimage around Kailas, since for most of its history Tibet has viewed the entry of foreigners into its territory with suspicion and hostility. Most who have ventured on to the remote plateau have had to don disguises and brave extremes of frost and heat, exhaustion, illness and possible capture, torture and death at the hands of Tibetan soldiers or bandits.

The first westerners to see Kailas, in 1715, were two Jesuit missionaries – the Italian Ippolito Desideri and the Portuguese Emanoel Freyre. But the sacred mountain impressed them only with its great height and girth. To Desideri, it was "always enveloped in cloud, covered with snow and ice, and most horrible, barren, steep and bitterly cold".

Throughout the 19th century, a number of British explorers, geographers and adventurers began to breach Tibet's borders from the safe haven of northern India under the control of the British Raj. They included the explorer and entrepreneur William Moorcroft and his companion, the Anglo-Indian adventurer Hyder Jung Hearsey. These two men entered Tibet in 1812 disguised as Hindu pilgrims, and

213

Moorcroft became the first Briton to see Kailas in the distance "tipped with snow". He also reached Lake Manasarovar before deciding to turn back to Nepal.

The British in general had little appreciation of the sacred connotations of Mount Kailas. However, this was not the case with Ekai Kawaguchi, a Japanese Buddhist monk who made the pilgrimage around Kailas in 1900. For Kawaguchi, the first sight of the mountain was inspiring. All hunger, thirst, freezing blizzards, exhaustion and lacerations experienced on his journey "seemed like dust, which was washed away and purified by the spiritual waters of the lake".

The Swede Sven Hedin, a lion-hearted, single-minded explorer who mapped thousands of miles of Tibetan territory was also moved by the mountain's sacred aura. In 1907, at the age of 42, Hedin became the first westerner to perform the *parikrama* around Kailas. Moving from monastery to monastery "set, like precious stones in a bangle", Hedin made his way around the mountain, "the finger which points up to the mighty gods throned like stars in unfathomable space".

Other pilgrims who have written classic accounts about Kailas during the 20th century include the Italian Tibetan scholar Giuseppe Tucci and the Austrian Herbert Tichy. Neither of their pilgrimages was without incident. Tucci's journey, made in 1935, was beset by stormy weather and an attack by bandits, who were scared off only

By the glittering waters of Lake Manasarovar, a Tibetan woman raises her hands in private worship beside a prayer flag. Known to Tibetans as Tso Rinpoche, the Precious Lake, Manasarovar is believed to have the power to heal. The woman has brought with her a canteen to take some of the holy water back home.

Two Tibetans *on the Kailas* parikrama *make offerings at one of the numerous sacred rocks that can be found along the route. Other pilgrims before them have attached various objects, such as photographs of themselves and money, thereby hoping to gain blessings.*

when Tucci's colleague pointed his tripod-mounted cine camera at them.

A year later, Tichy, disguised as a Hindu, almost came to grief when he was spotted at a Kailas monastery taking a surreptitious photograph. Hauled before Gorpon Sahib, the governor of western Tibet, who was staying in the same monastery, Tichy was impelled to remove his glasses and turban, revealing his blue eyes and dyed-black hair. The hair, at least, was convincing, and Tichy managed to bluff his way out of trouble through an interpreter.

The doyen of Kailas pilgrims, however, was Swami Pranavananda, who first visited the mountain in 1928. Over the next two decades, he made some 23 *parikramas* of the mountain and 25 of Manasarovar. His *Pilgrim's Companion*, published in 1938, combines flights of spiritually soaked prose with more mundane travel tips such as which medicines to take and how to avoid encountering bandits.

Another to have written vividly about the pilgrimage is the German-Bolivian Lama Anagirika Govinda. He became a Buddhist in Burma in 1928 and first visited Kailas 20 years later. His book, *The Way of*

the White Clouds, evokes the outer landscape of Tibet and also the pilgrim's "inner landscape", the receptive mental and emotional state the pilgrim arrives at through the hardships of travelling.

The fate of Tibet, and the Kailas pilgrimage, took a dramatic turn in 1950, when the Chinese annexed the country. In 1959, after repressive Chinese measures, the Dalai Lama, Tibet's spiritual and political leader, fled the country for India. The Hindu pilgrimage route through the Himalayas was closed. Then, in the years of China's Cultural Revolution (1966–76), religious worship in China and Tibet came under attack.

In the 1980s, China eased its stringent policy toward Tibet and allowed certain numbers of pilgrims to enter the country; in the 1990s, Tibet's political situation is still uncertain and volatile. Yet, for those who manage to reach the great sacred mountain, there is the prospect of "an immense peace", which, in the words of Lama Anagirika Govinda, "fills the heart of the pilgrim, making him immune to personal concerns, because, as in a dream, he feels one with his vision".

TIMEFRAME

A.D.

1040	BIRTH OF MILAREPA, WHO IN LEGEND RACED THE BON PRIEST NARO-BONCHUNG TO THE TOP OF KAILAS.
1715	JESUIT MISSIONARIES IPPOLITO DESIDERI AND EMANOEL FREYRE BECOME THE FIRST WESTERNERS TO SEE KAILAS.
1812	WILLIAM MOORCROFT OBSERVES KAILAS FROM AFAR – THE FIRST BRITON TO DO SO.
1900	PILGRIMAGE OF JAPANESE MONK EKAI KAWAGUCHI, WHO DISGUISES HIMSELF AS A CHINESE LAMA, OR SPIRITUAL TEACHER.
1907	THE SWEDISH EXPLORER SVEN HEDIN BECOMES THE FIRST WESTERNER TO PERFORM THE *PARIKRAMA* AROUND KAILAS.
1938	PUBLICATION OF SWAMI PRANAVANANDA'S *PILGRIM'S COMPANION*.
1950	CHINA ANNEXES TIBET.
1959	THE DALAI LAMA FLEES FROM TIBET TO INDIA.
1966–76	CHINA'S CULTURAL REVOLUTION, DURING WHICH RELIGIOUS ACTIVITY IN TIBET, INCLUDING THE KAILAS PILGRIMAGE, SUFFERS.

FRANCE

LOURDES

*"I raised my head and looked at the grotto,
I saw a lady dressed in white...."*

BERNADETTE SOUBIROUS ON SEEING THE FIRST
APPARITION AT LOURDES

IN A NATURAL GROTTO AT LOURDES during the mid-19th century, a young peasant girl saw a series of apparitions that transformed this small town in southwestern France into the greatest Christian pilgrimage centre in the world. Over a number of years, Lourdes changed from an isolated community nestling among rolling hills and streams near the Pyrenees to an international shrine. Now, up to three million pilgrims pour into the town each year. Many of them are sick and distressed and have come specifically to bathe in the spring water of Lourdes in the hope of a miraculous cure.

The seeds of Lourdes's transformation were sown on February 11, 1858, when the 14-year-old Bernadette Soubirous saw a vision of a white-robed lady, in a grotto in the rock face next to the Gave de Pau River that flows through the town. Over the next five months, the girl saw this mysterious figure in the same small cave 18 times.

At first, Bernadette did not know who the apparition was and simply referrred to her as Aqueró, meaning "That one" in the local patois. The lady apparently spoke to Bernadette on a number of occasions. One time, for example, she instructed Bernadette to uncover a spring of water

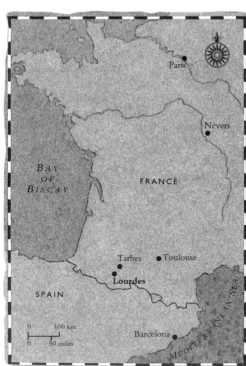

As if the stars had fallen to earth, tiny points of flickering candlelight move slowly in the darkness as Christian pilgrims walk in procession around the Domain of Our Lady, the spiritual core of Lourdes (ABOVE). At its epicentre lies the grotto (LEFT) where Bernadette Soubirous saw a series of apparitions of the Virgin Mary.

inside the grotto, and this water, which is now piped to a bathing house, was soon believed to have healing properties.

News of Bernadette's mystical encounters spread like wildfire around the town. And her appearances at the grotto began to draw large crowds of people, many of whom testified to the strange beauty of the girl's face during her ecstasies. But the local police and civic authorities, disturbed by the commotion that she was creating, interrogated Bernadette. They were, however, unable to shake her conviction in what she had seen. Even the local parish

priest, Father Peyramale, was not initially sympathetic. But he changed his attitude after the 16th apparition on March 25, when the lady dramatically revealed herself to Bernadette with the words: "I am the Immaculate Conception."

Peyramale was shaken by this. The words referred to the doctrine that Mary the mother of Jesus was born free from original sin: it was *not* the sort of phrase a simple uneducated child would invent. For Peyramale, it smacked of authenticity and pointed directly to the Blessed Virgin. From then on, he was Bernadette's keenest

The Domain of Our Lady, *an enclosed area set between hills and the river, embraces the principal churches and shrines of Lourdes. Dominating the site is the spire of the basilica which rises above three distinct churches. Access to them is provided by the ramps that sweep up from ground level. The grotto lies in the cliff face just to the right of the spire.*

The eldest child *of a local miller, Bernadette Soubirous was born in 1844. Throughout her life, she suffered from various ailments, especially asthma, and died at the age of 35. Her last words were: "Holy Mary, Mother of God, pray for me a poor sinner, a poor sinner."*

supporter. Four years later, an inquiry commissioned by the local bishop of Tarbes confirmed Peyramale's view that Mary had indeed appeared to Bernadette.

With this official endorsement – and despite internal wrangles among the clergy over areas of responsibility – the fame and popularity of Lourdes began to grow. This increased dramatically after 1866 when a railway line was built and trains brought in pilgrims in their thousands, many of whom were gravely ill or disabled. Lourdes soon became a town of two distinct halves, the purely spiritual complemented by the more worldly.

The spiritual part, known as the Domain of Our Lady, consists of a parcel of land that stretches up to and around the grotto. Iron railings mark the entrance to this sacred receptacle, and lawns, trees and statues beautify it, as does the glittering river bordering the domain's northern side.

Above the grotto stands a large, gleaming white basilica whose steepled spire is one of Lourdes's principal landmarks. The sanctuary is, in fact, divided into three distinct churches, ranged vertically above each other, and is connected with the ground by two curving ramps mounted on arches like an aqueduct's. The domain's most extraordinary structure, however, is the Underground Basilica of St. Pius X. Any resemblance to a concrete car park is immediately dispelled when it reverberates with the 20,000 worshippers it can hold.

Beyond the domain's precincts to the east lies the more worldly Lourdes. Here, more than 400 hotels and innumerable bars, cafés and restaurants cater for the needs of the flesh, while countless shops parade a

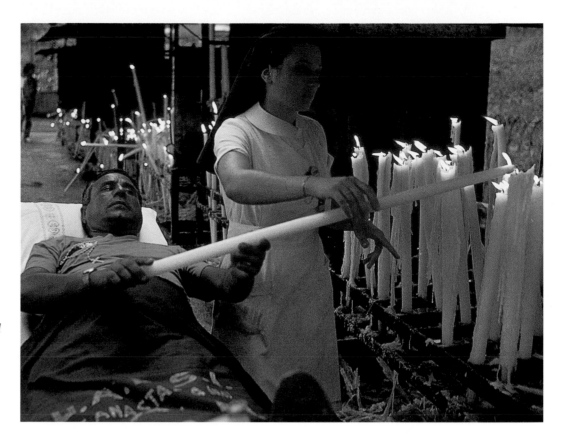

A paraplegic lights a candle from his bed with the assistance of one of the numerous nurses and volunteers who help the disabled at Lourdes. For many pilgrims, the shrine has brought hope or a strengthening of faith or even, in some cases, physical healing.

hodgepodge of souvenirs, ranging from rosary beads to Virgin Mary paperweights.

Yet Lourdes transcends any commercial vulgarity. The hopes and faith of millions of pilgrims continually spiritualize the atmosphere, especially around the grotto – the shrine's sacred heart. Here, the devout pray, light candles or simply contemplate the statue of the Virgin that stands approximately where Bernadette saw the apparition. The sick also usually proceed to the baths near by, where people are helped into enclosed pools filled with freezing water piped from Bernadette's spring.

Those who take the icy plunge hope for a God-given cure; and this is the most controversial aspect of Lourdes, arousing the emotions of believers and sceptics alike. Certainly, extraordinary cures have occurred, as even hardened opponents concede. But the cause of such cures is still hotly debated. Indeed, the shrine's religious authorities themselves set up a medical board in 1885 to scrutinize rigorously the claims of alleged cures.

One case that was passed by the board involved a young Frenchwoman named Lydia Brosse, who went to Lourdes on October 9, 1930, suffering from tubercular abscesses. Severely ill and in a "corpselike condition", she was bathed in the water of Lourdes and departed the next afternoon.

On the return train, even before nightfall, she was feeling better; and within hours her appalling sores were healing and she was able to sit and walk again. On October 12, she presented herself at her hospital, where doctors were astounded at the extent and rapidity of her return to health, which she maintained thereafter.

Bernadette herself seemed unconcerned about healing and suffered from bad health throughout her life. She continued to live in Lourdes for another eight years after her *annus mirabilis*. Then in 1866, she left for a convent in Nevers, hundreds of miles to the north. Here she remained, secluded from the prying gaze of the outside world, until she died in 1879, enduring great physical pain with fortitude.

Bernadette could never have imagined the vast throng that now annually converges on her small village from the four corners of the earth. But the more vulgar aspects of the pilgrimage trade apart, she would doubtless have approved of the outpourings of personal devotion, the many quiet prayers, and the hopes of the faithful borne heavenward on the flames of innumerable candles.

TIMEFRAME

A.D.
1844   BERNADETTE SOUBIROUS IS BORN AT LOURDES.

1858   FROM FEBRUARY TO JULY, BERNADETTE SEES A SERIES OF 18 APPARITIONS OF A LADY WHO IS EVENTUALLY IDENTIFIED AS THE BLESSED VIRGIN MARY.

1866   THE COMING OF THE RAILWAY BRINGS INCREASING NUMBERS OF PILGRIMS TO LOURDES; IN THE SAME YEAR, BERNADETTE LEAVES FOR A CONVENT IN NEVERS.

1879   BERNADETTE DIES IN NEVERS.

1885   A MEDICAL BOARD IS ESTABLISHED IN LOURDES TO INVESTIGATE ALLEGED CURES.

1933   POPE PIUS XI CANONIZES BERNADETTE AT ST. PETER'S, ROME.

1958   THE UNDERGROUND BASILICA IS COMPLETED DURING THE YEAR OF THE CENTENARY OF THE APPARITIONS.

GREAT BRITAIN

CANTERBURY CATHEDRAL

*"For the name of Jesus and the defence of
the Church I am willing to die."*

LAST WORDS OF THOMAS BECKET, MURDERED IN CANTERBURY CATHEDRAL IN 1170

As WINTER WAS WITHDRAWING ITS brief light on December 29, 1170, and the cold vaults of Canterbury Cathedral flickered with the tiny flames of candles, four armed knights loyal to Henry II, king of England, butchered the country's most important churchman: Thomas Becket, archbishop of Canterbury. The murder immediately turned Becket into England's most famous martyr and the cathedral into its holiest shrine, notably celebrated in *The Canterbury Tales* of the medieval poet Geoffrey Chaucer.

Founded in 602 by the missionary Saint Augustine, Canterbury Cathedral in south-eastern England is the home of English Christianity and the hub of Anglican churches worldwide. Its pinnacled tower,

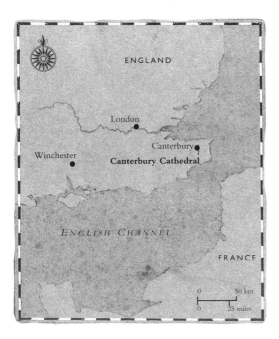

soaring nave and choir, and subsidiary chapels incorporate Norman and Gothic styles and are built on ancient Saxon foundations. Yet the cathedral's widespread fame in the Middle Ages was due not to its architecture but to Becket's murder, an event that shook western Christendom and turned Canterbury into one of the great pilgrimage places of Europe.

Formerly the boon companion of Henry and the chancellor of England, Becket fell foul of the king after he had been persuaded to become archbishop in 1162. The disagreement between them focused on whether churchmen accused of wrongdoing should be tried by the more lenient ecclesiastical courts favoured by Becket, or civil courts as Henry proposed. But the issue was a symptom of a greater struggle for supremacy between the medieval church and the crown.

The quarrel festered and intensified. Becket fled to France in 1164, returning six years later to rapturous acclaim from the common people. Meanwhile, in north-western France, where he was on military campaign, Henry became alarmed by this spontaneous show of public support for his enemy and reached the end of his tether. Turning to his entourage, the king barked out the fateful words: "Will no one rid me of this low-born [some say 'turbulent'] priest?" Four of his knights, de Tracy, FitzUrse, de Moreville and Brito, took the king at his word and set out for England, determined to resolve the problem of the "treasonous" churchman for good.

Winter sunlight *illuminates the stonework of Canterbury Cathedral, which became an important pilgrimage shrine in the Middle Ages after Archbishop Thomas Becket was murdered inside its holy precincts.*

After reaching Canterbury, the knights had a heated and inconclusive meeting with Becket, who was then persuaded by his monks to take refuge in the cathedral. But the knights forced their way in and cornered him. After a struggle, de Tracy struck Becket a glancing blow; then Brito applied the *coup de grâce*, cutting off his head and shattering his sword in the process. The knights then ran off shouting blood-curdling battle cries and proceeded to loot the archbishop's palace.

Stricken by this sacrilegious outrage, the monks went over to the corpse, cleaned up

the gory mess, and shifted the body to the high altar for the night. Later, they took it down to the crypt. Becket, the willful and courageous defender of the Church's rights, had died. But Thomas the Martyr, the miracle worker, was about to be born.

The power that radiated from Becket's tomb eventually attracted hundreds of thousands of pilgrims – including King Henry – and continued to do so for more than 350 years. Even on the night of Becket's murder, a blind man is said to have miraculously gained his sight and to have ascribed his cure to the archbishop.

Nor was it long before more miracle cures were reported, some of which are portrayed in the stained-glass windows of the 13th-century Trinity Chapel beyond the nave. Their rich colours tell of a forester,

shot by a poacher, who regained his health after drinking water from Saint Thomas's well; and of a carpenter who lacerated his leg while working and whose prayers to the saint were rewarded by the healing of the wound. There is also a workman who was buried alive while laying drainage pipes but was rescued and resuscitated thanks to Becket's intervention. As these miracles spread Becket's fame around Europe, Pope Alexander III officially canonized him in 1173, making December 29 his feast day.

Meanwhile Henry, realizing that most of Christian Europe believed that he had ordered Becket's murder, and fearing the pope's wrath, decided to make a public show of penance. In July 1174, he sailed to England from France and made a pilgrimage to the tomb of Saint Thomas.

The flame of a solitary candle *in the Trinity Chapel marks the spot where Becket's shrine once stood – before Henry VIII destroyed it in 1538. The shrine was transferred from the crypt to the chapel in 1220. A pulley, attached to the roof, was used to open its cover.*

On the outskirts of Canterbury, the king put on the penitent's traditional hair shirt, took off his shoes, and walked barefoot to the cathedral. Inside, he kissed the stone slabs where Becket had fallen and then proceeded to his tomb in the crypt. There, the king poked his head through one of the two large holes in each side of the outer tomb – designed so that pilgrims could touch the inner coffin – and received a scourging on his bare back from every bishop, abbot and monk present. Having thus received absolution, Henry stayed all night alone in the crypt and left next morning for London.

Over the next three hundred years, Canterbury became one of the most popular pilgrimage places in Europe. And, throughout Christendom, Saint Thomas was depicted in illuminations, stained glass and sculptures, and churches were dedicated to him.

Every springtime, pilgrims would set out with their long staffs, haversacks and wide-brimmed hats, and crowd the roads that led to the shrine from London, Winchester or coastal towns. Some went to petition the saint for a healing miracle. Others believed the journey would help to lessen or eradicate punishment in the

afterlife for sins committed in this one. For many, the trip served as an act of devotion combined with the pleasures of a holiday.

Pilgrims journeyed on horseback, in litters and carriages, and on foot, travelling in groups for protection against brigands and wild animals. One of the most famous parties of pilgrims is that described by Geoffrey Chaucer, whose *Canterbury Tales* is one of the greatest works of literature. The 14th-century poem describes the journey to Canterbury of a motley crew of pilgrims, including a prioress, a worldly monk, a scholarly clerk, a bagpipe-playing miller, a knight and a garrulous widow from Bath.

Setting out from the Tabard Inn in Southwark, London, the pilgrims agree to a storytelling contest to enliven the journey. These tales consist of a rich mixture of allegories, fables, sermons, courtly romances and bawdy stories. The Wife of Bath, for example, tells of her five late husbands and rails against the celibate life. By contrast, the "Pardoner's Tale" is a morality fable about three men who are seeking Death, who has killed one of their companions.

When they arrived at Canterbury, pilgrims fanned out through the narrow, dirty streets to find lodgings at one of the

Visitors to the cathedral *enter through the southwest porch (1) and emerge in the nave (2). To the north lies the Great Cloister (3), the library (4), and the chapter house (5), where clerical meetings took place. Becket's murder is commemorated in the Martyrdom (6) by a modern sculpture of a broken sword. Beyond the choir (7) lie the Trinity Chapel (8), the site of Becket's shrine, and the Corona Chapel (9), which is now dedicated to modern martyrs.*

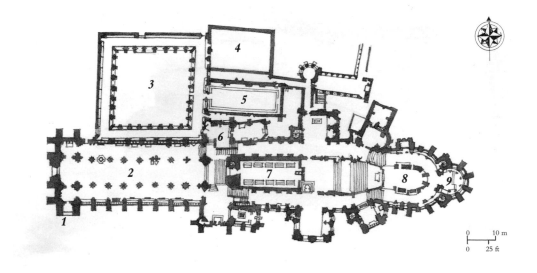

many inns and guesthouses or, if they were poor, at a convent or monastery. Once settled in, they made their way to the cathedral, where monks conducted them to the various pilgrimage stations.

They went first to the Martyrdom, the spot in the northwest transept where Becket was cut down, and which is now marked by a modern sculpture of a broken sword. Those who visited before a disastrous fire ravaged the cathedral in 1174 were then led, sometimes on their knees, up the steps to the high altar, where Becket's corpse was first laid after his death. They then went down to the crypt to the saint's sarcophagus and touched his coffin with their lips or hands through the two holes in the outer tomb.

However, after the fire and destruction of the choir, a new chapel, known as the Trinity, was built specifically to house the saint's tomb. (The steps leading up to it are noticeably worn by the tread of countless pilgrims.) And beyond this was raised the

Corona Chapel to display the "crown" of Becket's head – set in gold and encrusted with gems – which had been sliced off during his murder. Today, the chapel is dedicated to modern saints and martyrs, including Dietrich Bonhoeffer, the German theologian executed by the Nazis in 1945, and Martin Luther King, murdered in Memphis in 1968.

Both of the new chapels were completed in 1220 when, amid great ceremony and with King Henry III, the papal legate and Archbishop Stephen Langton in attendance, the saint's relics were "translated" to a new gold-plated chest resting on a marble base. The tomb was covered with a gold wire net that was weighed down with pilgrims' gifts, including various gems, brooches, gold cups and, most precious of them all, the Régale de France. This huge, glowing ruby was given by the French king Louis VII in 1179. According to one legend, the ruby actually leaped off the king's ring of its own accord

Flanked by angels, a powerful modern sculpture of Jesus Christ enthroned dominates the Christ Church gate, which gives access to the cathedral close from the south. The gate, completed in the early 16th century, houses two chambers that were originally the home of one of the six official cathedral preachers.

The statue of Christ stands in place of the original 16th-century one, which was used for target practice by fanatical Parliamentarian troops during the English Civil War. A year later, zealous Puritans lassoed the statue and dragged it down to destruction. The angels bear shields, now restored, which depict the instruments of Christ's passion.

Like fountains of stone, jets of fan vaulting spray upward along the four enclosed sides of the Great Cloister, which provided a shady retreat for Canterbury's monks to study and contemplate. In the side running parallel with the nave were small compartments, divided by wooden partitions, where monks copied or illuminated manuscripts.

Lit by chandeliers, the choir links the nave with the Trinity Chapel, beyond the altar. The choir was rebuilt after the fire in 1174 by the Frenchman William of Sens. But in 1178, he fell from scaffolding and was crippled. His place was taken by William the Englishman, a man "small in body, but in workmanship of many kinds acute and honest".

and fastened itself to the shrine "as if a goldsmith had fixed it there".

Apart from the Martyrdom, the high altar, the shrine itself and the Corona Chapel, pilgrims visited the well of Saint Thomas outside the cathedral. The well, which cannot now be traced, had been used by Becket during his lifetime and, after his death, the monks had cast into it dust soaked with his blood. Pilgrims queued up at the well to fill their small lead bottles, or ampullae, with the brew before departing homeward.

Modern scholars still debate how fervently pilgrims believed in the miraculous powers of shrines such as that at Canterbury, and at what point a more sceptical attitude developed. Some of Chaucer's characters display a this-worldly, if not cynical, outlook on life that would seem to be at odds with a belief in wonder working. And certainly, in the early 16th century, a marked rationalist suspicion was evident in the visit to Canterbury by the great Dutch humanist Erasmus and his English friend Dean John Colet.

Erasmus was proudly shown what was said to be the shoe of Saint Thomas and invited by a monk to kiss it. Erasmus obliged, but without any great relish. They were also shown dirty linen rags that had constituted a cloth used by the saint to wipe his nose and "the sweat of his face". When given one of these by the monk, Colet laid it down with such a theatrical grimace that even the sceptical Erasmus felt somewhat embarrassed.

Whether or not, by this time, the miracle-working relics of Saint Thomas were being increasingly questioned, the religious landscape of Europe was about to be rent by the Reformation, which ended up splitting Christendom into the Catholic and Protestant churches.

In England, Henry VIII declared himself the head of the Church of England and went on to dissolve the country's great

Arrayed in their finery, Canterbury pilgrims leave the city on horseback in this early 16th-century English illumination.

monasteries. In 1538, he destroyed the shrine of Saint Thomas, declaring him to have been a traitor and a rebel. Some 26 wagons were needed to shift the shrine's treasures to London, and the Régale de France, given as a sacred present, became a ring to adorn Henry's profane thumb. Overnight, the shrine of one of the great pilgrimages of Europe had been erased.

But Henry could not rub out Saint Thomas's memory. The saint's courageous stand against Henry II continued to exert a hold on the popular imagination. And it inspired later writers such as the British poets Lord Tennyson and T.S. Eliot and the French dramatist Jean Anouilh, all of whom wrote plays about Becket.

Today, modern pilgrims still flock to Canterbury, even though no miraculous relics or tomb, glittering with gold and jewels, hold out their attractions. The fact that they come in even greater numbers than their medieval counterparts, at a time when in many parts of the western world Christianity has faded to a ghost of its former self, is perhaps the final miracle that can be attributed to the remarkable powers of Saint Thomas.

TO BE A PILGRIM

The highways and byways of medieval Christian
Europe were constantly dotted with pilgrims making
their way to one of the great holy shrines of the day.
These were often housed within grand cathedrals and
contained holy relics, for example, the bones of a saint,
which were believed to confer supernatural benefit. Yet
the motives for pilgrimage were manifold. Some people
set out simply as an act of devotion, to pay homage to a

particular saint, while others wanted to give thanks,
perhaps for a healing or for good fortune. Some made
the trek walking barefoot or dressed in sackcloth as
an act of penance for a wrongdoing, while still others
went to petition the saint for a miraculous healing.

    The journey would usually begin with a blessing
from the local priest. Pilgrims would then set out
with their stout staffs, usually travelling in groups for

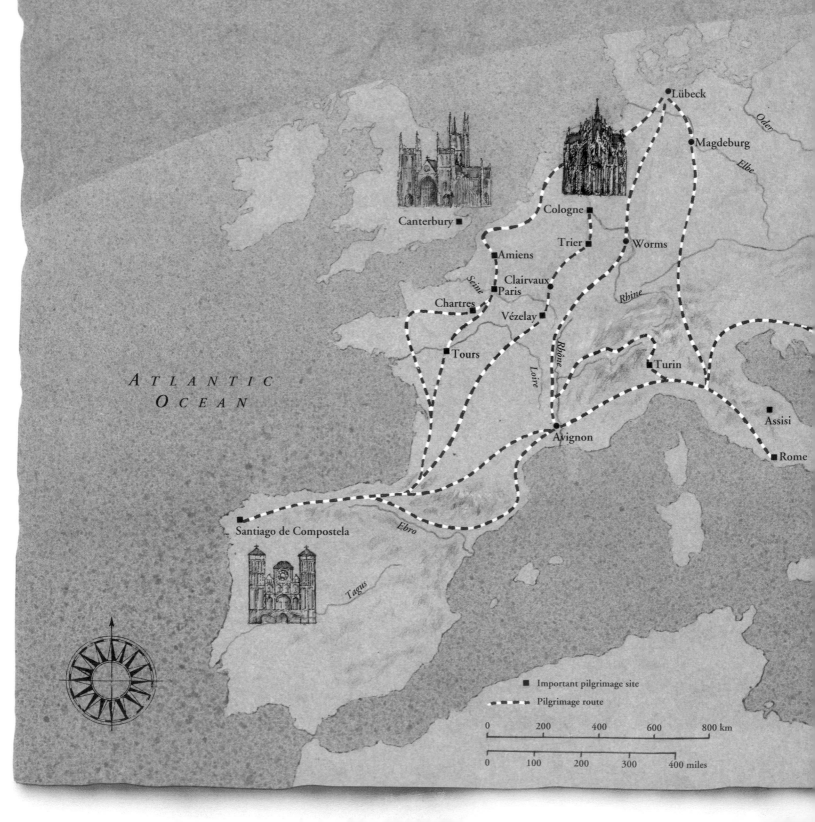

Important pilgrimage site

Pilgrimage route

protection from outlaws or wild animals. Along the way, they stayed in special pilgrim rest houses. At their destination, a variety of inns, taverns and hostels was available for rich and poor alike.

The map shows the principal pilgrimage routes of medieval Europe and farther abroad. Among the major shrines housing relics were: Canterbury Cathedral (Thomas Becket's bones); Cologne Cathedral (the bones of the three wise men); and Santiago de Compostela, the Spanish cathedral whose Romanesque doorways are shown below, (the bones of Saint James). Other sanctuaries were in Rome, where the bones of saints Peter and Paul were kept; Constantinople, with its church of Hagia Sophia; and Jerusalem, whose Church of the Holy Sepulchre was the traditional site of Jesus' crucifixion and last resting place.

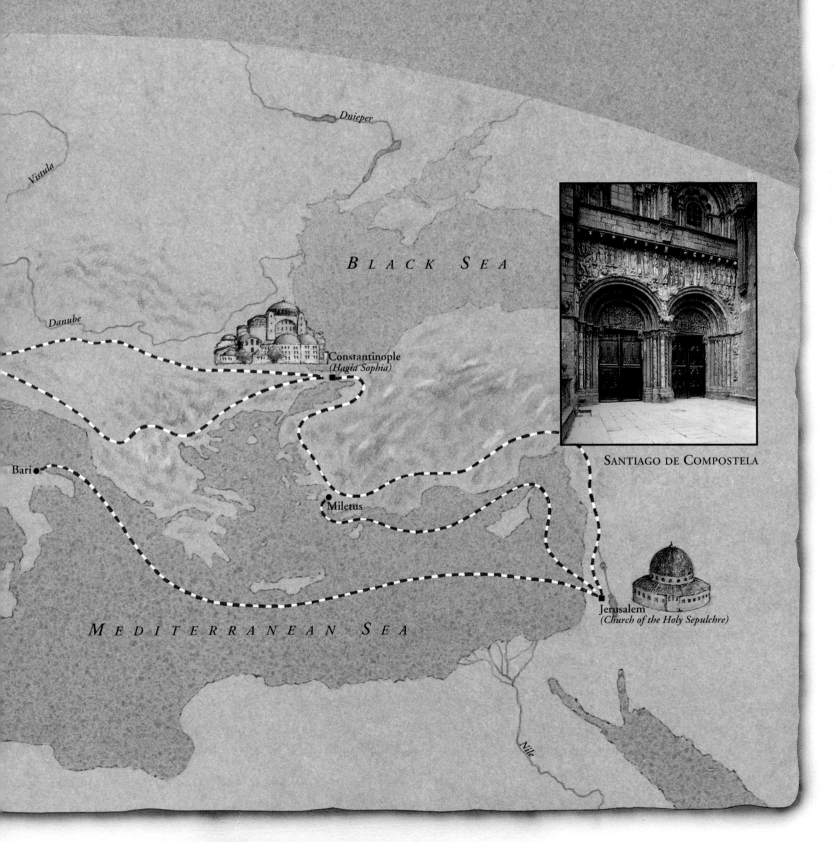

SANTIAGO DE COMPOSTELA

Dnieper

Vistula

BLACK SEA

Danube

Constantinople
(Hagia Sophia)

Bari

Miletus

Jerusalem
(Church of the Holy Sepulchre)

MEDITERRANEAN SEA

Nile

GAZETTEER

Practical advice regarding the places described in this book is given below. Local opening and closing times, however, should be checked before a visit.

BODH GAYA INDIA

The nearest town to Bodh Gaya is Gaya, 9 miles north, accessible by rail or air. Taxis and rickshaws can be rented from Gaya to the site; visitors are advised to agree fares in advance and avoid travelling at night. The monasteries situated near the Mahabodhi Temple offer accommodation as well as a variety of meditation courses and retreats from November to February.

Visitors may enter the inner shrine of the Mahabodhi Temple, in which is housed a huge gilded statue of the Buddha. The Bodhi tree and the 3rd-century A.D. stone which marks the spot where the Buddha sat are situated by the western side of the temple. The archaeological museum at the site displays original carvings and Buddhist images from the Mahabodhi Temple.

CAHOKIA UNITED STATES

Situated about 15 miles east of St. Louis, Missouri, the Cahokia Mounds State Historic Site is open daily from 8 a.m. to dusk, except on public holidays. Self-guided tour cassettes and booklets are available. Visitors may climb Monks Mound, the principal mound at the site, via its stairway.

The interpretive centre, which is open from 9 a.m. to 5 p.m. daily, except on public holidays, illustrates and explains Native American civilization using a variety of audiovisual displays, including a life-size reconstruction of a Cahokia settlement. Various events staged throughout the year include audiovisual presentations, lectures and re-creations of Native American ceremonies. For details, phone the interpretive centre. Children are well catered for at Cahokia, which provides play areas, playgrounds and restrooms.

CANTERBURY CATHEDRAL
GREAT BRITAIN

Visitors to Canterbury can reach the Cathedral via the city's medieval pilgrims' route, turning off the main street into Mercery Lane, where souvenirs, such as

healing water and medallions of St. Thomas, were once sold. Inside the cathedral, the place of Thomas Becket's murder is marked by a modern sculpture in the northwestern transept and his original shrine by an altar in the Trinity Chapel.

The sanctity of the cathedral can be best appreciated at choral evensong, held on weekdays at 5.30 p.m. and at weekends at 3.15 p.m. Services are held on Sundays at 11 a.m. and 6.30 p.m.

THE CATACOMBS OF ROME ITALY

Local buses from Rome city centre run to the Via Appia, a shady tree-lined Roman road where the most important catacombs are situated. The well-preserved catacomb of Saint Callistus is open Thursday to Tuesday, 8.30 a.m. to noon, and from 2.30 p.m. to 6.00 p.m. in summer. Custodian friars show visitors into the popes' crypt, where five 3rd-century popes were buried. Nearby is the 4th-century church of Saint Sebastian, whose catacombs lie underneath and are open Friday to Wednesday, 9 a.m. to noon, and from 2.30 p.m. to 5 p.m. in summer. To the west, the extensive catacombs of Domitilla, which contain important early Christian wall paintings, extend from the private cemetery of Emperor Domitian's kinswoman Domitilla. They are open daily 8 a.m. to noon, and from 2.30 p.m. to 5.30 p.m. in summer.

THE CAVES OF THE THOUSAND BUDDHAS CHINA

Dunhuang, the nearest town to the caves, is best reached by bus, which takes 2 hours from the train station at Liuyuan. The Caves of the Thousand Buddhas are then 16 miles away; buses leave at 7 a.m. and 1 p.m. daily and return at 11 a.m. and 5 p.m.

The caves are viewed by guided tour and visitors are advised to bring a torch as the interiors are not illuminated. Two kinds of ticket may be bought; one allows entry to just six specified caves, while the full ticket gives access to 40. Opening times are 8.30 a.m. to 11.30 a.m. and 2 p.m. to 4 p.m.

COLOGNE CATHEDRAL GERMANY

The main railway station in Cologne is directly opposite the cathedral. Admission to

the interior is free, but a donation to the upkeep of the building is appreciated. Guided tours are in German only.

The three main attractions (the Gero cross, the shrine of the Magi and the altar painting of the *Adoration of the Magi*) should not be missed. But there is much else to see; for example, the carved oak stalls and early Gothic statuary on the pillars in the choir, which is also the earliest part of the cathedral. For panoramic views of the city, the south tower can be climbed to an observation platform at the top.

DELPHI GREECE

A regular daily bus service links Athens to Delphi, which lies just over 100 miles northwest of the capital. Alternatively, visitors can take a train to Levadia and make the rest of the journey to Delphi by bus.

At least two days should be allowed to visit the site and the museum. It is possible to fit a quick tour into one day, but the terrain is precipitous and may prove tiring. The archaeological museum is best known for the lifesize bronze charioteer statue and the frieze of the Siphnian Treasury.

THE DOME OF THE ROCK ISRAEL

Temple Mount, where the Dome of the Rock is situated, lies on the east side of Jerusalem's old city. Non-Muslims are permitted to enter this sacred enclosure by just two gates, the *Bab el-Hadid* (Iron Gate) and the *Bab el-Magharibeh* (Moors' Gate), but may leave by any gate. Bags, cameras and shoes must be left at the entrance to the Dome before visiting the interior. Beneath the marble floor is a cave known to Muslims as *Bir el-Arwah* (Well of the Souls), where the voices of the dead are said to rise in prayer on their way to eternity.

The museum in the southwestern corner of Temple Mount contains relics from the Dome, notably the highly ornamental Great Doors dating from the late 15th century, as well as works of Islamic art.

EPHESUS TURKEY

The nearest town to Ephesus is Selçuk, which lies 2 miles away. The vast site is open daily until 6 p.m., and a tour is best begun at the Magnesia Gate. From here, the path descends along the Street of the Curetes and the Marble Street and commands views of the whole city. The most important remains are the Library of Celsus and the enormous theatre, from which the old harbour can be seen. The foundations of the temple of Artemis lie at the northeastern end of the site.

The archaeological museum at Selçuk contains the famous many-breasted statue of Artemis, along with other finds from the excavation site (open 8.30 a.m. to 6.30 p.m. daily); and the main road south leads to the House of the Virgin, 4 miles away.

THE GOLDEN TEMPLE INDIA

Situated in Punjab state, Amritsar is easily accessible from India's major cities. The Golden Temple is open to tourists, who must obey the rules regarding dress and cleanliness. Views from the upper stories are spectacular, and visitors can sit around the holy book on the ground floor and listen to or join in the religious singing from 4 a.m. to 11 p.m. in summer and from 5 a.m. to 10 p.m. in winter.

Sikh pilgrims circumambulate the pool in the temple precinct, where there are shrines and other places of devotion. Guest houses situated just behind provide free accommodation for pilgrims and visitors for a maximum of three days and nights.

GREAT MOSQUE OF CÓRDOBA SPAIN

Córdoba has two train stations and numerous coach terminals. Accommodation is plentiful around the Great Mosque, which is open daily between 10 a.m. and 1.30 p.m. and then from 4 p.m. to 5.30 p.m. in winter and until 7 p.m. in summer. There is an admission charge for entry to the spectacular *mihrab* (prayer niche) and the Christian cathedral, which are open from 11 a.m. onward. The 300-foot-high Renaissance belfry above the north wall, which replaced a 10th-century minaret, can be climbed.

Moorish influence in Córdoba can also be seen in the watermills and the old Turkish baths along the Guadalquivir River and in the Puente Romano, which was originally a Roman bridge but whose 16 arches date from the Moorish period.

IONA GREAT BRITAIN

The nearest embarkation point to Iona is Fionnphort on the island of Mull, where vehicles must be left in the car park. From here, a ferry departs every hour (crossing time 5 minutes) from Monday to Saturday, with a restricted service on Sundays and in winter.

The abbey is a short walk from the picturesque fishing village, where accommodation is available. A nearby museum houses an extensive collection of early Christian gravestones and effigies, including a stone known as "Columba's Pillow", possibly the saint's gravestone. The abbey provides accommodation from March to December, as well as week-long personal development courses run by the Iona Community, the Church of Scotland body responsible for the abbey's upkeep. For details, write to the abbey warden.

ISE JAPAN

The Inner and Outer shrines of Ise are 4 miles apart, connected by a regular bus service. Coming from Ise's train station, the first shrine encountered is Geku, the Outer Shrine, a 10-minute walk south of Ise town. The Outer Shrine's sacred area is enclosed by four fences; visitors may peer through only, but must first remove headgear and overcoats. The plot of land next to Geku is where the shrine is rebuilt every 20 years.

The Uji Bridge marks the entrance to the Inner Shrine precincts, and here Shinto pilgrims wash their hands and mouths in the river; it is respectful for western visitors to do the same. Again, the shrine's perimeter may not be crossed. A museum and small replica of the Inner Shrine lie near by.

ISFAHAN IRAN

Since 1990, Iran has become more open to western tourists, and visiting Isfahan has been facilitated by a new international airport situated 12 miles away.

The Royal Mosque stands at the south end of the Maidan – the main square. It is traditional to stamp on the few black paving stones below the dome in the east sanctuary to create seven clear echoes. The nearby Lutfullah Mosque is now a museum and is open daily to visitors, while Isfahan's huge

bazaar, where carpets, shoes, samovars and other traditional crafts can be bought, is situated at the north end of the Maidan. North of the bazaar is the Friday Mosque, the oldest parts of which were built by the Seljuks in the 11th century; it opens daily.

LOURDES FRANCE

A modern airport at Tarbes, 12 miles from Lourdes, provides access for the millions of pilgrims who arrive during the pilgrimage season from Easter to mid-October. Lourdes is particularly crowded during the most important pilgrimage on August 15, when there are huge torchlit processions at night.

In addition to the grotto and other churches and shrines that lie within the Domain of Our Lady, there is a small museum with mementoes of Saint Bernadette's life and an illustrated history of the pilgrimages. Many also visit the saint's birthplace and the rooms where her family lived (open in summer, daily 9.30 a.m. to 11.45 a.m. and 2.30 p.m. to 5.45 p.m.).

MECCA SAUDI ARABIA

Non-Muslims are strictly forbidden access to Mecca, and checkpoints on the roads into the city allow entry only to Muslims with appropriate visas. Muslims must obtain either a *hajj* (annual pilgrimage) or an *umrah* (individual pilgrimage) visa, for which return tickets to and from the country of departure must be shown, as well as proof of physical fitness and, where there may be doubt, proof of adherence to Islam. Muslim countries organize pilgrimages at low rates, while Muslims from non-Muslim countries must make travel arrangements individually.

Accommodation is arranged by special guides for *hajjis* in Mecca and at all the other holy places on the pilgrimage; this includes tents on the plain of Arafat. Individual pilgrims should book a hotel in Mecca well in advance of the *hajj* season.

MOUNT KAILAS TIBET

Visitors are advised to contact the Chinese Embassy regarding access to Tibet, which is sometimes restricted, and travel with an organized tour group is recommended. The capital, Lhasa, is best reached by air, and from here the journey by road to Burang, the nearest village to Mount Kailas, takes more than a week. The journey on foot from Burang to Lake Manasarovar at the southern foot of the mountain, where the pilgrimage starts, takes another two days.

Pilgrims walk around the lake in a clockwise direction, which takes two or three days. The circuit around the mountain can be performed by Tibetans in one day, but less experienced westerners should plan for at least three days. Monasteries provide shelter, although food is rarely available.

MOUNT SINAI EGYPT

There are regular flights from Cairo to Mount Sinai Airport, which is situated about 12 miles east of Jebel Musa. Visitors may stay at St. Catherine's Tourist Village, a mile from the monastery.

St. Catherine's monastery is open Monday to Thursday and Saturday from 9 a.m. to 1.30 p.m. Its oldest part is the Chapel of the Burning Bush, in which a silver plate marks the place of Moses' vision. The library contains more than 2,000 rare manuscripts, while the museum's treasures date from the 6th to the 15th centuries.

A number of routes ascend Jebel Musa, the most famous of which is the "path of our Lord Moses" with more than 3,000 steps. Another path has only 800 steps, but either way takes three hours there and back.

MYCENAE GREECE

Buses run from Athens to Mycenae, and trains from the capital go to Mycenae station, close to the village of Fikhtia, 2 miles from the site. Mycenae is open all year round and the admission charge to the main citadel area includes entrance to the Treasury of Atreus outside it.

Many of the treasures and artefacts found by Heinrich Schliemann, including the "mask of Agamemnon", are now on display in the National Archaeological Museum in Athens. Other finds, including armour and pottery, are housed in a museum at Argos, just 8 miles to the south.

NEWGRANGE IRELAND

The passage grave of Newgrange lies 7 miles southwest of Drogheda on the eastern coast of Ireland and is open all year round.

Admittance to the mound's interior is by guided tour, which takes about 25 minutes. The best time to visit is at the winter solstice (December 21 or 22), when the sun enters the passageway through the roof-box. The public, however, are admitted only during the few days before or after the solstice, and early reservations, either with the Newgrange office or the Office of Public Works in Dublin, is advisable. The guided tour includes a re-creation of the solstice sunrise by means of an electric light.

In addition to Newgrange, the nearby mounds of Dowth and Knowth are also worth a visit, although the interiors are not open to the public. A guided tour of Knowth operates from May to October.

THE OLGAS AUSTRALIA

The town of Yulara, situated 23 miles east of the Olgas, provides accommodation, including a campsite. The nearest airport is at Comellan, 3 miles north; buses also run from Alice Springs to Yulara. Daily buses run from Yulara to Uluru National Park, where the Olgas and Uluru (Ayers Rock) are situated. Guided tours can be arranged at the rangers' office, where visitors' passes (valid for a week) must also be bought.

There are several walking trails around the Olgas, with the Valley of the Winds one of the most popular. Another way to see the Olgas is by light aircraft or helicopter; tours can be booked in Yulara. Children between the ages of 3 months and 8 years can be left at the Yulara Child Care Centre.

OLYMPIA GREECE

The site of Olympia is a short walk from the town, which is on the main Peloponnese railway line to and from Athens. Buses also run to and from the capital until 9 p.m.

Nothing evokes the ancient games more than the running track in the stadium, in which the original starting and finishing lines as well as judges' and spectators' seats can be seen. The temple of Zeus, marked today by scattered Doric columns, still dominates the Altis as it did in the 5th century B.C. The temple of Hera, located in the northwestern corner of the Altis, is the most complete sanctuary on the site, with more than 30 columns partly standing.

The archaeological museum, situated about 200 yards north of the site, contains the magnificent 4th-century limestone head of Hera and the marble statue of Hermes by Praxiteles, as well as other relics such as weights, discuses and weightlifters' stones.

OSEBERG NORWAY

The site of the Oseberg mound, where the Viking ship burial took place, lies just northeast of Tonsberg, 40 miles south of Oslo. There are good rail and road connections between Oslo and Tonsberg.

The Oseberg ship, along with the boat found at the site of Gokstad, is displayed in the Viking Ship Museum situated on the Bygdøy peninsula, 4 miles west of Oslo. Bus 30 runs from Oslo to the peninsula, and a ferry service departs every half hour in the summer. Artefacts found in the burials are on display, and special towers allow a bird's-eye view into the ships' hulls. The museum is open daily until 6 p.m. in summer and 3 p.m. in winter.

PAGAN MYANMAR (BURMA)

Visas are required for travel within Myanmar; they are issued for a maximum of 14 days and are relatively inexpensive. Flights to Pagan airport are irregular and difficult to book. The nearest train station is at Thazi, about 80 miles south of Pagan, and from here the last part of the journey can be made by bus or by boat.

The Pagan area includes a number of villages at the centre of which lies Pagan itself, with the greatest concentration of temples and pagodas. The important Ananda, Dammayangyi and Gawdawpalin temples can be entered, and steps ascend to upper levels, affording magnificent views. A museum illustrates the history with exhibits covering all styles of Burmese religious art.

THE PYRAMIDS OF GIZA EGYPT

Approached by local bus, the pyramids are situated at Giza, 6 miles southwest of central Cairo. Visitors pay one admission charge for the pyramids and the Sphinx and another for the Solar Boat Museum, where the wooden funeral boat uncovered south of the Great Pyramid is displayed. The interiors of the pyramids may be visited, but the steep descent and cramped conditions require a certain degree of fitness; climbing the pyramids is no longer permitted. The Great Pyramid is entered via a passage on the north side that leads to the pharaoh's tomb chamber and his red granite sarcophagus.

The pyramids and the Sphinx are flood-lit at night and *son-et-lumière* performances are given in English, French, German and Arabic on different nights of the week.

THE ROCK OF CASHEL IRELAND
Visitors to the Rock of Cashel should take the train to Tipperary, 12 miles southwest of the site, and make the rest of the journey by bus or guided excursion. The Rock is a 10-minute walk from Cashel town centre.

There is a small admission charge for the site, which is open daily until 7.30 p.m. in summer (4.30 p.m. in winter). Inside the main entrance is a visitor centre and small museum situated in the Hall of the Vicars Choral, where the original St. Patrick's Cross, a 4th-century high cross, is on display (the one outside is a replica). The round tower and walls may be ascended with permission from a warden.

SAN VITALE ITALY
Ravenna is accessible by rail from Italy's main cities. San Vitale is open daily in summer from 8.30 a.m. to 7 p.m. and in winter from 9 a.m. to 4.30 p.m., as is the Mausoleum of Galla Placida, which contains the oldest mosaics in Ravenna. A single ticket for both these sites also admits visitors to four others; these include the 5th-century Neonian Baptistry (named for Bishop Neon) with its 13th-century font large enough for the immersion of adults, and the Archiepiscopal Museum housing the throne of Bishop Maximian.

The mosaics in the 6th-century Sant'Apollinare Nuovo rival those in San Vitale for extensiveness and should not be missed. The church is open daily in summer from 9.30 a.m. to 5.30 p.m.

THE SÜLEYMANIYE TURKEY
Easily reached from Istanbul city centre, Süleyman the Magnificent's mosque stands within a complex of buildings, including four *medrasahs*, or theological colleges, a medical school, hospice and huge *imaret*, or public kitchen. The mosque is still used for worship, and visitors must be particularly respectful at these times.

The superbly tiled octagonal *türbes* (mausolea) of Süleyman and his queen Roxelana are situated in the cemetery on the eastern side of the mosque (open Wednesday to Sunday from 9.30 a.m. to 4.30 p.m.).

THE TEMPLE OF KARNAK EGYPT
The town of Luxor (ancient Thebes), where the temples of Karnak and Luxor are situated, lies about 420 miles south of Cairo.

In summer, Karnak should be visited only in the morning and late afternoon to avoid the intense midday heat, and at least two days are required to see all the many temple buildings. The highlight of a visit is the Great Hypostyle Hall, with its 134 towering columns. *Son-et-lumière* performances in various languages – including English – are held several times every evening.

A museum in Luxor houses exhibits from the sites, and from here boats depart for the West Bank, where the Valley of the Kings and other temples and tombs may be seen. Tickets must be obtained at the ferry docking office on arrival at the West Bank.

TEOTIHUACÁN MEXICO
Tour buses run the 30 miles from Mexico City to Teotihuacán, which is open from 8 a.m. to 5 p.m.; entry is free on Sundays. A museum at the main entrance gives a useful overview of the site. About 1½ miles in length, Teotihuacán can be seen in a day, and the main structures, including the pyramids of the Sun and Moon, can be climbed. Murals and carvings are housed in Mexico City's Anthropology Museum.

Son-et-lumière performances are held every night except Monday, at 7 p.m. in English and at 8.15 p.m. in Spanish, setting ancient myths to traditional Indian music.

THE TOMB COMPLEX OF SHI HUANGDI CHINA
Xi'an is the nearest large town to the tomb complex and has an airport and train station.

Buses run daily from Xi'an city centre to the site, which lies 17 miles to the east. The emperor's 130-foot-high burial mound on the lower slopes of Mount Li may be climbed via a stepped path lined with souvenir stalls.

The pits containing the terracotta army lie about a mile east of the mound, although only Pit 1 is currently open. It is covered by a hangar and has walkways around its sides from which visitors may view the immense army below. Maps, photographs of the excavation work and other exhibits are displayed in the side wings, including two magnificent bronze chariots, in a hall to the right of the pit.

VARANASI INDIA
Reached by air, rail or road, Varanasi (Benares), in Uttar Pradesh state in northern India, is best described as one big shrine. Many unexpected temples are situated in the old town's labyrinthine streets, including the Vishvanatha temple, whose inner shrine with its *lingam* may be viewed by non-Hindus from the house next door for a small fee. The *ghats* are best seen at dawn from rented boats, although photography is not permitted at the funeral *ghats* of Manikarnika and Harishchandra.

Also worth visiting is Sarnath, 6 miles from Varanasi, where the Buddha preached his first sermon. The spot is marked by the huge Dhamekh Stupa set among the remains of Sarnath's ancient monastery.

WAT PHRA KEO THAILAND
Bangkok's Royal Palace, which encloses Wat Phra Keo, is open daily – except on Buddhist holidays – from 8.30 a.m. to 3.30 p.m. with an hour's break from noon. Wat Phra Keo is closed at weekends. A ticket for the Royal Palace includes admission to Wat Phra Keo. Trousers or dresses must be worn in the Royal Palace, shoes must be removed before entering the shrine of the Emerald Buddha, which lies at the heart of Wat Phra Keo, and photography is prohibited.

On the western side of the Royal Palace is the Wat Phra Keo museum, housing the magnificent Manangalisa Throne and a scale model of the Royal Palace and Wat Phra Keo complex.

BIBLIOGRAPHY

The following is a selection of volumes used in the making of this book, and recommendations for further reading.

INTRODUCTION
Burckhardt, Titus *Sacred Art in East and West* (trans. Lord Northbourne) Perennial Books Ltd, Bedfont, 1967
Eliade, Mircea *The Sacred and the Profane* (trans. Willard R. Trask) Harcourt Brace Javanovich, New York, 1959
Otto, Rudolf *The Idea of the Holy* (trans. John W. Harvey) Oxford University Press, Oxford, 1923

BODH GAYA
Bechert, Heinz and **Richard Gombrich** (eds.) *The World of Buddhism* Thames and Hudson, London, 1984
Harvey, Peter *An Introduction to Buddhism* Cambridge University Press, Cambridge, 1990
Michell, George *The Penguin Guide to the Monuments of India; Volume One: Buddhist, Jain, Hindu* Viking, London, 1989
Shearer, Alistair *The Traveller's Key to Northern India* Harrap Columbus, London, 1987

CAHOKIA
Fowler, Melvin *Cahokia: Ancient Capital of the Midwest* Addison-Wesley, Massachusetts, 1974
Gellman Mink, Claudia *Cahokia: City of the Sun* Cahokia Mounds Museum Society, Illinois, 1992
Korp, Maureen *The Mound Builders: Mysteries of the Ancient Americas* The Reader's Digest Association, Inc., New York, 1986
Silverberg, R. *The Mound Builders of Ancient America* New York Graphic Society Ltd, Greenwich, 1968

CANTERBURY CATHEDRAL
Adair, John *The Pilgrims' Way* Thames and Hudson, London, 1978
Boyle, John *Portrait of Canterbury* Robert Hale, London, 1974
Keates, Jonathan and **Angelo Hornak** *Canterbury Cathedral* Summerfield Press Ltd, and Philip Wilson Publishers Ltd, London, 1980
Loxton, Howard *Pilgrimage to Canterbury* David and Charles, Newton Abbot, 1978

THE CATACOMBS OF ROME
Gough, Michael *The Origins of Christian Art* Thames and Hudson, London, 1973
Hertling, Ludwig and **Engelbert Kirschbaum** *The Roman Catacombs and their Martyrs* Darton, Longman and Todd, London, rev. ed. 1960
Hibbert, Christopher *Rome: The Biography of a City* Penguin Books, Harmondsworth, 1985
Stevenson, J. *The Catacombs* Thames and Hudson, London, 1978
Toynbee, J.M.C. *Death and Burial in the Roman World* Thames and Hudson, London, 1971

THE CAVES OF THE THOUSAND BUDDHAS
Blunt, Wilfred *Golden Road to Samarkand* Hamish Hamilton, London, 1973
Giles, Lionel *Six Centuries At Tunhuang* The China Society, London, 1944
Hopkirk, Peter *Foreign Devils on the Silk Road* John Murray, London, 1980
Stein, Sir Aurel *On Ancient Central-Asian Tracks* Macmillan and Co., Limited, London, 1933

COLOGNE CATHEDRAL
Baum, Julius *German Cathedrals* Thames and Hudson, London, 1956
Bentley, James *The Rhine* George Philip, London, 1988
Wolff, Arnold *The Cologne Cathedral* Vista Point Verlag, Cologne, 1990

DELPHI
Hoyle, Peter *Delphi* Cassell, London, 1967
Lewis, Neville *Delphi and the Sacred Way* Michael Haag, London, 1987
Parke, H.W. *Greek Oracles* Hutchinson University Library, London, 1967
Pausanias *Guide to Greece: Central Greece* (trans. Peter Levi) Penguin Books, Harmondsworth, 1979

THE DOME OF THE ROCK
Cragg, Kenneth *The Dome and the Rock* S.P.C.K. Press, Cairo, 1964
Kolleck, Teddy and **Moshe Pearlman** *Jerusalem Sacred City of Mankind* Steimatzky's Agency Limited, Jerusalem, 1968 (rev. ed. 1972)
Landay, Jerry *Dome of the Rock* The Reader's Digest Association Inc., New York, 1972

EPHESUS
Brownrigg, R. *Pauline Places* Hodder & Stoughton, London, 1989
Freely, John *The Companion Guide to Turkey* Collins, London, 1979
Lloyd, Seton *Ancient Turkey* British Museum Publications Ltd, London, 1989
Morton, H.V. *In the Steps of Saint Paul* Methuen, London, 1936

THE GOLDEN TEMPLE
Edwardes, Michael *Indian Temples and Palaces* Paul Hamlyn, London, 1969
Tully, Mark and **Satish Jacob** *Amritsar: Mrs Gandhi's Last Battle* Jonathan Cape, London, 1985

GREAT MOSQUE OF CÓRDOBA
Gautier, Théophile *A Romantic In Spain* Alfred A. Knopf, New York and London, 1926
Gilmour, David *Cities of Spain* John Murray, London, 1992
Read, John H. *The Moors in Spain and Portugal* Faber & Faber, London, 1974

Sordo, Enrique *Moorish Spain* Elek Books, London, 1963

IONA
Adamnan *Life of Saint Columba* (ed. William Reeves) Llanerch Enterprises, Dyfed, 1988
Dunbar, John G. and **Ian Fisher** *Iona* HMSO, Edinburgh, 1983
Finlay, Ian *Columba* Richard Drew Publishing Ltd, Glasgow, 1990
McNeill, F. Marian *Iona: A History of the Island* Blackie & Son Ltd, Glasgow, 1959

ISE
Collcutt, Martin, Marius Jansen and **Isao Kumakura** *Cultural Atlas of Japan* Phaidon Press Ltd, Oxford, 1988
Kishida, Prof. Hideto *Japanese Architecture* Board of Tourist Industries, Japanese Government Railways, 1935
Morton, W. Scott *Japan: Its History and Culture* David and Charles, Newton Abbot, 1975
Popham, Peter *Wooden Temples of Japan* Tauris Parke Books, London, 1990

ISFAHAN
Blunt, Wilfred *Isfahan Pearl of Persia* Elek Books, London, 1966
Byron, Robert *The Road to Oxiana* Penguin Books, London, 1992
Payne, Robert *Journey to Persia* William Heinemann, London, 1951
Stevens, Roger *The Land of the Great Sophy* Methuen & Co. Ltd, London, 1965
Upham Pope, Arthur *Persian Architecture* Thames and Hudson, London, 1965

LOURDES
Ashe, Geoffrey *Miracles* Routledge & Kegan Paul, London, 1978
Cranston, Ruth *The Mystery of Lourdes* Evans Brothers Ltd, London, 1956
Marnham, Patrick *Lourdes: A Modern Pilgrimage* Heinemann, London, 1980

MECCA
Burton, Captain Sir Richard F. *Personal Narrative of a Pilgrimage to Al-Medinah and Mecca* Dover Publications, Inc., New York, 1964
Kaïdi, Hamza *Mecca and Medinah Today* (trans. Marianne Sinclair) les éditions j.a., Paris, 1980
Peters, F.E. *Jerusalem and Mecca: The Typology of the Holy City in the Near East* New York University Press, New York., 1986
Stewart, Desmond *Mecca* Newsweek, New York, 1980

MOUNT KAILAS
Allen, Charles *A Mountain in Tibet* Futura Publications, London, 1982

Johnson, Russell and **Kerry Morgan** *Kailas: On Pilgrimage to the Sacred Mountain of Tibet* Thames and Hudson, London, 1989
Snelling, John *The Sacred Mountain* East West Publications, London and The Hague, 1983

MOUNT SINAI
Anderson, Bernard W. *The Living World of the Old Testament* (2nd ed.), Longman, London, 1967
Gayley, John *Sinai and the Monastery of St. Catherine* Chatto & Windus, London, 1980
Kamil, Jill *The Monastery of Saint Catherine in Sinai* The American University in Cairo Press, Cairo, 1991

MYCENAE
Chadwick, J. *The Mycenaean World* Cambridge University Press, Cambridge, 1976
Payne, Robert *The Gold of Troy* Robert Hale Ltd, London, 1958
Schliemann, H. *Mycenae and Tiryns* John Murray, London, 1878
Senior, Michael *Greece and its Myths* Victor Gollancz, London, 1978
Taylour, Lord William D. *The Mycenaeans* Thames and Hudson, London, 1983

NEWGRANGE
Brennan, Martin *The Stars and the Stones: Ancient Art and Astronomy in Ireland* Thames and Hudson, London, 1983
Harbison, Peter *Pre-Christian Ireland* Thames and Hudson, London, 1988
O'Kelly, Michael J. *Newgrange: Archaeology, Art and Legend* Thames and Hudson, London, 1982
Ó'Ríordáin, Sean P. and **Glyn Daniel** *Newgrange and the Bend of the Boyne* Thames and Hudson, London, 1964

THE OLGAS
Dutton, Geoffrey *Australia's Last Explorer: Ernest Giles* Faber & Faber, London, 1970
Isaacs, Jennifer *Australian Dreaming: 40,000 Years of Aboriginal History* Landsdowne Press, Sydney, 1980
Mountford, C.P. *Brown Men and Red Sands* Robertson & Mullins, Melbourne, 1948
— *Nomads of the Australian Desert* Rigby, Adelaide, 1976

OLYMPIA
Anderson, Patrick *The Smile of Apollo* Chatto & Windus, London, 1964
De Jongh, Brian *The Companion Guide to Southern Greece* Collins, London, 1972
Melas, Evi (ed.) *Temples and Sanctuaries of Ancient Greece* Thames and Hudson, London, 1964
Pausanias *Guide to Greece; Volume 2: Southern Greece* (trans. Peter Levi) Penguin Books, London, 1988

Pentreath, Guy *Hellenic Traveller* Faber & Faber, London, 1964

OSEBERG
Brøndsted, Johannes *The Vikings* Penguin Books, London, 1965
Magnusson, Magnus *Vikings!* BBC Books and Bodley Head, London, 1980
Roesdahl, Else *The Vikings* Penguin Books, London, 1991
Sjøvold, Thorleif *The Viking Ships* Dreyers Forlag, Oslo, 1954
Wilson, David M. *The Vikings and their Origins* Thames and Hudson, London, 1989

PAGAN
Courtauld, Caroline *Collins Illustrated Guide to Burma* Collins, London, 1988
Hall, D.G.E. *Burma* Hutchinson's University Library, London, 1950
Maung Htin Aung *A History of Burma* Columbia University Press, New York and London, 1967
Scott, Sir J.G. *Burma from the Earliest Times to the Present Day* Alfred A. Knopf Inc., New York, 1924
Swaam, Wim *Lost Cities of Asia* Elek, London, 1966

THE PYRAMIDS OF GIZA
Edwards, I.E.S. *The Pyramids of Egypt* Penguin Books, London, 1991
Hobson, Christine *Exploring the World of the Pharaohs* Thames and Hudson, London, 1987
James, T.G.H. *An Introduction to Ancient Egypt* British Museum Publications Ltd, London, 1979
Spencer, A.J. *Death in Ancient Egypt* Penguin Books, Harmondsworth, 1982

THE ROCK OF CASHEL
Gleeson, Rev. John *Cashel of the Kings* James Duffy & Co. Ltd, Dublin, 1927
MacGowan, Kenneth *The Rock of Cashel* Kamac Publications, Dublin, 1985
Moody, T.W. and **F.X. Martin** (eds.) *The Course of Irish History* The Mercier Press, Cork, 1987
St. Patrick's Rock, Cashel National Parks and Monuments Service, Dublin.

SAN VITALE
Beckwith, John *Early Christian and Byzantine Art* Penguin Books, Harmondsworth, 1970
Bovini, Giuseppe *San Vitale, Ravenna* (trans. Basil Taylor) "Silvana" Editoriale d'Arte, Milano/André Deutsch, London, 1956
Kitzinger, Ernst *Byzantine Art in the Making* Faber & Faber, London, 1977
Sherill, Charles H. *Mosaics in Italy, Palestine, Syria, Turkey and Greece* John Lane/The Bodley Head Ltd, London, 1933

THE SÜLEYMANIYE
Hoag, John D. *Islamic Architecture* Faber & Faber/Electra, London, 1987.
Kelly, Lawrence *Istanbul: A Traveller's Companion* Constable, London, 1987
Sumner-Boyd, Hilary and **John Freely** *Strolling Through Istanbul* KPI, London and New York, 1987

TEMPLE OF KARNAK
Baines, J. and **J. Malek** *Atlas of Ancient Egypt* Phaidon Press Ltd, 1980
Cerny, J. *Ancient Egyptian Religion* Hutchinson, London, 1952
Davies, J.G. *Temples, Churches and Mosques* The Pilgrim Press, New York, 1982
Frankfort, J. *Ancient Egyptian Religion: An interpretation* Harper, New York, 1961
Kamil, Jill *Luxor* Longman, London and New York, 1983

TEOTIHUACÁN
Bray, W.M., **E.H. Swanson** and **I.S. Farrington** *The Ancient Americas* Phaidon Press Limited, Oxford, 1989
Castro Leal, Maria *Archaeological Mexico* (trans. Erika Pauh) Casa Editrice Borechi, Florence and Monclem Ediciones, Mexico, 1990
Heydon, Doris and **Paul Gendrop** *Pre-Columbian Architecture of Mesoamerica* Faber and Faber, London, 1980

THE TOMB COMPLEX OF SHI HUANGDI
Cotterell, Arthur *The First Emperor of China* Macmillan London Ltd, London, 1981
FitzGerald, Patrick *Ancient China* Elsevier-Phaidon, Oxford, 1978
Topping, Audrey "China's Incredible Find" *National Geographic Magazine*, April 1988
Wood, Frances *Blue Guide to China* A. and C. Black Publishers Ltd, London, 1992

VARANASI
Eck, Diana L. *Banaras: City of Light* Princeton University Press, Princeton, New Jersey, 1982
Newby, Eric *Slowly Down the Ganges* Hodder & Stoughton, London, 1966
Sherring, Rev. M.A. *The Sacred City of the Hindus* Trübner & Co., London, 1868

WAT PHRA KEO
Bartlett, Norman *Land of the Lotus Eaters* Jarrolds Publishers Ltd, London, 1959
Nicol, Gladys *Thailand* B.T. Batsford Ltd, London/Hippocrene Books, New York, 1980
Shearer, Alistair *Thailand: The Lotus Kingdom* John Murray, London, 1989
Van Beek, Steve and **Luca Invernizzi Tettoni** *The Arts of Thailand* Thames and Hudson, London, 1991

INDEX

ACKNOWLEDGMENTS

The publishers would like to thank the following people for their help in the making of this book:

EDITORIAL: Maggi McCormick, Tim Probart, Judy Batchelor (index), Jazz Wilson, Pennie Jelliff

DESIGN: Karine Bai, Vicky Holmes

ILLUSTRATIONS: David Atkinson (maps); Debbie Hinks (symbols); Sue Sharples (ground plans); Stephen Conlin (reconstruction artworks); Eileen Batterberry and Tim Heard (map annotation).

PICTURE CREDITS

l = left; *r* = right; *c* = centre; *t* = top; *b* = bottom

1 A. Abbas/Magnum Photos; 2/3 Sarah Stone/Tony Stone Images; 6 Jean Kugler/ Spectrum Colour Library; 10 S.H. & D.H. Cavanaugh/Robert Harding Picture Library; 12 Robert Harding Picture Library; 12/13 Erich Lessing/Magnum Photos; 14*t* Spectrum Colour Library; 14*b* The Bridgeman Art Library; 15 Ann & Bury Peerless; 17 The Bridgeman Art Library; 18 Ann & Bury Peerless; 19 J.H.C. Wilson/Robert Harding Picture Library; 20*t* Picturepoint; 20*b* Ann & Bury Peerless; 21 Jean-Louis Nou/Explorer; 22 Erich Lessing/Magnum Photos; 22/23 Robert Harding Picture Library; 24 Images Colour Library; 25*l* Michael Short/ Robert Harding Picture Library; 25*r* E.T. Archive; 26 Adam Woolfitt/Robert Harding Picture Library; 27 D. Lennon/Spectrum Colour Library; 28 Picturepoint; 30 G.L. Carlisle/Spectrum Colour Library; 31 Spectrum Colour Library; 32 James Harpur; 33 Ghigo Roli/Robert Harding Picture Library; 34*t* The Bridgeman Art Library; 34*b* James Harpur; 35 The Mansell Collection; 36/37 Zefa Picture Library; 38*t* Fred Mayer/Magnum Photos; 38*b* Zefa Picture Library; 39 Robert Harding Picture Library; 40/41 The Bridgeman Art Library; 41 Michael Holford; 42 The Mansell Collection; 42/43 Fred Mayer/Magnum Photos; 44 David Hamilton/The Image Bank; 46/47 Adam Woolfitt/Robert Harding Picture Library; 48 Office of Public Works, Dublin; 49 Bob Hobby/Impact Photos; 51 Louis Salou/ Explorer; 52/53 Robert Harding Picture Library; 54 Zoe Dominic; 55*t* The Mansell Collection; 56 F.H.C. Birch/Sonia Halliday Photographs; 57 Images Colour Library; 58*t* Trevor Wood/Robert Harding Picture Library; 58*b*/59 National Archaeological Museum,

Athens/The Bridgeman Art Library; 60 G. & P. Corrigan/Occidor; 61/62 Robert Harding Picture Library; 63 Mauro Carraro/Colorific!; 64/66*l* Robert Harding Picture Library; 66*r* John G. Ross/Robert Harding Picture Library; 67 E.T. Archive; 68 F. Jack Jackson/Robert Harding Picture Library; 69 James Harpur; 70 Mary Evans Picture Library; 71 R.K. Pilsbury; 72 University Museum of Oslo/The Bridgeman Art Library; 72/73 David Hurn/Magnum Photos; 74 The Image Bank; 75*t* Knudsens Fotosenter; 75*b* University Museum of National Antiquities, Oslo; 78/81 Scala; 82 Tom Owen Edmunds/The Image Bank; 84 Spectrum Colour Library; 84/85 Zefa Picture Library; 86 Telegraph Colour Library; 87 David Tokeley/ Robert Harding Picture Library; 88 Chris Haigh/Tony Stone Images; 89 Richard Passmore/Tony Stone Images; 91*l* James Harpur; 91*r* E. Chalker/Spectrum Colour Library; 92 Hugh Sitton/Tony Stone Images; 93 Mary Evans Picture Library; 94 Michael Holford; 95 Friedrich Damm/Zefa Picture Library; 98/99 Spectrum Colour Library; 100*t* Nick Saunders/Barbara Heller Archive; 100*b* National Museum of Anthropology, Mexico/ Werner Forman Archive; 102 Colorific!; 103 Tony Morrison/South American Pictures; 104 Michael Holford; 104/105 Sonia Halliday Photographs; 106 Spectrum Colour Library; 107*l* Michael Holford; 107*r* Images Colour Library; 108*t* James Harpur; 108*b* British Museum; 109 Archiv für Kunst und Geschichte; 110 James Harpur; 111 Mary Evans Picture Library; 112 Werner Forman Archive; 112/113 David Muench; 114 Otis Imboden/National Geographic Society; 116 Museum of the American Indian, Heye Foundation, New York/Werner Forman Archive; 117 Joslyn Art Museum, Omaha, Nebraska. Gift of the Enron Art Foundation; 118 Dr. Georg Gerster/ Comstock; 120/122 Robert Harding Picture Library; 123 Spectrum Colour Library; 124 Nigel Blythe/Robert Harding Picture Library; 125*t* J.J. Augustin Incorporated Publisher; 125*b* Zaw Lwin; 126/127 Dallas & John Heaton/ Spectrum Colour Library; 128 Hulton Deutsch Collection; 129 Mick Sharp; 131 James Harpur; 132 Chris Fairclough Colour Library; 133 British Museum/Robert Harding Picture Library; 134 Tom Nebbia/Aspect Picture Library; 135 Chris Fairclough Colour Library; 136 Simon Wescott/Robert Harding Picture Library; 138 Mika Kansas/The Image Bank; 140 Roland Michaud/The John Hillelson Agency; 141 Picturepoint; 142/143*t* Robert Harding Picture Library; 143*b* Museum für Islamische Kunst/Bildarchiv Preussischer Kulturbesitz; 144 Frank Spooner Pictures; 145 Picturepoint; 146/147 Luca Tettoni/Photobank Photolibrary; 148*l* Ann & Bury Peerless; 148*r*/149 Luca

Tettoni/Photobank Photolibrary; 150 Hackenberg/Zefa Picture Library; 150/152 Arxiu Mas; 153*l* Robert Harding Picture Library; 153*r* E.T. Archive; 154 Biblioteca Apostolica Vaticana; 155 George Wright/ Comstock; 156 The Image Bank; 157 Jake Rajs/The Image Bank; 158*l* Mary Evans Picture Library; 158*r* The Bridgeman Art Library; 159/160 Robert Harding Picture Library; 161 A. Abbas/Magnum Photos; 162 The Bridgeman Art Library; 163 J.H.C. Wilson/Robert Harding Picture Library; 166/167 Spectrum Colour Library; 168 Raghu Rai/Magnum Photos; 169 Ann & Bury Peerless; 170/173 Scala; 174 Michael Holford; 174/175 Orion Press; 176 Pan-Asia Newspaper Alliance; 177 Orion Press; 178/179 British Museum/The Bridgeman Art Library; 180 Erich Lessing/ Magnum Photos; 181 Terry Williams/The Image Bank; 182 Friedrich Damm/Zefa Picture Library; 183*l* Hulton Deutsch Collection; 183*r* Erich Lessing/Magnum Photos; 184 P. & G. Bowater/The Image Bank; 185 Erich Lessing/ Magnum Photos; 186 Russell Johnson; 188 Robert Harding Picture Library; 188/189 Tim Bieber/The Image Bank; 190 Adam Woolfitt/ Robert Harding Picture Library; 191*t* W.R. Davis/Spectrum Colour Library; 191*b* Adam Woolfitt/Robert Harding Picture Library; 192 Raghubir Singh/Colorific!; 193 Ross Greetham/Robert Harding Picture Library; 194/195 K. Kerth/Zefa Picture Library; 196*l* James Harpur; 196*r* Dave Longley/Mick Sharp; 198*l* Bildarchiv Preussischer Kulturbesitz; 198*r* Images Colour Library; 199 K. Kerth/Zefa Picture Library; 200*t* James Harpur; 200*b* Sandra Lousada; 201 Sonia Halliday Photographs; 202 Mohamed Amin/Camerpix; 202/203 Nabeel Turner/Tony Stone Images; 204*l* Edinburgh University Library; 204*r* Sonia Halliday Photographs; 205 Mohamed Amin/Camerpix; 206*l* A. Abbas/Magnum Photos; 206*r* Mohamed Amin/Camerpix; 210/211 Russell Johnson; 212 The Bridgeman Art Library; 213/214 Russell Johnson; 215 Allan Bramley/Tony Stone Images; 216 Superstock; 217/218*l* Steve McCurry/Magnum Photos; 218*r* Hulton Deutsch Collection; 219 Steve McCurry/ Magnum Photos; 220/221 A.F. Kersting; 222 Picturepoint; 223 David Lomax/Robert Harding Picture Library; 224 Images Colour Library; 225 Spectrum Colour Library; 226 George Rodger/Magnum Photos; 227 Michael Holford; 229 Scala.